AND THE ROY
...CINE AND DI
...ER STREET, L
7110

WITHDRAWN
FROM STOCK
QMUL LIBRARY

MORAL UNCERTAINTY
AND ITS CONSEQUENCES

MORAL UNCERTAINTY AND ITS CONSEQUENCES

Ted Lockhart

New York   Oxford

Oxford University Press

2000

SBRLSMD

CLASS MARK	W 50 LOC
CIRC TYPE	1 w/k
SUPPLIER	CISL 28/1/02 £33.50
BINDING	

Oxford University Press

Oxford   New York
Athens   Auckland   Bangkok   Bogotá   Buenos Aires   Calcutta
Cape Town   Chennai   Dar es Salaam   Delhi   Florence   Hong Kong   Istanbul
Karachi   Kuala Lumpur   Madrid   Melbourne   Mexico City   Mumbai
Nairobi   Paris   São Paulo   Singapore   Taipei   Tokyo   Toronto   Warsaw

and associated companies in
Berlin   Ibadan

Copyright © 2000 by Ted Lockhart

Published by Oxford University Press, Inc.
198 Madison Avenue, New York, New York 10016

Oxford is a registered trademark of Oxford University Press

All rights reserved. No part of this publication may be reproduced,
stored in a retrieval system, or transmitted, in any form or by any means,
electronic, mechanical, photocopying, recording, or otherwise,
without the prior permission of Oxford University Press.

Library of Congress Cataloging-in-Publication Data
Lockhart, Ted, 1946–
Moral uncertainty and its consequences / Ted Lockhart
p.   cm.
Includes bibliographical references and index.
ISBN 0-19-512610-6
1. Decision making—Moral and ethical aspects.
2. Uncertainty.   I. Title.
BJ1419 L63   1999
17021—dc21   99-017331

9 8 7 6 5 4 3 2 1

Printed in the United States of America
on acid-free paper

In honor of my father,
Clifford Odell Lockhart
(1921–1992)

Preface

In this book, I urge reforming our thinking about moral decision-making in three ways. I argue that most ethicists' views about the role our moral beliefs should play in our choices of action are inadequate in several important respects and in need of repair. If adopted, the reforms that I shall offer would greatly alter how we make moral decisions.

Chapter 1 begins by posing the question, "What shall I do when I am uncertain what I morally ought to do?" For urgent, problematic moral decisions, this is the *practical* quandary that we often face. I show that how we should act under moral uncertainty is not necessarily, and is often not in fact, how we morally ought to act. A surprising corollary is that even if moral considerations have paramount importance, we should not always do what we know is morally right. Whether moral considerations actually have this exalted status is a controversial issue in contemporary ethics, and I consider the possibility that they do not. However, in either event, the problems of decision-making under moral uncertainty that we face are essentially the same, whether or not we view moral considerations as always preempting nonmoral considerations.

It is reasonable to ask why, if decision-making under moral uncertainty is as important and as ubiquitous a problem as I claim, ethicists have paid virtually no attention to it? In chapter 1, I explore several possible explanations of their lack of interest and conclude that none of them entitles us to ignore the problem or to fail to recognize its critical importance for our moral choices.

In chapter 2, I maintain that when we make moral decisions we should take our moral uncertainties into account no less than, and in much the same way that, we should take our ordinary factual uncertainties into account. How, in general, we should do this is the substance of my first reform—a maximize-expected-moral-rightness criterion for our moral decisions. Most ethicists accept what I call the binary hypothesis—the view that actions cannot be partially right or wrong but must be either right or wrong *tout à fait*. I show that if we accept the binary hypothesis, the maximize-expected-moral-rightness criterion directs us to choose actions that have the maximum probability of being morally right. I illustrate this decision strategy by applying it to several forms of moral uncertainty. I also explain why the criterion cannot coherently be regarded as a criterion of moral rightness, and I defend it against several possible objections.

In chapter 3, I demonstrate the utility of the maximize-expected-moral-rightness criterion by applying it to several kinds of abortion decisions. We see that in the vast majority of cases the criterion allows us to disarm such seemingly intractable problems as the personhood of fetuses and the moral significance of a right to life. I explain how, for practical purposes, we may circumvent our moral uncertainties by factoring them into the deliberation process. However, for a couple of particularly problematic abortion cases that I consider, the criterion is more difficult to apply. To solve the problems they raise, I formulate and defend a second-order criterion that presides when we lack the information we need to employ the original maximize-expected-moral-rightness criterion. The second-order criterion sanctions actions that have the greatest likelihood of satisfying the first-order criterion. I then apply the second-order criterion to those problematic abortion decisions.

In chapter 4, I adduce reasons for rejecting the binary hypothesis in favor of a many-valued concept of moral rightness. This is the second of the three reforms. I argue that for at least some prominent moral theories, like utilitarianism, it is semantically natural to adopt such a view. More important, adopting a many-valued concept has practical, as well as semantic, significance. I explain how if we use the maximize-expected-moral-rightness criterion to choose our actions, the many-valued concept of moral rightness will often make a difference in what we ultimately should do. I illustrate this difference with several examples, and I argue that for some decisions under moral uncertainty we do not get the correct answers unless we employ the many-valued concept.

One possible challenge to my claim that we should always *maximize* expected moral rightness is based on the concept of supererogation. The idea is that if supererogatory actions are "optional" even though they are morally "better" than other morally right actions, then perhaps we are sometimes justified in choosing actions that do not maximize expected moral rightness. Chapter 5 gives reasons for doubting that the maximization of expected moral rightness can be "optional" even if supererogatory actions are possible. However, I go further and undermine the argument against maximization by showing that the two essential characteristics of supererogatory actions—namely, their "optionality" and their superiority in moral value—are mutually incompatible and, therefore, the notion of supererogation is incoherent. I explain also how we can account for the idea that we are not morally "required" to be saints or heroes within a framework of decision-making under moral uncertainty and without recognizing a special category of supererogatory actions.

In chapters 6 and 7, I present examples of real-world decisions that illustrate how the many-valued concept of moral rightness would, if adopted, affect our choices of action. In chapter 6, I examine a case in medical ethics and demonstrate how the maximize-expected-moral-rightness criterion in combination with the many-valued concept can be used to guide decision-making. There we see how using the many-valued concept can complicate the application of the criterion to individual decisions and even make it impossible to apply directly. Again the solution is to employ a second-order principle that advises us to choose some action that has maximum likelihood of satisfying the first-order principle. We also find that this approach sometimes serves another purpose—namely, resolving *disagreements* about which actions should ultimately be chosen. I explain how disputants may sometimes be able *rationally* to agree on what should be done, all things considered, even when their disagreement about what it would be most right to do cannot be resolved.

In chapter 7, I take up the *Roe* v. *Wade* Supreme Court decision and show how my methods can handle the kinds of uncertainties intimated in Justice Blackmun's opinion for the majority. Here I demonstrate how my methods can be adapted to situations where the normative issues are of a nonmoral character. Again it turns out that there are better (i.e., more reasonable) ways of dealing with the pertinent uncertainties than ignoring them or pretend that they have been resolved. I show how a group of individuals who must render a collective decision and who disagree about underlying normative issues, by carefully identifying areas of agreement and disagreement and by assessing their degrees of confidence in the premises and inferences of their respective arguments, may be able to reach consensus on what, for practical purposes, matters most—that is, deciding what is to be done.

The third reform, which I propose in chapter 8, is that we should view moral rightness as a characteristic of what I call "courses of action" as well as a characteristic of individual actions. By "course of action" I mean a sequence of actions by an individual moral agent that occur over a span of time. I explain how some courses of action can possess greater expected degrees of moral rightness than others. Particularly important are our own future *lifetime* courses of action. I contend that, ultimately, we should select lifetime courses of action that have the highest possible expected degrees of moral rightness.

Since each individual action initiates a future lifetime course of action, the standard for our course-of-action choices is also a standard for our individual action choices. This norm, I argue, is properly the ground for all of our moral decision-making. Here again I provide examples to illustrate the correct application of the standard. I also speculate about its implications for collective action and, in particular, for courses of action aimed at bringing about utopian results. It turns out that we are sometimes morally justified in carrying out utopian projects on the basis of the course-of-action moral standard even if some of our actions would violate the maximize-expected-moral-rightness standard for individual actions. Since the former standard overrides the latter, we are *morally* justified in pursuing suitable utopian goals. Paradoxically, we are sometimes *morally* justified in performing morally suboptimal individual actions in order to implement morally optimal courses of action.

If my arguments are sound, then it follows that the methods of practical reasoning that we should use in making moral decisions are very different from those that ethicists usually assume. In large measure their methods suppose that moral decision-making should consist of implementing a judgment about the moral rightness or obligatoriness of a particular action alternative. They are often unhelpful in real-world decision-making because the difficulty of resolving the pertinent moral questions leaves us without any moral judgment to implement. And they often dispense bad advice because they ignore the significance of the variations in strength among our moral opinions. As a result, moral agents receive little or no useful, credible advice about *what to do*. It is not difficult to understand why some decision-makers have concluded that moral philosophy is, on the whole, a rather academic and useless enterprise.

The approach to moral decision-making that I propose in this book virtually guarantees that practical guidance is available to agents, since no amount of moral uncertainty can silence the decision criterion. For the maximize-expected-moral-rightness standard, moral uncertainty is a constraint under which decision-making operates, rather than a lacuna in its sphere of operation. This built-in practicality is an important advantage that my approach has over other approaches.

In many of the examples in which I apply the maximize-expected-moral-rightness criterion and its variations to different sorts of moral decisions, I freely use some of the technical methods of decision theory. The reader will be able to see how these methods enable us to reason about moral uncertainty with much greater than usual precision. This precision is quite often *mathematical* precision. Unfortunately, the price of purchase is considerable complexity in some of the details of the analyses that I shall employ. Motivated and attentive readers should be able to digest enough of those details to understand in more-or-less general ways the decision strategies that I shall propose. I have relegated expositions of some of the more complicated mathematical tasks to endnotes. (And even there, I present some of the relevant information only in schematic form.) Thus readers who wish not to be distracted from the more "philosophical" aspects of the discussion may conveniently skim over the mathematical technicalities. Even so, mathematical expressions and decision tables are numerous in the text, and some appreciation of their significance will be necessary if the reader is to have any but a superficial understanding of how the general decision principles I propose apply to actual decisions. Also, it will be helpful for readers to have some knowledge of probability and decision theory, especially expected utility theory. Those who are completely uninitiated may consult an introductory text such as Michael D. Resnik's *Choices: An Introduction to Decision Theory* (Minneapolis: University of Minnesota Press, 1987).

Some readers may view the kinds of mathematical methods that I shall employ as inappropriate for moral philosophy. They may feel that while such methods are suitable for such applications as predicting the weather or planning investment strategy, they are ill-suited for moral decision-making, which, it will be said, is an activity of a very special, qualitative character.

With this point of view I have some sympathy. In the course of writing this book, I became acutely aware of the limits of my own ability to be completely objective and calculating in making difficult moral choices. For moral agents who face difficult decisions and who fully experience the intense emotional pull of conflicting moral forces, questions about *rational* decision-making may seem out of place. However, to shun decision-theoretic methods as "too rational" for moral decision-making obliges us to explain how they differ *significantly* from the often dry, emotionless cogitations that ethicists typically engage in. How may we regard mathematical methods as excessively rationalistic while we consider the methods of ordinary deductive logic to be entirely appropriate for moral deliberation? Moreover, the kinds of reasoning required in order to rigorously apply moral theories to difficult moral decisions seem almost as intricate and calculating as those necessitated by the decision-theoretic methods that I shall employ. This is true even for intuitionist moral perspectives—prima facie duties moral theories, for example—which assign moral intuition the task of identifying the conflicting obligations but not of determining which obligations have the greatest weight. For the latter purpose, elaborate argumentation and analysis may be needed. Thus, as a means of evaluating moral alternatives, formal decision-theoretic methods appear not to be significantly more rationalistic than the customary methods of normative ethics. I shall comment further on this subject in chapter 3.

I, of course, hope that readers will find merit in the analyses and arguments that they find in the following pages. The territory that I have chosen to explore is largely uncharted, however, and I suspect that some readers will find my arguments inadequate to their tasks. Perhaps they will see fit to correct my errors and propose better arguments. My more limited objective is to provide reason and motivation for philosophers to recognize the questions that I have raised as important questions for moral philosophy. If my efforts serve that purpose, then they will not have been entirely in vain.

Houghton, Michigan
August 1999   T. L.

Acknowledgments

Most of this book was written during sabbatical leaves from Michigan Technological University for the 1985–1986 and 1992–1993 academic years. Some parts have been expanded from previously published material: Chapter 6 is a somewhat longer version of my essay "Professions, Confidentiality, and Moral Uncertainty," which appeared in *Professional Ethics* 1: 3 and 4 (1992), pp. 33–52. Chapter 7 is expanded from "A Decision-Theoretic Reconstruction of *Roe* v. *Wade*," which appeared in *Public Affairs Quarterly* 5:3 (July 1991), pp. 243–258. Its editor, Robert Holmes, has kindly permitted me to reprint here. Portions of chapter 8 are taken from my essay "Technological Fixes for Moral Dilemmas," which was part of the Spring 1996 issue of the *Society for Philosophy and Technology Electronic Journal*. I am grateful to the editor, Paul Durbin, for permission to include those sections.

Some of the ideas in this book were presented and discussed at conferences and colloquia. Several of the analyses and arguments in Chapter 3 are similar to those I presented under the title "Abortion and Moral Uncertainty" at the University of Florida on October 20, 1985, as a department of philosophy colloquium. An abbreviated and revised version of that paper, titled "Abortion, Moral Uncertainty, and Rational Decision-making," was presented as a colloquium paper at the central division meeting of the American Philosophical Association in Chicago on May 1, 1987. A few of the arguments in chapter 8 are essentially the same as those contained in my essay "Utopia as an Ethical Paradise," which I read at the

Society for Utopian Studies annual conference at Pennsylvania State University in Media, Pennsylvania, on October 10, 1987. An early draft of "Professions, Confidentiality, and Moral Uncertainty" was presented at the National Conference on Ethics and the Professions at the University of Florida in Gainesville on January 30, 1992. The discussion of supererogation in chapter 5 is revised from my essay "Shall I Act Supererogatorily?," which I read at the Central States Philosophical Association meeting at Washington University in St. Louis, Missouri, on November 8, 1991. Finally, the discussion of technology in chapter 8 closely follows my essay "Technological Fixes for Moral Dilemmas," which I presented at the Seventh Biennial Congress of the Society for Philosophy and Technology at the Centro de Estudios de Peñíscola in Valencia, Spain, on May 22, 1993. I am grateful for all the helpful comments that I received on those occasions.

I particularly wish to thank Derek Parfit, who read the entire book in draft form and recommended it for publication. I also want to express my appreciation to an anonymous reviewer for Oxford University Press whose incisive comments and thoughtful suggestions helped me see where I needed to improve my arguments and my exposition of them.

I have had useful discussions with a number of people over the years during which I have thought about the problems that this book addresses and have formed the views that I offer in the following pages. Those people include Robert Baum, Tom Donaldson, Lee Erlebach, R. M. Hare, Terry Kent, Richard Montgomery, Henry Richardson, Kristin Shrader-Frechette, Bill Sewell, Harvey Siegel, Ted Talbot, and Laurie Whitt. I am grateful to all of them and to others whom I have forgotten to acknowledge. I regret that Michael Bayles's death prevents me from expressing to him my sincere gratitude for his generous counsel and encouragement.

I particularly wish to express my gratitude to Otto Ruehr for devising a method for carrying out many of the mathematical calculations that I use in this book. His discovery enabled me to computerize those calculations and thus saved me considerable time and labor. I also want to acknowledge commentaries by Donald Hubin and Hud Hudson on my papers "Abortion, Moral Uncertainty, and Rational Decision-making" and "Shall I Act Supererogatorily?," respectively. Both were of significant help to me in improving the formulation of my ideas. In less specific but no less important ways, I am indebted to Robert Baum, Kristin Shrader-Frechette, and Harvey Siegel, who at various times and in various ways energized my efforts to bring this project to completion. I also owe special thanks to Harvey for bringing the passage in Russell Banks's novel *Cloudsplitter* to my attention.

I particularly want to thank my wife, Deborah, for exposing the incomprehensibility of some of my sentences and for sustaining me throughout this endeavor with her love and support.

Contents

MORAL UNCERTAINTY
AND ITS CONSEQUENCES

We were obliged to oppose slavery, then, not merely to preserve and perfect the Republic, although that alone was a worthy enough task, but to defeat Satan. It was our holy, our peculiarly American, obligation.

Simple. Or so it seemed. For even though I understood Father's logic well enough, I didn't always understand his applications of that logic to the specific circumstances, contingencies, and conditions that arose in our daily lives. Which meant that, on a day-to-day basis, I sometimes did not know right from wrong.

Russell Banks,
Cloudsplitter

One

Decision-making under Moral Uncertainty

What shall I do when I am uncertain what I morally ought to do? Philosophers have paid little attention to this sort of question. Yet moral uncertainty lurks in the background of many of our moral decisions. And given the notorious difficulty of answering moral questions, moral uncertainty is often fitting and proper. It is not difficult to find reputable ethicists and plausible arguments on opposite sides of important ethical issues. In fact, certainty about the moral propriety of one's actions may betray one's philosophical naiveté or, worse, an attitude of narrow-mindedness or fanaticism. This is true not only of highly conspicuous moral controversies, such as those about abortion, physician-assisted suicide, sexual behavior, capital punishment, and so on. A heightened sensitivity to moral considerations may produce a realization that their scope is much broader than we formerly appreciated. We may come to understand that they extend even to our decisions about how we shall use the time and resources at our disposal. At this moment, instead of writing this page, I could be collecting donations for a Third World relief organization or teaching an illiterate person to read.

In this chapter, I shall argue that not to take moral uncertainty into account in practical deliberations is a serious omission, the recognition of which invalidates much of what philosophers have assumed about moral decision-making. It is also a significant source of missed opportunities to provide practical guidance to ordinary moral agents. Later I shall offer some explanations as to why this oversight

3

has occurred and continues to occur in moral philosophy. In the meantime, I shall explain why it is important for us to take our moral uncertainties into account in making our moral decisions. In doing so, I shall show that reasonable action choices need not always coincide perfectly with morally permissible ones.

Moral Uncertainty as a Practical Problem

Suppose I find myself in a situation of the following kind:

Example 1.1
I must choose among alternative acts x, y, and z. I believe that x would be morally wrong for me to perform and that both y and z would be morally right. However, I have complete confidence in the moral rightness of z, whereas I am not completely certain of that of y.

If my objective is to do what is morally right, which action should I choose?

The intuitively obvious answer is that I should choose z. If my ultimate objective is to do what is morally right, it makes no sense at all for me to choose x. And by choosing y, I risk moral failure, while doing z avoids any such risk. Since z is one of my options, I can avoid the moral risk associated with y. If my sole purpose is to do what is right, it makes no sense to accept an avoidable moral risk. Therefore, in this situation z is the best choice.

We might compare the decision of Example 1.1 to someone's choice of strategy in a game of chess. Suppose that Ann has three defenses that she uses when she plays chess. Whenever she plays against Betty she usually loses whenever she uses the French defense and usually wins whenever she uses the Lopez defense. However, Ann *always* wins against Betty whenever she uses the Sicilian defense and is completely sure that she would win again if she chose that defense in this particular game. If winning is paramount to Ann, then obviously it would make no sense for her to choose either the French or Lopez defense since she is sure to win if she uses the Sicilian defense and risks losing if she uses any other defense. Although Ann might win if she chose the French defense and probably would win if she chose the Lopez defense, acting in accordance with the "spirit" of her "winning is paramount" credo means choosing the strategy that affords her certainty of victory. Similarly, acting in accordance with the "spirit" of a "morality is paramount" doctrine entails choosing actions the moral rightness of which we are certain over actions the moral rightness of which we are unsure.

Example 1.1 shows that there is more to consider in moral decision-making than the moral rightness or wrongness of our alternatives. In the example, z is *the* reasonable choice of action. I should choose neither x nor y.[1] But the reason I should decline y is not because I believe that y would be morally wrong. In fact, I believe, perhaps justifiably, the opposite. I believe that y would be morally right; I just am not absolutely certain that this is so. If my belief that y would be morally right is correct, then it is false that I ought (morally) to choose z. It would be morally right for me to choose z, but I would not be morally *obligated* to do so. Rather, I ought (morally) to choose either y or z. It follows that what is reasonable for me to do is not the same as what is morally right for me to do.

In Example 1.1 and in the rest of this book, I use "morally right" as generally equivalent to "morally permissible."[2] Although some ethicists have seen reason to distinguish between the meanings of "ought (morally) to do" and "is (morally) obligated to do," I shall use them interchangeably. I also assume that what one ought (morally) to do on a particular occasion is to perform any of the action alternatives x_1, x_2, . . . that would be morally right for me to perform on that occasion. This means that if x_1 and x_2 are the only alternatives that would be morally right for me to perform, then I ought (morally) to perform either x_1 or x_2. It, of course, does not follow either that I ought (morally) to do x_1 or that I ought (morally) to do x_2. A locution of the form "x is *the* right thing to do" may imply that x is the *only* morally right alternative in the situation. In that event, the statement would imply that x is obligatory as well as right.

Example 1.1 also shows why we cannot simply *define* "morality" as reasonableness in action. Our conclusion that z would be *the* reasonable choice rides only on the assumptions that moral considerations are paramount and that the decision-maker is uncertain about the moral rightness or wrongness of x and y. We could avoid that conclusion only if we could somehow rule out the possibility that such a situation could arise—that is, if it were impossible for anyone to have to make a decision under moral uncertainty for which moral considerations are paramount. There is no reason to believe morality loses its paramountcy whenever moral uncertainty enters the picture. If moral considerations can be supreme, then morality cannot be exactly the same thing as reasonableness in action.

Our discussion of Example 1.1 shows that for decision-making under moral uncertainty the question of what it is reasonable to do can sometimes be addressed separately from the question of what it is morally right to do. This is so even under the assumption that moral considerations are paramount. Why is this important? Because it offers us some hope that it may be possible to develop decision strategies that mediate between the *practical* importance that moral considerations have for (at least) some of our decisions and the moral uncertainty that often suffuses those situations. A skeptic might note that there will likely be a number of such strategies and that we would probably encounter uncertainty all over again in selecting one candidate over the others. Therefore, according to this objection, we would gain nothing in attempting to develop a rational strategy for decision-making under moral uncertainty. However, even if we were unable to become completely sure which general strategy is the correct strategy in every detail, Example 1.1 shows us that at least in some cases of unresolved moral uncertainty, it may be quite clear how decision-makers should decide. We should not assume at the outset that we shall not often find it much easier to tell what would be reasonable for us to do in situations of moral uncertainty than to resolve that uncertainty.

In Example 1.1, I, the decision-maker, am certain of the moral rightness of at least one of my alternatives. Many and perhaps most moral decisions lack this characteristic. Situations in which philosophically sophisticated moral agents are 100% sure of the moral rightness of any of their options are probably quite rare. We sometimes have no alternative the moral rightness of which we are totally certain. Example 1.1 is useful in exposing an important blind spot in philosophers' treatment of moral decision-making. Ethicists usually regard the critical question to be about the moral rightness or wrongness of a particular kind of action—for example, having or performing an abortion, killing enemy soldiers in wartime, breaking a promise for the good of the promisee, and so on. They tacitly assume that whether the action alternative under consideration would be right or wrong is the central *practical* question. If they were to consider a concrete instance of Example 1.1, they might focus on the question of y's rightness or wrongness and try to reach some conclusion. They would see their job as evaluating the arguments on both sides of that issue in order to determine which moral judgment was supported by the strongest arguments. They would sanction my choosing y if they found the strongest argument to support the moral rightness of y. Otherwise, they would advise me not to perform y.

Our discussion of Example 1.1 shows what is wrong with this customary approach to applied ethics. Since my overriding purpose is to do what is morally right, unless the moral rightness of y can be established with certainty, I should choose z over y. If the question of y's rightness or wrongness is particularly controversial or difficult, I may have no real prospect of achieving certainty about the answer. Under such circumstances, the strength as well as the content of the agent's moral beliefs are significant. As we shall see in our discussion of abortion in chapter 3, philosophers have largely been oblivious to the sort of practical reasoning illustrated here.

One might object to my analysis of Example 1.1 on the grounds that in such a situation I, the decision-maker, should continue to deliberate until I have eliminated my uncertainties about the moral rightness or wrongness of *all* of my alternatives before deciding what to do. Once *all* my moral uncertainty has been dispelled, I may then choose an alternative the moral rightness of which I am certain. However, it is unrealistic to suppose that it is always possible to eliminate *all* one's moral uncertainties before the decision must be made. Decisions cannot be indefinitely postponed. Sooner or later the moment of decision arrives and action must be taken. I must then act under whatever moral uncertainty remains.

Some might argue that it is always possible to do nothing and thus to avoid decision in that way. However, "doing nothing" is often not morally neutral. "Doing nothing" in a situation in which I decide whether to administer CPR to the person who has just collapsed in front of me clearly has moral ramifications. I may even recognize "doing nothing" as one of my alternatives, and I may have beliefs about its rightness or wrongness. Perhaps in Example 1.1 x is the "do nothing" alternative. Then, for the reasons just given, "doing nothing" would not be a reasonable choice. Moreover, even if further reflection would eventually clear up my doubts about the moral rightness or wrongness of x and y, I could never become more certain about the rightness of x or y than I am about that of z. If moral rightness is my paramount concern, I can do no better than to pick z. Pondering further about x and y would be superfluous.

Another argument against my contention that we should recognize decision-making under moral uncertainty as an important problem is that although ethicists debate seemingly intractable moral issues, they are issues that most of us rarely confront as decision-makers. According to this assessment, the moral decisions that we most commonly face are not especially difficult to make, and it is not unreasonable to believe that we can resolve our moral uncertainties in those situations. Therefore, decision-making under moral uncertainty is not a topic that urgently needs investigation.

However, this assessment underestimates the complexity of the moral problems of everyday life. We must continually decide how we shall use the resources under our control—our money, for example. The contemporary debate about our moral obligations as individuals to contribute to the relief of poverty and suffering in the world-at-large demonstrates the complexity of those issues.[3] Some ethicists contend that our obligations to alleviate suffering are much greater than even the more altruistic among us recognize. Perhaps the radicals who argue that average middle-class Americans and Western Europeans ought to divest themselves of most of their material wealth in order to feed the world's hungry children are mistaken. But unless we are completely certain that they are mistaken, moral uncertainty infects our decisions about how we shall use our wealth.

Part of the reason moral controversies and quandaries occur so frequently is that there is still no consensus among ethicists about which moral theory, moral principles, or canons of moral reasoning we should use to ground our moral beliefs and judgments. Several years ago, Alasdair MacIntyre lamented:

> Methods of justification for individual [moral] rules or principles are over-abundant: we have utilitarian justifications, contractarian justifications, universalizability justifications, intuitionist justifications, and each of these in more than one variety. But from Ross to Rawls the treatment of priority questions is notoriously weak. For it always presupposes some prior unargued position about how our values are to be organized.[4]

Some philosophers have recently argued for abandoning the traditional foundationalist doctrine that moral judgments can be justified only by appealing to established moral theories or principles. The reformers have proposed alternatives based on communitarian views and casuistical models, among others.[5] It is very unlikely, however, that adopting these new approaches would eliminate moral uncertainty entirely. Difficulties in applying them to concrete situations will engender doubts about the rightness or wrongness of actions—doubts that will be compounded by any uncertainties about the accuracy of the proposed methods.

In any event, the significance of Example 1.1 does not hinge on the correctness of ethical foundationalism. Moral decisions that are relevantly similar to that of the example may arise even for someone who rejects all universal moral theories or principles.[6] For the description of the situation says nothing about the source of the agent's uncertainties. It makes no mention of moral theories, moral principles, or rules of moral reasoning. Therefore, the problem of moral decision-making that it raises is a general one that does not presuppose a particular paradigm of moral reasoning.

Some philosophers have yet other reasons to dispute my claim that decision-making under moral uncertainty is as serious and pervasive a problem as I am suggesting. They would claim that the resources currently available to moral philosophy are sufficient for practical decision-making purposes, even though controversies continue to rage about such topics as abortion, capital punishment, affirmative action, and animal rights. The argument is that for many controversial issues the most plausible moral theories, like utilitarian and Kantian theories, support compatible moral judgments about the moral rightness of certain actions and thus afford moral agents sufficient guidance about what to do. Accordingly, our uncertainties about which theory is correct do not stand in the way of identifying morally acceptable alternatives, since there is sufficient overlap among the competing theories.[7]

The claim that the common ground among moral theories is large enough to encompass practical solutions to contentious moral problems is plausible only if we rule certain perspectives, like ethical egoism, out of court. However, even if we accept this dubious "overlap thesis," it does not mean that decision-makers are out of the woods, since they still must apply the competing theories to the moral decisions they face. In a concrete situation, it is often difficult to tell whether a particular action would be morally right according to a given theory. Some of our uncertainties about the rightness or wrongness of one of our alternatives emanate from our difficulties in applying the theory to the situation. Just as two rule utilitarians may come to very different conclusions about the morality of capital punishment, a third individual may be unsure which of the two has applied the theory correctly. The difficulties of applying moral theories to concrete situations may allow proponents of the "overlap thesis" to deflect their critics' counterexamples. However, the sword is double-edged, since those same difficulties may defeat their own efforts to verify the thesis.

I also doubt that it is even *in principle* possible for us to reach universal agreement on the fundamental principles of moral obligation—at least, not by using completely rational methods.[8] I doubt, for example, that it is possible to settle all *rational disputes* about the extent to which we may favor our own interests and those of our families, friends, and compatriots over the interests of the world at large. (By "rational disputes" I mean disagreements in which all the parties are sincere and are able and willing to follow the arguments to their logical conclusions.) And if some disagreements about the basic standards of moral obligation cannot be rationally settled, then it is likely that we shall sometimes be unsure which standard we should base our moral decisions on. Perhaps some moral questions are like unsolvable problems in mathematics and are not subject to rational resolution. Or maybe ethical skepticism is true in the sense that we can never be (epistemically) justified in accepting any comprehensive moral theory or account of moral reasoning. This may partly explain why some issues have remained contentious throughout the history of moral philosophy.[9]

However, we need not embrace moral skepticism in order to see that decision-making under moral uncertainty is often unavoidable. For there is virtually no prospect that all important moral problems will be conclusively solved in the foreseeable future. In the meantime, many of us (professional ethicists included) will have to act under moral uncertainty. Moral uncertainty is especially likely to beset the moral decisions of individuals who recognize and appreciate the complexities of the pertinent moral and philosophical questions. Although philosophical inquiry is open-ended and can continue for centuries without producing consensus, decision-making cannot be indefinitely postponed. Sometimes I must decide what to do *now*. And unless it does not matter what I do (on those occasions), not all answers are equally reasonable.

The pressing *practical* question then is how we should use whatever information is available about the moral rightness or wrongness of our action alternatives in order to make reasonable action choices. To ignore the question of how we should make such decisions is to ignore the landscape of moral uncertainty in which many of our moral decisions are situated. If moral philosophy is to provide real, *practical* guidance to real-world moral agents, it has no choice but to address this question.

Rationality and Moral Uncertainty

In Example 1.1, my overriding purpose as agent is to do what is morally right. In the view of many philosophers, this *should* be my purpose. According to this traditional view, not regarding moral considerations as always trumping non-moral considerations is a serious mistake—one that misunderstands the nature of morality itself. This view is controversial, however. An influential minority of philosophers have challenged the morality-is-paramount view and have argued that, in some instances, moral considerations should be subordinated to nonmoral ones. Bernard Williams is one prominent contemporary philosopher who supports this view. In the next chapter, I shall defend the traditional morality-is-paramount view against Williams's "moral luck" argument. However, I have no illusions that I shall settle this enduring issue once and for all. My objective in this section is to show that even if we accept the thesis that moral considerations are not always paramount, decision-making under moral uncertainty is still an important problem for philosophers to address.

Let us suppose, for the moment, that in Example 1.1 I am correct in believing that moral considerations have exclusive importance *for my decision*. In that event, for the reasons already discussed, z is the only action choice that "makes sense." If morality is paramount in the situation, then x would be the worst choice and, given the my uncertainty about the moral rightness of y, it makes no sense to choose y over z. Thus, *all things considered*, or *in the final analysis*, I should choose z.

In this section and in the remainder of this book, it will be convenient to use the following terminology. Let us say that an agent who does what is reasonable *all things considered* or *in the final analysis* acts "rationally." And conversely, one who acts "rationally" does what she should do *all things considered*. Thus, as I shall use the term *rational*, to assert that it is rational for someone to do x is to claim final, all-things-considered justification for her doing x.[10]

The reader should note that my use of "rational" varies from other, more common uses by philosophers. Many ethicists associate rational action with self-interested behavior. And many philosophers disqualify self-interest as a possible moral consideration on conceptual grounds. As Derek Parfit has reported, "We have expelled Egoism from Ethics, and we now doubt that acting morally is 'required by Reason.'"[11] Other ethicists enjoin us to adopt a "moral point of view," from which we are debarred from giving special consideration to our own interests.[12] Egoism resurfaces, however, as a *nonmoral* decision criterion that sometimes overrides moral rightness as the governing criterion for action choice.

Moral rightness and rationality in action end up as separate and often conflicting standards between which agents must somehow choose.[13]

Unfortunately, philosophers who accept this rubric have offered little clear advice about how we are to choose between the two when they conflict. Even if we are able to resolve our moral doubts, we may encounter other impasses about the relative importance of morality and rationality. For I may find myself in a situation in which I should (morally) do x and I should (rationally) do y and I must decide whether to do x or y. There is no reason to expect this problem to be easier to solve than that of determining when self-interest is the dominant *moral* consideration under the traditional, expansive concept of morality. If morality and rationality are competitors, then, in order to decide what to do, I may need some decision criterion that would tell me *in each instance* how to choose between acting morally and acting rationally. Such a criterion, which would tell me what to do *all things considered*, would pick the winner in each morality-versus-rationality contest.

The tradition that contemporary moral philosophy has largely abandoned (unwisely, in my view) regarded ethical egoism as a bona fide theory of moral rightness and also recognized self-interest as a possible *moral* consideration. Assuredly, there are plausible arguments against ethical egoism that we should consider carefully before subscribing to it. However, it is unclear why similar criticisms would not work equally well against egoism as a nonmoral decision criterion or self-interest as a nonmoral consideration in decision-making.

In the conceptual scheme that I adopt here, rationality in action is the all-things-considered decision criterion. Therefore, its principles would inform us of the role that moral rightness should, in the final analysis, play in our action choices. As I shall use "rational," there is no question whether morality or rationality is more important for a particular decision. Acting rationally is *necessarily* what we should do, all things considered. Consequently, if moral rightness conflicts with rationality, we should, all things considered, choose rationality. From this perspective, to ask about the proper role of moral considerations in decision-making is to ask about the relationship between morality and rationality. My use of "rational" simply provides a convenient way of expressing judgments about what we should do, all things considered. Other notions of rationality leave us in need of a suitable expression.

Let us return to the discussion with which this section began: Williams and other philosophers regard moral rightness as just one standard for action choice and evaluation among others. They contend that for many decisions nonmoral considerations are more important than, or at least as important as, moral considerations.[14] If they are right, then my claim that I should always choose an action the moral rightness of which I am sure over any action the moral rightness of which I am unsure is much too sweeping and must be qualified. They would argue that in Example 1.1 my having as my primary aim doing what is morally right may itself be a mistake. For if the situation is one in which nonmoral considerations outweigh moral considerations, I would err if I chose z solely on the grounds that I was certain of its moral rightness.

For the moment, let us accept the hypothesis that morality can be overridden by nonmoral standards of action choice. There are two ways in which we might conceive this occurring: First, there may be a ranking among moral and nonmoral standards where some nonmoral norms rank higher than moral norms. Here higher ranking norms are to be applied to one's action alternatives before lower ranking norms are consulted. Lower ranking norms are used only to break ties among multiple alternatives that satisfy the higher ranking norms. For example, if norm N_1 takes precedence over norm N_2 and x, y, and z are action alternatives, then if z does not satisfy N_1 we are to apply N_2 only to x and y. The higher ranking standard N_1 eliminates z from further consideration. Let us call this the *lexicographical* version of the morality-can-be-overridden thesis.[15]

The second way in which we might think of morality as subject to being overridden by nonmoral considerations is to regard rationality in action as maximizing weighted sums of the form $R(x) = w_1R_1(x) + w_2R_2(x) + \ldots + w_nR_n(x)$, where $R_1, R_2, \ldots, R_n$ are the relevant moral and nonmoral decision criteria, the $R_i(x)$s are the respective degrees to which alternative x would satisfy the n criteria R_i in the situation, the w_is are the respective degrees of importance that the n criteria R_i have for the decision, and $R(x)$ may be thought of as x's "degree of rationality." An action x is rational if $R(x)$ is at least as great as $R(y)$ for any other alternative y. Nonmoral considerations override moral considerations whenever one or more morally wrong action alternatives would maximize R. Let us call this the weighted sum version of the morality-can-be-overridden thesis.[16]

It is not hard to see why the two versions of the morality-can-be-overridden thesis differ. For the weighted sum version, moral rightness will be one of the R_is, say R_1. On some occasions, it may turn out that x would be morally right and that w_1, the weight that moral rightness has in the situation, is greater than any of $w_2, w_3, \ldots, w_n$, and yet that $R(x) < R(y)$ for some y because of the values of the other terms in the expressions for $R(x)$ and $R(y)$. Hence, according to the weighted sum version of the morality-can-be-overridden thesis, moral rightness can be outweighed by the nonmoral criteria even if its weight is greater than that of any other single criterion. This is not true for the lexicographical version. Another difference between the two versions is that the weighted sum version allows for degrees of satisfaction of the criteria $R_1, R_2, \ldots$ whereas the lexicographical version assumes all-or-nothing satisfaction of the criteria.

It may appear that either version of the morality-can-be-overridden thesis significantly palliates the difficulties of decision-making under moral uncertainty. For when it would be rational for us to choose our actions on the basis of nonmoral criteria, we need not worry whether our actions are right or wrong. Thus, it might seem, the problem of decision-making under moral uncertainty is much less serious and important than I have alleged.

One who denies that morality is *always* paramount might nevertheless grant that morality is *sometimes* paramount in situations, like Example 1.1, in which the decision-maker is uncertain about the moral rightness or wrongness of some of her alternatives. If such situations are not uncommon, then this is sufficient to make the case that rational decision-making under moral uncertainty is a problem that warrants philosophical examination. I suspect that decisions of this sort are not exceptional.

I wish to make a stronger point, however: even if there are situations in which moral considerations are not paramount, determining what one should do *all things considered* may necessitate taking moral uncertainty into account. To see why, let us look at situations of the following type:

Example 1.2

I must choose among alternative acts *x*, *y*, and *z*. I have the same information about their moral rightness or wrongness as in Example 1.1—namely, that *x* would probably be morally wrong, that *y* would probably be morally right, and that *z* would certainly be morally right. However, there is a nonmoral norm (e.g., self-interest) that, for this situation, exceeds morality in importance and that I know, with certainty, would proscribe *x* and would permit both *y* and *z*.

Table 1.1 summarizes Example 1.2.

What would be the rational choice of action in Example 1.2? If morality had no bearing in the situation, then I should simply follow the nonmoral standard *N*, which would mean that *y* and *z* would both be rational choices. Let us suppose, however, that morality is pertinent in the situation, though less so than the nonmoral norm, and that no other standards have any relevance for my decision. Without the modifiers "probably" and "certainly" in Table 1.1, the nonmoral norm *N* and the moral norm *M* would have the same implications for the alternatives *x*, *y*, and *z*. Both *y* and *z* would be rational choices, according to both versions of the morality-can-be-overridden thesis. With the modifiers in place, however, *z* is the sole rational choice for the following reasons: *x* fails to satisfy the higher ranking norm *N* and thus is eliminated, according to the lexicographical version, and, furthermore, since *y* and *z* both satisfy *N*, *M* comes into play. At this stage, the situation is essentially the same as in Example 1.1, and the reasons for choosing *z* over *y* are the same as before. For the weighted sum version, since *N* outweighs *M*, no alternative proscribed by *N* could be a reasonable choice. This eliminates *x*. The remaining alternatives, *y* and *z*, differ only in that there is certainty that *M* is satisfied only in the case of *z*. This makes *z* the reasonable choice.

In presenting Example 1.2, I have used the phrases "probably right" and "probably wrong" in relation to the agent's alternatives. And throughout this discussion and much of the rest of this book, I shall employ the notion of the *probability* that an action alternative would be morally right or wrong. Some may question whether such a notion makes sense. In Example 1.1, I portrayed the agent as *believing* that an alternative would be right or wrong and as being *completely confident* in an alternative's moral rightness. However, in Example 1.2, I presented the relevant information in terms of each alternative's being "probably" right/

Table 1.1   Decision Table for Example 1.2

	nonmoral norm (*N*)	moral rightness/wrongness (*M*)
x	proscribed	probably wrong
y	permitted	probably right
z	permitted	certainly right

wrong or "certainly" right/wrong. Thus I appear to conflate the agent's *believing* that an alternative A would be right (wrong) with A's being *probably right (wrong)* and the agent's being *completely confident* of A's rightness (wrongness) with A's being *certainly right (wrong)*.

Does this mean that I am a subjectivist about probability? Not necessarily! An agent may base her beliefs about the moral rightness or wrongness of her alternatives on her other beliefs—for example, her beliefs about the alternatives' consequences or about the moral status of certain affected entities. And she may regard it as a *fact* that the latter beliefs *justify* her moral beliefs to degrees commensurate with their strength. If such epistemic facts exist, then she could conceivably be mistaken in believing that an alternative x_1 would *probably* be morally right or that alternative x_2 would *probably* be morally wrong. That is, the *true* probabilities may deviate from her beliefs. I do not rule out the possibility that the relevant moral probabilities for decision-makers are at least sometimes *objective* probabilities and that we may sometimes challenge their probability assessments. Moreover, decision-makers may have doubts about the accuracy of their own assessments. Later we shall consider situations in which the decision-makers are uncertain about the magnitudes of the relevant probabilities as well as about the moral rightness or wrongness of their action alternatives. We shall see how this second-order uncertainty can sometimes affect what agents should, in the final analysis, do. For the moment, the important message is that we need not commit ourselves to any particular philosophical view about probability, except to exclude those views according to which talk about the probability of an action's being morally right or morally wrong is nonsense. The empirical fact that moral uncertainty occurs, and occurs in varying degrees, is enough to show that an intelligible and important notion of probability can properly be applied to our moral judgments.

We should not, however, confuse the issue of the subjectivity or objectivity of moral probabilities with the quite different issue of whether moral judgments themselves are fact-stating assertions. For some noncognitivists, R. M. Hare for example, moral reasoning is no less important in enabling us to arrive at *justified* moral judgments than it would be if moral judgments were capable of stating facts. An agent's doubts about whether the judgment that alternative A would be morally right was justified would differ in no significant *practical* respects from doubts about whether alternative A would be morally right. If such doubts can be "too large" or "too small," then, epistemically speaking, there is a correct degree of doubt—a level of doubt that the agent "should" (epistemically) have. Such a "correct degree of doubt" would suggest the existence of a true, "objective" probability. None of this would require the moral judgment about A to be a fact-stating assertion.

Example 1.2 shows how the problem of decision-making under moral uncertainty can arise even if moral considerations are subordinate to nonmoral ones. There is no reason to suppose that moral problems become more tractable when moral norms are secondary to or are outweighed by nonmoral norms. Nor is there any reason to believe that morality declines in significance as our moral uncertainties increase. Therefore, unless we are ethical nihilists or amoralists, we cannot avoid the necessity of taking moral uncertainty into account.

It is interesting to see what happens under the weighted sum version of the morality-can-be-overridden thesis when degrees of satisfaction of the R_is enter the picture. For instance,

Example 1.3

As in Example 1.2, I must choose among alternative acts x, y, and z. As before, x would probably be morally wrong, y would probably be morally right, and z would certainly be morally right. Again, there is a nonmoral norm N that, for this situation, has more importance than morality. However, here it is possible to satisfy N to varying degrees between 0 (minimum possible satisfaction) and 1 (maximum possible satisfaction).

Table 1.2 represents the situation.

For the weighted sum version, we are interested in which alternative maximizes the "degree of rationality" R, which we calculate using the preceding weighted sum expression. We shall ignore, for now, the practical problems of measuring the w_is and the R_i quantities in the expression for R. We imagine that I am somehow able to obtain exact measurements of all of the w_is and $R_i(\_\_)$s except for the $R_i(\_\_)$s that represent the moral rightness or wrongness of my alternatives. This means that I am uncertain of the value of some of the $R_i(\_\_)$ terms—namely, those that represent the moral rightness or wrongness of the alternatives x and y. Since we are assessing "degrees of rationality," we shall have to represent the moral rightness or wrongness of the alternatives as numerical quantities—for example, by letting 1 represent moral rightness and 0 represent moral wrongness.[17] Thus we are supposing that I am uncertain whether the values of $R_i(x)$ and $R_i(y)$ are 1 or 0 for some i.

In Example 1.3, if I wish to maximize R, which alternative should I choose? The answer, of course, depends on the magnitudes of the w_is for this particular situation and on those of the R_is for each of the alternatives. Here there are two norms, N and M. We assume that the degrees of satisfaction of N and M are scaled so that they range between 0 and 1.[18] This means that the degrees of satisfaction of the moral norm M for each alternative will be either 0 or 1, since moral rightness comes in only two "sizes"—right and wrong. It is easy to show that for some values of w_1, w_2, $N(x)$, $N(y)$, and $N(z)$, the values of $M(x)$, $M(y)$, and $M(z)$ would have no effect on which alternative maximized R. For example, if $w_1 = .9$, $w_2 = .1$, $N(x) = 1$, $N(y) = .2$, and $N(z) = 0$, then $R(x) = .9 + .1M(x)$, $R(y) = .18 + .1M(y)$, and $R(z) = .1M(z)$. Since $M(x)$, $M(y)$, and $M(z)$ are all either 0 or 1, the minimum possible value of $R(x)$ would be .9 while the maximum possible values of $R(y)$ and $R(z)$ would be .28 and .1, respectively. Thus $R(x)$ would be larger than either $R(y)$ or $R(z)$, regardless of the M values.

Table 1.2   Decision Table for Example 1.3

	nonmoral norm (N)	moral rightness/wrongness (M)
x	$N(x)$	probably wrong
y	$N(y)$	probably right
z	$N(z)$	certainly right

However, it is also easy to think of values of the w_i and R_i terms where the magnitudes of $M(x)$, $M(y)$, and $M(z)$ are critical. For example, let $w_1 = .4$ and $w_2 = .6$, and let $N(x) = .6$, $N(y) = 1$, and $N(z) = .4$. Under these assumptions, $R(x) = .4M(x) + .36$, $R(y) = .4M(y) + .6$, and $R(z) = .4M(z) + .24$. Since ex hypothesi I am certain that z would be morally right, $M(z) = 1$ and therefore $R(z) = .64$. And since $M(x)$ and $M(y)$ are each either 0 or 1, the two possible values of $R(x)$ are .36 and .76 and the possible values of $R(y)$ are .6 and 1. Therefore, which R value is larger obviously depends on $M(x)$ and $M(y)$. If y is highly likely to be morally right and x is unlikely to be morally right, then the probability that the true value of $R(y)$ is the larger of its two possible values is much greater than the probability that the true value of $R(x)$ is its larger possible value. This also means that the true value of $R(y)$ is very likely to be greater than .64. Under these conditions, it might be reasonable to choose y over both x and z. However, if the moral rightness of both x and y is doubtful, then the rational choice may be z.

Perhaps some will object to the preceding analysis on the grounds that it fails to consider other ways in which moral uncertainty could enter into our practical deliberations. For example, for the lexicographical version of the morality-can-be-overridden thesis, one might simply ignore any norm in our hierarchy of norms if she is unsure of its content or of its implications for her decision. This would mean that if one is faced with a decision for which moral rightness is on the list of relevant norms and she is uncertain of the moral rightness or wrongness of some of the alternatives, then she would ignore moral considerations altogether and make the decision on the basis of the other criteria. However, this decision strategy would give counterintuitive results for the decision in Example 1.1. In that situation, I am 100% sure that z would be morally right; my moral uncertainty is about x and y only. It would make little sense to ignore moral rightness altogether if I were sure of the moral rightness of one of my alternatives. To insist on perfect certainty about the moral rightness or wrongness of *all* of my alternatives as a necessary condition for taking morality into consideration would be unreasonably stringent. If I can do what I am sure would be morally right and doing what is morally right is very important, then why not take that information into account?[19]

The purpose of this somewhat technical discussion of Examples 1.2 and 1.3 is to show that regardless of how we construe the morality-can-be-overridden thesis, rational decision-making requires us to take our moral uncertainties into account. How to make decisions under moral uncertainty is an important problem, whether or not we regard moral considerations as always overriding nonmoral ones. In general, if we should weigh moral considerations against nonmoral considerations in deciding what to do, there will be fewer occasions on which our moral uncertainties should affect our action choices than if moral considerations should always govern our decisions. However, if moral considerations usually or often outweigh nonmoral factors, then moral uncertainties should often make a difference in our actions.

Taking the problem of rational decision-making under moral uncertainty seriously also means reconsidering the traditional identification of morality with rationality in action. The view, first enunciated by Kant and, until recently, the prevailing view among moral philosophers, regarded the two as equivalent in the sense that all morally right actions turn out to be rational actions, and conversely.[20] A variation on this view holds that morality is a proper subset of rationality in action, since not all decisions that present opportunities for rational or irrational action involve moral considerations.[21] It follows from either view that *necessarily* we should always do what is morally right when we make moral choices. Lawrence Becker expresses this Kantian thesis in terms of moral justification:

> What the demand for a moral justification of an act does is to "detach" the act from its connection with special or restricted assumptions about what sorts of considerations are relevant and ask for a justification of it no holds barred. If that is so, then a valid moral judgment is by definition overriding. Its action-guidance is "inescapable" or "binding" in the sense that there is nothing more to consider—nothing which might be introduced to enlarge the inquiry further and make the prescription subject to withdrawal.[22]

Becker describes moral judgments as "final" in the sense that when "valid" they are based on all relevant considerations and thus nothing more need enter into our deliberations. His view implies that we should think of moral considerations not merely as outweighing nonmoral considerations but rather as *preempting* them in our action choices. Henceforth, I shall refer to this claim about the all-inclusiveness of moral considerations as the "finality thesis."[23]

Example 1.1 shows what is wrong with the finality thesis. My uncertainty about the rightness of y makes it irrational for me to choose y over z, the rightness of which I am certain. Therefore, even if my moral judgment about y is "valid" (in Becker's terms), I should not choose y. There is something more to consider—namely, the degrees of certainty with which I am able to judge the rightness of y and that of its principal competitor, z. On my view, moral considerations are still "overriding" insofar as my primary aim is to do what is morally right. However, I must take into account how certain or uncertain I am about the moral rightness of my alternatives. I should, all things considered, choose an action the rightness of which I am certain over any other action the rightness of which I am uncertain. The flaw in the finality thesis is that it ignores the need to take our moral uncertainties into account.

Why Have Ethicists Ignored Decision-making under Moral Uncertainty?

If the question "What shall I do when I am uncertain what I morally ought to do?" is as important and urgent as I have claimed, it is remarkable that philosophers have had so little to say about the question. How can we account for their lack of interest? There are at least four plausible explanations. One is that philosophers view their assigned task as answering *moral* questions—that is, questions about right and wrong, good and bad, just and unjust, and so forth—and not as answering questions about rational action (in my sense of the term). On this view, their contribution to solving the problem of moral decision-making is to resolve as much moral uncertainty as possible so that it will not hinder moral agents any more than necessary. Of course, ideally they would like to eliminate moral uncertainty altogether. However, as we have already seen, this is an excessively narrow view of ethicists' role. Since the total elimination of moral uncertainty is an unrealistic goal, at least in the short run moral agents need practical advice about what to do in situations in which they have no alternative the moral rightness of which they are completely sure. If moral philosophy is to meet that need, then it must provide an adequate normative account of moral decision-making— one that does not ignore moral uncertainty.

A second possible reason ethicists are unconcerned about the problem of decision-making under moral uncertainty is that some of them regard the continuing resistance of basic moral problems to rational solution as evidence for the inherent subjectivity or relativity of morality. If fundamental moral quandaries and disagreements occur because "moral truth" is a matter of individual or societal determination, then there are no preexisting, objective moral facts about which we can be uncertain. According to this view, it is a mistake to see moral uncertainty and ordinary nonmoral factual uncertainty as two varieties of the same phenomenon. It is a confusion, one might argue, to think of moral uncertainty as uncertainty about some independent truth that is external to or independent of human beings and human communities. "Moral uncertainty" is a misnomer that misleads us into thinking that there is objective moral truth that we can, at least in principle, discover. We must understand that moral uncertainty is to be resolved by decision rather than by rational inquiry. And posing the problem as one of rational decision-making under moral uncertainty perpetuates the misrepresentation.

The arguments against moral subjectivism and moral relativism are well known, and I shall not rehash them here. I find some of them quite convincing, and I believe that they pose insuperable obstacles for subjectivists and relativists. However, the principles for decision-making under moral uncertainty that we shall discuss in the following chapters are not inconsistent with either position, for those principles assume no particular metaethical position on the nature of morality or moral truth. Unless subjectivists and relativists are willing to say that any choice of action by a moral agent is as "good," morally speaking, as any other, their evaluations of alternative actions can be taken into account in applying the principles we shall consider. And it is clear that subjectivists and relativists do recommend some action choices over others. Simplistically stated, subjectivists claim that my belief that a certain action would be right for me to choose makes it morally right for me. Similarly, for me to choose an action that I judge to be wrong would be wrong for me. Since I am the person who must make my decisions, subjectivism provides a moral criterion for my action choices. Furthermore, if I am uncertain whether moral subjectivism is correct, I can register that uncertainty in applying a decision principle to my decisions. In fact, it would be irrational for me to do otherwise. Similar observations may be made about ethical relativism. Therefore, neither subjectivism nor relativism presents any serious difficulties for the decision principles we shall discuss.

The empirical fact that moral agents, both individually and collectively, have moral uncertainties raises an interesting question about the tenability of the subjectivist and relativist positions. For suppose I am a subjectivist and I must decide whether to do x or y on a particular occasion. My subjectivist principle tells me that whatever I judge about the moral rightness or wrongness of x and y is, ipso facto, correct. But suppose I am completely ambivalent about the rightness or wrongness of x and y. What then should I do, all things considered, if I wish to decide on moral grounds? Subjectivists appear not to have an answer. Perhaps some will say that I should simply decide ex nihilo about the moral rightness of x and y. After all, if it is my judging that an alternative is morally right or wrong that makes it so for me, then it really does not matter what I judge as long as I judge something. But can I really generate moral judgments ex nihilo? I can, of course, say to myself such things as "x is morally right" or "y is morally wrong." But merely saying such things is not actually to judge their rightness or wrongness, unless I believe what I say. Judging involves more than just pronouncing or thinking the words. And can I really believe something about the rightness or wrongness of x or y simply by choosing to do so? If ethical subjectivism is correct, the only adequate evidence that I could have for a moral judgment is that I already believe it. Thus the flight from complete ambivalence about the moral rightness or wrongness of x and y to judgment of their rightness or wrongness would never get off the ground.

A subjectivist might claim that it is extremely rare for a moral agent to be completely ambivalent about the moral rightness of all of her alternatives. It is much more likely that for my decision between x and y in the preceding paragraph I shall be at least a little inclined to judge x or y one way or the other. But if this is true, I may encounter decisions similar to my decision in Example 1.1. That is, I may have to choose among alternatives x, y, and z toward which I have the following attitudes: I am inclined to judge x as morally wrong and y as morally right, but I am totally committed to the moral rightness of z. For such a decision what should I do, all things considered? From a subjectivist perspective, do I view y and z as equivalent, since I judge both to be morally right? But if it is my judging that one of my alternatives is right or wrong that makes my judgment true for me, then it would seem that the more strongly inclined I am toward a judgment that an alternative is morally right, the more strongly inclined I should be toward performing that action. And if I wish to take the strength of my inclinations toward moral judgments into account, then it appears that I am tacitly appealing to a decision principle that advises me to choose actions that I am most strongly inclined to judge as morally right.

Ethical subjectivists would perhaps deny that, properly speaking, decision-makers can be certain or uncertain of their judgments about the moral rightness or wrongness of their alternatives, since they would deny the existence of any objective moral facts about which agents can be certain or uncertain. However, clearly decision-makers are ambivalent toward or "committed" to such judgments to varying degrees, and the proper role of degrees of commitment or ambivalence in moral decision-making from a subjectivistic perspective would seem to be analogous to that to be played by moral certainty or uncertainty in the decision principles we shall develop in the following chapters.[24]

Essentially the same point can be made about moral decision-making from a relativistic perspective. We can easily imagine a society in which opinion on a particular moral question is evenly divided. We might think of such a society as a whole as having no opinion on that issue. Of course, if ethical relativism is true, then there is no fact other than the views of the members of that society that can determine the correctness of moral judgments about that issue. Individuals whose decisions involve that issue in significant ways are left, it seems, with no way of deciding *on moral grounds* what to do. And even if we can rule out such a division of moral opinion in the real world, there will still be moral decisions for which, although the society approves each of two alternatives, it approves one of them more strongly (e.g., with greater popularity) than it approves the other. And for such cases, some decision principle that takes strength-of-approval into account would apparently be needed.

A critic might argue that at least one metaethical perspective—ethical nihilism—is incompatible with any general approach to decision-making under moral uncertainty. If ethical nihilism is true, then no moral judgments about the moral rightness or wrongness of actions can ever be true or justified. If so, then probabilities that actions are morally right or wrong are counterfeit currency and decision-makers should not deal in them. However, we need not worry about criticisms based on such an implausible doctrine as ethical nihilism. Surely there are actions that we know with virtual certainty to be morally wrong. We know, for example, that it is wrong for someone to torture to death an innocent child for trifling personal amusement. Perhaps it is debatable which moral theory or account of moral reasoning ultimately grounds such a judgment, but that it is true or, at least, justified is not in doubt. And if we know this with virtual certainty, then we also know with virtual certainty that ethical nihilism is false. Even if a decision-maker wished to entertain some minuscule doubt about the falsity of ethical nihilism, rationality would advise choosing actions according to some decision principle that accommodates that kind of moral uncertainty.

A third possible reason why ethicists have failed to address the problem of decision-making under moral uncertainty is that some of them have recently concluded that questions about the moral rightness of our actions are less important and less central to moral philosophy than questions about the goodness of persons and their lives and the excellence of their characters. MacIntyre and other recent proponents of "virtue ethics" have argued that philosophers should pay more attention to the latter questions and less attention to the former. MacIntyre's main thesis in *After Virtue: A Study in Moral Theory* is that the social roles and cultural traditions that we inherit are our proper moral touchstones and that we should take as our primary ethical concern the entire "narrative" of our lives, rather than our choices of individual actions. It is virtue, he claims, that sustains us in our individual and collective pursuit of the good. This means that ethicists should regard virtue, rather than obligation, as the primary subject matter of normative ethics.

For MacIntyre, "the notion of 'an' action, while of the highest practical importance, is always a potentially misleading abstraction."[25] It is misleading, he says, because "I can only answer the question 'What am I to do?' if I can answer the prior question 'Of what story or stories do I find myself a part?' "[26] Many of us would agree that long-term decisions about such things as one's career, lifestyle, and role in society are the most important moral choices that we make. Contemporary moral philosophy perhaps devotes too little attention to them and too much attention to sensationalized issues that most moral agents face infrequently or never (e.g., decisions about physician-assisted suicide). And few ethicists would deny that what we envision as the purposes and ultimate goals of our lives should play a central role in how we conduct our current affairs. Clearly it should, and I shall attempt in the final chapter of this book to describe that role in some detail. But we execute plans for our lives only by performing the requisite individual actions. And since we cannot make ourselves virtuous merely by acts of will, even acquiring or reinforcing a virtuous character requires choosing appropriate and effective individual actions. Perhaps the phrase "while of the highest practical importance" in the preceding quotation expresses MacIntyre's admission of the importance of individual action choice. But if so, then he is admitting either that his "virtue ethics" approach does not address the main practical question or that it constitutes yet another view about how we should make moral decisions—one we might add to the list of such methods that he provides in the passage quoted previously. And unless we are totally convinced that his is the correct method— that is, the one that when employed yields morally acceptable choices of actions— some of our moral uncertainty will remain unresolved. Moreover, even if we were totally convinced of the method's correctness, we would still have to apply it to concrete decisions. And there is little evidence that "virtue ethics" theories are significantly easier to apply to real-world decisions than utilitarian, Kantian, and other prominent moral theories.[27]

Perhaps some will say that the whole question of how to choose individual actions is relatively unproblematic and therefore less important for ethics than the question of what kind of life one should live or what kind of person one should be.[28] Ethicists of this persuasion would claim that once the latter questions are answered, problems of action choice will be straightforwardly solved. However, we should have no great difficulty seeing that this is not the case. In order to live a life of a certain kind, obviously I must act in certain ways. For example, if I choose to lead a life of altruism, then I must act altruistically in individual cases. I must therefore make decisions about which persons I shall seek to benefit and to what extent I shall sacrifice my own material well-being in that pursuit. I may also decide whom to take as my role model(s). Do I choose Mother Teresa? Karl Marx? Jonas Salk? Winston Churchill? And how do I go about patterning my behavior after him or her? These and myriad other details must be settled in order to implement my choice of lifestyle.

Similar questions arise about how to realize one's aspirations to be a particular kind of person. If I desire to become a person of great wisdom and courage, I must decide how to go about becoming that sort of person. Again, details are important. Do I study the writings of great philosophers? Do I undergo psychotherapy in order to try to understand why I am presently unwise and cowardly? Do I seek to cultivate courage and wisdom in myself by performing acts like those that courageous, wise people perform? And, for the last method of transformation, do I put myself in situations in which I have opportunities to act courageously? Do I, for example, volunteer for military service? May I instill courage in myself by killing enemy soldiers in a just war? And, if so, how do I tell whether a particular war is just? These questions appear no easier to answer than those that concern the rightness or wrongness of individual actions.

The point of these remarks is that we do not avoid the problem of individual action choice by adopting a "virtue ethics" perspective. Unless we act in effective ways, we shall not realize in ourselves the character traits that we value. And unless we deliberate carefully before acting, our actions will not effect the changes we seek. The notion of an individual action, far from being an unimportant abstraction, is an essential part of the conceptual apparatus that we need if our vision of the good life is to have any effect on how we actually live.

A fourth possible reason ethicists have not recognized decision-making under moral uncertainty as an important topic is that they believe the solution to that problem is implicit in the positions that they take on the moral questions that they address. It is implicit, they might argue, because the moral judgments that they offer should be understood as provisional and subject to future revision or refutation. If, for example, a philosopher argues that abortion as a means of birth control is morally justified, usually she neither claims nor insinuates that she is completely sure of the "truth" of that moral judgment. Except perhaps for mathematical reasoning, we should not expect our arguments to establish their conclusions with perfect certainty. Whatever uncertainties we have about our premises are transmitted to our conclusion. Successful arguments justify us in accepting their conclusions but, in general, do not assure us that their conclusions are true. This is no less true for moral arguments than for nonmoral arguments. And this, according to the view we are considering here, is enough for practical decision-making purposes. If A argues successfully that it would be morally right for her to do x, then A has sufficient reason not only to believe that it would be morally right for her to do x but also to decide to do x. None of this requires that A be certain about what it is morally right for her to do. Thus there is no need to consider moral uncertainty explicitly or to make it an ingredient of the deliberation process.

This, I suspect, is essentially the defense that most philosophers would offer for not addressing the question "What shall I do when I am uncertain what I morally ought to do?" It makes two assumptions: (1) In our moral reasoning, we need not take into account how certain or uncertain we are about the premises of our arguments as long as we have sufficient reason to accept those premises, and (2) we may, all things considered, perform any action that we have adequate reason to believe to be morally right. Both claims, I shall later argue, are false. They are false because in order to act rationally we must maximize the probabilities that our actions are morally right. Doing so requires that we take into account the likelihood that the premises of our moral argument are true. And maximizing the likelihood that our actions are morally right means that we shall sometimes decline alternatives that we have good reason to believe would be morally right.

The task now before us is to find acceptable decision strategies that take our moral uncertainties into account. We hope to discover a principle or set of principles that will enlighten us about how to make rational choices in situations in which we are uncertain what we morally ought to do. This will be our main objective in chapter 2.

SBRLSMD (Whitechapel)

Two

Principles for Decision-making under Moral Uncertainty

In chapter 1, we saw that in the real world the urgent practical problem for decision-makers is how to choose among action alternatives the moral rightness or wrongness of which they are uncertain. The problem is especially serious when moral considerations are paramount. No attempt to avoid or finesse the problem can succeed. However, so far we have said little about what *in general* we should do, all things considered, when we find ourselves in such situations. It will be our task in this chapter to discover and defend a principle or set of principles that we can apply to the vast array of moral decisions that we face.

In order to keep our discussion as uncomplicated as possible, we shall postulate that only *moral* considerations are relevant for the decisions we shall be concerned with, unless we indicate otherwise. This stipulation is not as limiting as it might appear. We can easily adapt our conclusions to the lexicographical version of the morality-can-be-overridden thesis in the following way. Under the lexicographical version, we apply the various decision criteria, R_1, R_2, and so forth, one at a time, in accordance with their order in the ranking. Thus an agent would apply moral rightness as a decision criterion *separately*, at some stage of deliberation, to the action alternatives that are still viable at that stage. At that point, she faces a decision where essentially moral considerations alone are relevant. If moral uncertainty is present, the agent's decision problem is fundamentally the same as the one we shall inquire about. For the weighted sum version of the morality-can-be-overridden thesis, matters are a bit more complicated, since the decision criteria are all "applied" simultaneously. Even though I shall not detail a decision strategy for the weighted sum version, the reader should have little difficulty extrapolating the arguments and analyses given in this chapter to that context.

Our main question is this: What principle(s) should we consult in order to make decisions under moral uncertainty? We might begin by asking what clues we get from the previous discussion of Example 1.1 and my decision among x, y, and z. What sort of principle would advise me to choose z in that situation? One possibility is the following:

PR1

In a situation of moral uncertainty, I (the decision-maker) should (rationally) choose some alternative the moral rightness of which I am certain.

By "situation of moral uncertainty" I mean a situation in which a decision-maker is uncertain of the moral rightness of at least one of the alternative acts under consideration. Let us note that PR1 (Principle of Rationality 1) does not approve every morally right alternative. For my decision among x, y, and z, PR1 would not support my choosing y even if y would be morally right for me. PR1 would not support y even if I *knew*, but with less than complete certainty, that y would be morally right. This shows what is wrong with the modus operandi of all, or almost all, applied ethicists, which presumes that it is always rational for us to choose actions that we know to be morally right.[1] And if moral considerations preempt nonmoral considerations, then we should always choose actions the moral rightness of which we are certain over actions the moral rightness of which we are in doubt.

Perhaps the reader will protest that in Example 1.1 I, the decision-maker, may be mistaken in my moral beliefs about x, y, and z. My doing x may in fact be morally right, and my doing y or z may be morally wrong. The job of moral philosophy, it might be argued, is to straighten out my erroneous moral beliefs rather than to accommodate my choice of action to those beliefs. This criticism, however, overlooks the fact that ultimately we must choose our actions in light of whatever beliefs we happen to have when we make our decisions. It is true that my beliefs should ideally encapsulate the information that is available to me during my deliberations. I should take moral decision-making seriously and be sure to consider arguments on all sides of the relevant issues, at least to the extent that time permits. However, this does not guarantee that I shall come to the correct moral conclusions. Even if I am aware of and understand the most sophisticated philosophical analyses and arguments, there is no assurance that the moral conclusions that I draw will turn out to be true. To say otherwise would be to say that moral conscientiousness makes for moral infallibility.

Let us hypothesize that in Example 1.1 my deliberations about x, y, and z take into account all pertinent information available to me and that I deliberate in as careful and reasonable a fashion as I am capable. I may, of course, determine later that my judgments about x, y, and z were mistaken and that my doing z was morally wrong. An ethicist might even assist me in identifying the errors in my reasoning that led to my mistaken moral beliefs. Nevertheless, with respect to those beliefs, I "do the best that I can" by choosing z. I would properly be regarded as incoherent if I said that in spite of my moral beliefs about x, y, and z and particularly my belief that x was probably wrong for me to do, I chose x on the grounds that x was *in fact* the morally right thing for me to do. I cannot *rationally* justify my actions on the basis of moral claims that I disbelieved at the moment of decision. I may be faulted for any improper reasoning that led to my false moral beliefs about x, y, and z. I may also be judged to have acted immorally in choosing z. However, an observer who "puts himself in my shoes" and assumes my moral beliefs at the moment of decision must admit that my decision to do z was, at the time, the most reasonable decision for me to make.

Readers who are bothered by the element of subjectivity in my discussion of Example 1.1 may hypothesize that my beliefs about the moral rightness or wrongness of x, y, and z are held with epistemically appropriate degrees of confidence. We may pretend that I am an expert on the moral issues that my decision raises and that I have reflected at great length on the moral merits of x, y, and z. For this amended example, we make an even stronger case for my choosing z, even if z is, in fact, morally wrong for me to do. Unless expert moral opinion is infallible—a claim that is disproved by the fact that the experts often disagree on specific moral issues—it is sometimes rational to choose actions that may in fact be morally wrong.

In a similar way, we can defend PR1 against the complaint that it does not consider whether one's beliefs about the moral rightness or wrongness of her alternatives are reasonable. Some critics might argue that actions cannot be rational if they are based on unjustified beliefs, whether or not those beliefs are true. However, we must not confuse epistemic rationality with rationality in decision-making. We must choose our actions on the basis of the beliefs that we actually hold, whether or not we have good reason to hold those beliefs in the first place. Moreover, we still have an interesting and important problem of moral decision-making if, for my decision in Example 1.1, we simply hypothesize that my beliefs about the moral rightness or wrongness of my alternatives are *epistemically* justified by the information available to me, whether or not those beliefs are correct. This is so because decision-making under moral uncertainty is an important *practical* problem, even if we confine our attention to situations in which the decision-maker's moral beliefs and moral uncertainties are epistemically justified.

An objection closely related to the preceding one is the following: If we say that whether a decision-maker may rationally perform a certain action x depends on her beliefs about the moral rightness of x and not on whether x is in fact morally right, then we remove any incentive for the rest of us to inform her that her moral beliefs about x are false. After all, if she is doing the best that she can by acting appropriately on the basis of the information available and if doing the best she can is all that anyone can reasonably expect of her, then we cannot hope to improve her decision-making by giving her more information. Therefore, according to PR1 it makes no sense to correct someone's mistaken moral beliefs. But (the objection goes) surely it does, in general, make sense to do so. Thus something must be wrong with our thinking about what she should (rationally) do.

To answer this objection, it may be helpful to compare the decision in Example 1.1 to a case of decision-making under ordinary factual uncertainty. Suppose Doris is certain that by doing x she would produce maximum utility U, but she is uncertain whether by doing y she would produce U or some lesser utility u. Therefore, given Doris's information, Doris would "do the best that she can" with respect to utility maximization by choosing x. However, Charles has information heretofore unavailable to Doris that shows that in fact Doris would produce maximum utility U by doing y instead of x. What reason would Charles have to correct Doris's false beliefs about the consequences of her action? Doris, of course, has an interest in having her beliefs corrected, since in this way she may produce greater utility. However, let us suppose that Doris does not know about Charles's information and therefore does not request it from Charles. Why then should Charles volunteer it to Doris? This is the puzzle we are to solve.

The best answer in the utility maximization case appears to be that by increasing the utility of Doris's action, Charles may also be maximizing the utility of his own action. If, as we are hypothesizing, maximizing utility is the ultimate objective, then enabling Doris to increase the utility of her action *may* be how Charles himself maximizes utility. From this maximize-utility perspective, Charles has good reason to do so.

May we translate this sort of reasoning to the question of correcting someone's false moral beliefs? The analogous argument would say that by causing Doris's action to be morally right, Charles achieves moral rightness in his own action. The trouble with this proposal, however, is that it is debatable whether we generally make our own actions morally right by facilitating the morally right actions of others. And from some moral perspectives, it may be the exception rather than the rule. For example, a perspective that enjoins us to respect the moral autonomy of others might direct Charles not to foist unwanted moral advice on Doris, even if Charles's doing so would increase the frequency with which Doris acts rightly. Therefore, we may not simply assume without further argument that correcting Doris's false moral beliefs is usually the morally right thing for Charles to do.

A different argument for Charles's informing Doris that her moral beliefs are mistaken considers the rationality, rather than the morality, of doing so. The major premise is that it is *rational* for us to concern ourselves not only with the moral rightness of our own actions but also with the moral rightness of everyone else's actions. To see matters in this light would be to amend our views about the relationship between morality and rationality in action. Instead of endeavoring only to make our own actions morally right, we would also take into account the effects of our actions on the moral rightness of the actions of others. The relevant question is whether, generally speaking, we should simply do what is morally right or we should also seek to get others to do what is morally right. These objectives do not necessarily coincide. However, I shall not try to answer this question here. I shall be in a better position to address it in chapter 8, where I shall discuss the topic of moral optimization. For the moment I shall leave this as a loose end, which I shall try to tie up at a later stage.

It is interesting to compare my predicament as a decision-maker in Example 1.1 with that of someone who, forced to choose among three alternatives u, v, and w, consults a variety of professional ethicists for their advice about what to do. Let us imagine that only 20% of the ethicists claim that u would be morally right, 60% assert that v would be morally right, and all unanimously advise that w would be morally right. If the decision-maker wishes to follow the ethicists' advice as closely as possible, which alternative should she choose? It is clear that w would be the appropriate choice. Of course, it is possible that the minority is correct and that u would be morally right. However, if one goes by the expert opinion, it is more likely that v would be morally right and it would be taking an unnecessary chance of doing what is morally wrong to choose u over v. And, by the same token, the body of expert opinion would favor w over v. Of course, the experts are fallible and there is no guarantee that w is morally right. However, ceteris paribus, it makes more sense to do what the consultants unanimously approve than to do what a significant portion of them disapprove. If moral rightness were the decision-maker's overriding and all-encompassing aim, w would be the rational choice.

Let us now modify Example 1.1 slightly. I still have options x, y, and z, and I still believe that x would be morally wrong and that both y and z would be morally right. And I continue to have more confidence in the rightness of z than in that of y. But now let us suppose I also have some doubt about z's rightness. If I regard moral considerations as having paramount importance, what would be most reasonable for me to do in the situation? For the same reasons as before, it would make no sense for me to choose x. Furthermore, if only moral considerations are relevant, there can be nothing about y that would compensate for its inferior likelihood, compared with that of z, of being morally right. Clearly it would make more sense for me to choose z than to choose y, given my exclusive objective of acting morally.

Again we may compare the decision in this modified Example 1.1 to a choice of strategy in a modified version of the game of chess we discussed in chapter 1: Ann is our chess player for whom "winning is everything." As before, she has three defenses that she uses when she plays chess. Whenever she plays against Betty, she wins 40% of the time when she uses the French defense, 60% of the time when she uses the Lopez defense, and now 80% of the time when she uses the Sicilian defense. If "winning is everything" to Ann, then obviously it would make no sense for her to choose either the French or the Lopez defense, since the Sicilian defense affords her the best chance of reaching her objective. Although she may lose if she employs the Sicilian defense in a particular game against Betty and may win if she chooses one of the other defenses, using the Sicilian defense is clearly the reasonable choice. Ann cannot guarantee that she will win the chess match, but acting in accordance with the "spirit" of the "winning is everything" credo requires her to choose the strategy that affords her the greatest likelihood of winning. Similarly, acting in accordance with the "spirit" of a "morality is everything" doctrine for moral agents requires them to maximize the probabilities that their actions are morally right.

The preceding examples expose the defect in PR1: PR1 does not cover situations in which decision-makers are not certain of the moral rightness of any of their alternatives. Since this is often, if not usually, the situation, such a flaw in a principle of rationality is serious. Perhaps then we should modify PR1 as follows:

PR2
In situations of moral uncertainty, I (the decision-maker) should (rationally) choose some action that has the maximum probability of being morally right.

We might argue for PR2 as follows: If one's objective were to maximize utility and she were uncertain which action(s) would do so, decision theory would tell her to maximize *expected* utility (EU). The analogous principle for moral uncertainty would prescribe maximizing *expected* moral rightness (EMR). But what is "expected moral rightness"? The expected utility of an act x is defined as the weighted sum of the quantities of utility that x would produce under various possible states of affairs, where the weights are the respective probabilities that those states of affairs actually obtain in the situation. Symbolically, $EU(x) = p(c_1, x) \cdot u(c_1) + p(c_2, x) \cdot u(c_2) + \ldots + p(c_n, x) \cdot u(c_n)$, where $c_1, \ldots, c_n$ are the possible states of affairs (e.g., possible sets of consequences of x) that could affect the utility produced by x in the situation, $p(c_1, x), p(c_2, x), \ldots, p(c_n, x)$ are the respective probabilities that those states of affairs would accompany the performance of x, and $u(c_1), u(c_2), \ldots, u(c_n)$ are the respective utilities that would be produced if $c_1, c_2, \ldots, c_n$ were to exist. Analogously, the EMR of an action x would be the weighted sum of the degrees of moral rightness that would result from the performance of x under various possible sets of morally significant conditions, where the weights are the respective probabilities that those conditions would obtain if x were performed. In symbols, $EMR(x) = p(c_1, x) \cdot mr(x, c_1) + p(c_2, x) \cdot mr(x, c_2) + \ldots + p(c_n, x) \cdot mr(x, c_n)$ where $p(c_1, x), p(c_2, x), \ldots, p(c_n, x)$ are the respective probabilities that the sets of morally significant conditions $c_1, c_2, \ldots, c_n$ would obtain if x were performed, and $mr(x, c_1), mr(x, c_2), \ldots, mr(x, c_n)$ are the respective degrees of moral rightness that x would have if $c_1, c_2, \ldots, c_n$ occurred in the situation.[2] For example, c_1 might be the condition that a certain moral theory T_1 is true, and c_2 might be the condition that some other moral theory T_2 is true. Then $p(c_1, x)$ and $p(c_2, x)$ would be the probabilities that T_1 and T_2, respectively, are true, and $mr(x, c_1)$ and $mr(x, c_2)$ would be the degrees of moral rightness that x would have if T_1 and T_2, respectively, were true.[3]

But what sense can be made of the phrase "degrees of moral rightness"? Normally we assume that moral rightness comes in only two possible "sizes"—right and wrong. Let us call this the binary hypothesis. As before, we shall let 1 and 0 signify moral rightness and moral wrongness respectively. Then all the $mr(x, c_i)$s in the preceding expression will be either 1 or 0, and $EMR(x)$ will equal the sum of the probabilities of the conditions under which x would be morally right. Since the conditions $c_1, c_2, \ldots, c_n$ are mutually exclusive and collectively exhaustive, this means that $EMR(x)$ will be the overall probability that x is morally right. Hence, $EMR(x)$ will be a maximum if and only if the probability that x is morally right is maximized. Obviously, this result does not depend on the arbitrary choices of 1 and 0 for moral rightness and wrongness. Thus the maximize-expected-utility (MEU) idea, when adapted to decision-making under moral uncertainty in a natural way, lends support to PR2.[4]

A critic might charge that PR2, since it tells us always to "play it safe," morally speaking, expresses a kind of moral conservatism that we should question. In directing us always to *maximize* the probabilities that our actions are morally right, PR2 tells us always to minimize our risks of doing what is wrong. And in order to minimize moral risks we would often choose to act insipidly or passively. We would forfeit the benefits that greater moral boldness would sometimes avail us. Let us consider the following example:

Example 2.1

I am to choose between alternatives x and y in a situation in which the only morally relevant considerations are the effects of my action on two individuals, Enrico and Felicia. If I choose x, then I am certain to neither benefit nor harm them. If I choose y, then I am certain to benefit Enrico greatly and there is a 40% likelihood that I shall also greatly benefit Felicia. However, there is a 60% chance that I shall harm Felicia to a small but not negligible degree if I choose y. Since by choosing x I ensure that I shall harm neither Enrico nor Felicia, and since by choosing y I am likely to harm Felicia, the "morally safe" choice is x. But by choosing x I am sure to benefit neither, while if I take a moral risk by choosing y the expected benefits are substantially greater.

According to the argument against PR2 we are considering, the more reasonable choice in this situation is y, the morally riskier alternative. Since PR2 tells me to choose x, it offers the wrong advice for my decision.

This argument against PR2 suggests that we should sometimes sacrifice a degree of moral security in order to promote the benefits that a little moral boldness may procure. The argument does not advocate moral recklessness, of course. We must be judicious in weighing benefits against risks. However, the argument says that in some instances it is reasonable for us to accept moral risks in order to obtain certain benefits, even when we are able to avoid the risks altogether. Since PR2 always tells us to play it as safe as possible, morally speaking, it is too cautious a principle of rational decision-making under moral uncertainty.[5]

In order to see what is wrong with this argument, we must pay attention to what sorts of "benefits" and "risks" are being weighed against each other. Apparently, the risks that the critic has in mind are the risks of harm to Felicia. And it is possible, of course, to view moral rightness and wrongness in such a way that moral rightness consists of not harming others. But if this is the moral perspective, then the "benefits" that Enrico and Felicia may receive if I choose y have no moral significance, since the moral perspective with which we are operating gives me no moral credit for benefiting others. And since we have hypothesized that morality is paramount and that it preempts all nonmoral considerations, the fact that a particular alternative would produce benefits that have no bearing on its rightness or wrongness cannot, *in the final analysis*, support the choice of that alternative. Morally irrelevant characteristics of our actions are *necessarily* irrelevant, *all things considered*.

Perhaps, however, it is a different moral perspective that the critic has in mind. Perhaps he is assuming that benefits done to others, as well as harms done to them, affect the moral rightness or wrongness of our actions. There are two ways in which this might work: (1) Our moral obligation is always to maximize the (actual? expected?) difference between the total benefits and the total harms done to others. (2) Our moral obligation is always to maximize the (actual? expected?) total benefits done to others, *provided that no one is harmed*. Thus there are really four possibilities here, corresponding to whether we have "actual" or "expected" in mind for (1) and (2).

Suppose it is actual benefits and harms we are talking about. Then, according to (1), the clear choice is y, since even if I harm Felicia, that harm is outweighed by the greater benefit I provide to Enrico. Therefore, PR2 tells me to choose y and thus there is no conflict between the kind of moral cautiousness that PR2 may embody and any ideal of moral boldness instantiated by y. According to (2), however, there appears to be conflict, since the requirement that I harm neither Enrico nor Felicia makes x more likely to be right than y. Hence PR2 tells me to choose x, the morally safer alternative. But what is the nature of the benefits that I would seek to produce by choosing y? Would they be *morally* significant? If the answer is "No," then they would not affect what I should do, *all things considered*, given our hypothesis that moral considerations are preemptive. In that event, no rational purpose would be served by pursuing those benefits.

One might argue that the benefits would be morally *insignificant* as follows: According to the "actual benefits" version of (2), which alternative, x or y, would be morally right in Example 2.1 depends entirely on whether by choosing y I would harm Felicia. If by choosing y I would harm Felicia, then x would be morally right. Otherwise, y would be the morally right choice. Since there is a greater probability that I would harm Felicia by choosing y than that I would benefit her, x is more likely to be morally right. The appeal of y is that *if* by choosing it I would not harm Felicia, *then* the total benefits that it would produce would be much greater than those that x would produce. However, it is easy to be misled here. Even though the *possible* total benefits-minus-harms for Enrico and Felicia that y would produce are greater than those that x would produce, the possible *moral rightness* of y is no greater than that of x—at least not if the binary hypothesis is true. For according to the binary hypothesis, moral rightness/wrongness comes in only two "sizes"—viz., right and wrong. One right action can be no more and no less right than any other right action. And since the moral rightness of our actions is our paramount, preemptive objective, the difference in the benefits-minus-harms that would be produced by x and y should not affect my decision, except for the possible harm to Felicia. Thus the "moral benefits" that y would afford are illusory.

But what if the binary hypothesis is false? What if not all right actions are equally right and there are degrees of moral rightness between "right" and "wrong"? Then the door is open to recognizing the possibly greater benefits that y would produce as morally significant. But clearly PR2 is not adequate as a rational decision principle if we recognize degrees of moral rightness intermediate between "right" and "wrong." We should recall that the decision-theoretic argument for PR2 that we used explicitly appealed to the binary hypothesis. If we reject the binary hypothesis, then we shall have to find a replacement principle for PR2—one that may prescribe y in Example 2.1. Thus it is important for us to consider carefully whether the binary hypothesis is true, which we shall do in chapter 4. For the moment, however, we shall continue to assume the binary hypothesis.

Let us now consider the "expected benefits and harms" version of moral perspectives (1) and (2) and their implications for Example 2.1. For (1) there is no need for me to take moral risks in order to achieve maximum moral benefits, since clearly I would maximize the total expected benefits-minus-harms for Enrico and Felicia collectively by choosing y. Therefore, (1) prescribes y, which ipso facto is also prescribed by PR2. For (2) I am to maximize total expected benefits-minus-harms for Enrico and Felicia provided that I harm neither of them. I am certain that I would satisfy the "do no harm" requirement by choosing x, but x would never maximize expected benefits-minus-harms for Enrico and Felicia. This is because even if by choosing y I harmed Felicia, the total benefits-minus-harms for the two of them together would be greater than 0, which is all that x would produce. However, there is only a 40% probability that y would satisfy the "do no harm" condition. Since according to (2) doing no harm is a *necessary* condition for the rightness of y, y has a 40% probability of being morally right. Consequently x has a 60% probability of being morally right, which means that PR2 advises me to choose x.

Is there a case to be made for y here? Can I justify choosing y on the grounds that the moral risks that it poses are outweighed by the moral benefits that it may produce? For reasons similar to those given earlier, the answer is "No" if we assume the binary hypothesis. If all morally right actions are equally right and moral rightness is our final, overriding objective, the greater benefits-minus-harms that y may produce are irrelevant to what I should do, *all things considered*. Again, the "moral benefits" of choosing y are illusory. However, if the binary hypothesis is false, then PR2 may give us the wrong answer. But we have already acknowledged that without the binary hypothesis PR2 is inadequate as a rational decision principle.

Thus we may say at this point that, provided that the binary hypothesis is correct, the criticism of PR2 based on the charge that it is excessively conservative, morally speaking, is unsuccessful. At least, that is true if the situation described in Example 2.1 is the sort of decision for which this criticism of PR2 is strongest and most plausible. The general flaw in the argument against PR2 is that in casting PR2 as a principle of moral conservatism and inciting moral boldness against moral cautiousness, the argument appeals to a narrow "do no harm" notion of moral rightness. It ignores our hypothesis that moral rightness is the paramount, preemptive norm for our decisions. According to that premise, any factor that bears on what we should do, *all things considered*, in any situation to which moral questions pertain must be a moral consideration. Consequently, any benefits or values to be pursued by exercising "moral boldness," if at all relevant to our moral choices, are *ipso facto* morally relevant. Within that conceptual scheme, nothing precludes moral rightness from advising us sometimes to risk harms or evils in pursuit of benefits or values. And some moral theories, such as utilitarian theories, call for precisely such risk-taking. Of course, what is being risked is not moral rightness itself but rather certain values that may have moral significance. Morality itself may be bold in the sense that it may approve or even require the taking of such risks.

We can highlight the shortcomings of the preceding "conservatism" argument against PR2 by considering more "liberal" principles of decision-making under moral uncertainty. One very liberal principle would allow us to choose any action that is probably morally right (i.e., has a probability of being morally right greater than .5) in the situation. However, as we have seen, if only moral considerations are relevant, then we have no good reason to settle for an action whose probability of being morally right is less than that of some other action. And such a principle would suffer a serious incompleteness problem. In some situations, there may be no alternative whose probability of being morally right is greater than .5. For example, if the probabilities that x, y, and z would be morally right were measured to be .3, .25, and .45 respectively, there would be no single alternative that would probably be right, although we might be certain that at least one of the three would be right. In such a case, the liberal principle would leave the decision-maker without any advice about what to do, whereas PR2 would prescribe picking an action with the greatest likelihood of being morally right, even if that probability were less than .5. If no more information were available, this would be the best the decision-maker could do.

A defender of the liberal principle might respond to my incompleteness criticism by pointing out that in the situation I described there are alternatives with probability greater than .5 of being morally right—namely, doing not-x, doing not-y, and doing not-z, for which the probabilities are .7, .75, and .55, respectively. However, this response makes the dubious assumption that the logical complement of an alternative is necessarily an alternative. It would imply that if, for example, x were the alternative of making a certain true statement, then not making *that* particular statement would also be an alternative in the situation. Doing not-x could be accomplished by making a different true statement, making any false statement, or making no statement at all. Therefore, prescribing not-x would provide no satisfactory guidance to the agent whose primary concern is deciding what to do rather what not to do. Furthermore, the agent may well have ways of doing not-x other than by doing y or z—ways of acting that she may view as much less promising, morally speaking, than x, y, or z and that she may already have eliminated from consideration.

It is difficult to say in general what things qualify as action alternatives and what things do not. Decision-makers seem to have intuitions about what their most plausible alternatives are, even though they may sometimes overlook the best alternatives. Nevertheless, it is clear that they do not recognize every logical complement of an alternative as an alternative. It is also clearly false that if the probability of x's moral rightness is p, as long as one does not-p she has a $1 - p$ chance of acting rightly.

The preceding decision among x, y, and z is a special case—a situation in which the probabilities add up to 1. Since there can be more than one morally right alternative in a situation, the sum of the probabilities will sometimes be greater than 1. And if alternatives other than x, y, and z exist, the sum might be less than 1. If x, y, and z exhausted the set of possible actions, then doing not-x would amount to doing the disjunctive act y-or-z. How does one perform a disjunctive act? Presumably by performing one or the other *but not both* of the component acts, since it will generally not be possible to do both. But if so, it is illusory to think that doing not-x has a rightness probability of .7. Since the agent cannot do both y and z, the maximum rightness probability she can attain by doing not-x—that is, doing y-or-z—is .45, which she achieves by choosing z. She has no way of acting such that the probability of her action's turning out to be morally right is greater than .45. This is the fallacy in the liberal principle's defender's argument.

Some may wish to argue that moral considerations become less important when the moral issues are murky and the moral agent has relatively little confidence in the moral rightness of each of her options. Thus if none of an agent's options have greater than an even chance of being morally right, then she may discount moral considerations or perhaps ignore them altogether and act on the basis of what she regards as nonmoral factors. This view assumes the importance of a norm to depend on the degree of confidence with which one is able to judge the norm's implications for her decision. However, this is a mistake. It would be like supposing that if a patient must decide whether to undergo a risky, complicated surgical procedure for which the outcome is highly uncertain, medical issues diminish in importance. The complexity of moral considerations does not affect their importance.

Previously in our discussion of Example 1.1, we entertained the suggestion that for the lexicographic version of the morality-can-be-overridden thesis a decision-maker should consult nonmoral decision criteria whenever she is uncertain of the moral rightness or wrongness of some of her alternatives. This made no sense for Example 1.1, since one of the alternatives was certain to be morally right. However, in Example 2.1, no such alternative is available. And since we are assuming that only moral considerations are relevant, there is no nonmoral decision criterion to which the decision-maker can appeal. PR2 tells us to maximize the probabilities that our actions are morally right. This can mean taking into account not only our uncertainties about how different moral considerations apply to the situation but also our uncertainties about which of those considerations should carry the most weight. For example, I might recognize utility maximization and justice as determining the rightness or wrongness of my alternatives in a particular situation. I may be unsure not only which of my alternatives would maximize utility and meet the demands of justice but also which of the two considerations is the stronger determiner of my moral obligation.

To illustrate the point just made, let us consider the following example:

Example 2.2

I must choose between action alternatives x and y. There are two moral factors, C_1 and C_2, that I regard as possibly relevant. I believe that C_1 prescribes x and that C_2 prescribes y, but I am not certain that this is so. In my judgment there is a 60% probability that C_1 prescribes x and a 40% probability that it prescribes y, while there is a 70% probability that C_2 prescribes y and a 30% probability that it prescribes x. (I shall assume that there is a 0% probability that either C_1 or C_2 approves both x and y.) However, not only am I uncertain about which actions C_1 and C_2 prescribes, but I am also unsure which factor is the more stringent. I judge there to be a 55% probability that C_1 outranks C_2 and a 45% probability that C_2 outranks C_1. I must determine which alternative, x or y, I should (rationally) choose.

Table 2.1 Decision Table for Example 2.2

	C_1 outranks C_2. ($p = .55$)		C_2 outranks C_1. ($p = .45$)	
	C_1 prescribes x. ($p = .60$)	C_1 prescribes y. ($p = .40$)	C_2 prescribes y. ($p = .70$)	C_2 prescribes x. ($p = .30$)
do x	1	0	0	1
do y	0	1	1	0

Table 2.1 summarizes the preceding information.

It is a simple matter to determine that the probability that doing x would be morally right is .465 and the probability that doing y would be morally right is .535. Hence, PR2 prescribes y even though x is more likely to accord with C_1, the factor more likely to be the dominant one. Had we not considered the agent's uncertainty about which factor he should apply, we would have come to a different conclusion.

Of course, in general, the more strongly we believe something, the greater should be its impact on our decisions. This is true simply because the greater the probability that a morally relevant condition holds, the greater will be its impact on the probabilities of actions' rightness or wrongness. But our recognizing the greater potency of the more probable conditions does not mean that we are compromising moral rightness as a decision criterion. In moral decision-making, as in bridge, we must play the hands we are dealt. We do not abandon our principal objective just because we have a diminished likelihood of achieving it. We do the best we can with the information we have. And doing the best we can where our ultimate objective is to do what is morally right means that we maximize the probabilities that our actions will be morally right.[6]

A variation on the liberal decision principle described earlier would allow us to choose any action whose probability of being morally right is greater than .5 but would direct us to maximize probable moral rightness if no such alternative was available. In effect, such a principle would say that any probability greater than .5 is "enough" as far as moral rightness is concerned. However, we may appropriately ask, "Enough for what?" If only moral considerations are relevant, as we have hypothesized, we have no reason to "balance" moral aspects against nonmoral ones. For example, we have no reason to balance moral considerations against those of self-interest. If self-interest is at all relevant to one's decision, then, according to our hypothesis, it must *be* a moral consideration. Although I have criticized Becker's "finality thesis" for not appreciating the practical significance of moral uncertainty, PR2 says in effect that our moral decisions should be guided by the "spirit" of that principle. PR2 implies that there can be no rational justification for not getting as "close" to moral rightness as we are allowed by the available information. In practical terms, this means that we must choose some action or other that has maximum probability of being morally right.

Another principle of rationality would instruct us always to remove our initial moral uncertainty, or at least to reduce it as much as possible, *before* taking action and *then* to select some action that has been identified as having the greatest probability of being morally right. We should note, however, that PR2 does not rule out actions aimed at reducing one's moral uncertainties and in fact prescribes such actions whenever they have maximum probability of being morally right. But when the situation is urgent, there may be no time to pursue any further the resolution of the moral issues themselves, and the agent may have to act on the information available at the time of the decision. Furthermore, deciding whether to invest a significant amount of time and energy in reflecting on those issues may itself raise moral questions. We should not assume that prolonged moral deliberation is always a morally right or rational choice.

Some commentators on the methodology of applied ethics have counseled against ethicists' making specific recommendations to moral agents about what they should do when they face difficult moral choices. These commentators contend that ethicists should limit their advice to such matters as identifying action alternatives; raising pertinent moral problems and issues; clarifying moral concepts and statements; and formulating, analyzing, and evaluating moral arguments.[7] According to this view, ethicists should not advise moral agents what to do or judge the rightness or wrongness of specific actions. It is not far from this position to the view that ethicists should not use PR2, or any other principle of rationality, to recommend specific choices of action to moral agents.

Surely no one should deny that ethicists should be circumspect in their public statements and not cavalierly offer advice about what others should do. However, if ethicists are to avoid the danger of at least appearing to be useless for the tasks of real-world decision-making, their conclusions must enable moral agents to avoid some of the errors that they might otherwise make and thus improve their chances of doing what is morally right. But if this is our rationale for doing *applied* ethics, then it suggests that we who act under moral uncertainty should strive to maximize the probabilities that our actions are morally right. And this reinforces PR2 as a principle of rational action.

If moral uncertainty is possible, as it surely is, there will sometimes be conflict between PR2 and whatever moral principles or theories are actually true. This is so because acts that, with respect to decision-makers' moral beliefs, have maximum probability of being morally right may in fact be morally wrong. As we have seen, there is something incongruous about a moral agent who attempts to excuse her action on grounds that it turned out to be morally right, although at the time she acted she believed it to be morally wrong. This would be like attempting to justify having bet one's life savings on a 100-to-1 shot at the racetrack on the grounds that the improbable actually happened and the horse won the race. With respect to the information available, the original bet was irrational, notwithstanding the fortunate outcome. Perhaps a similar observation may be made about "moral luck."[8]

PR2 also shows how it can sometimes be irrational to perform actions that one *knows* to be morally right. Since one can know that p without being certain that p, it is possible for a decision-maker to know that x is morally right and yet have doubts about x's rightness. In such a situation, if the decision-maker has smaller doubts about the moral rightness of some other action y than about that of x, then according to PR2 she should choose y over x. *All things considered*, she should *not* choose x.

One might argue that PR2, which I have characterized as a principle of *rationality*, really amounts to a principle of subjective moral obligation. An agent's *objective* moral obligations are those that depend on what the pertinent facts are, regardless of whether the agent knows them, or could have known them, at the time of her decision. However, one's *subjective* moral obligations are relative to what the agent knows or could reasonably be expected to know at the moment of decision. For example, act utilitarianism, understood as a principle of objective moral obligation, directs us to *produce* maximum utility and faults us if we fail to do so, even if we have no way of knowing with certainty which of our alternatives will bring about this result. Act utilitarianism, as a principle of subjective moral obligation, instructs us to maximize *expected* utility and thus factors in our uncertainties about the relevant facts. PR2, if understood as a principle of subjective *moral* obligation, would direct us to maximize the probability that our action will be objectively morally right.

As a principle of subjective moral obligation, however, PR2 is inadequate. The following example from Donald Hubin shows why:

> Imagine that I have promised my daughter that I will buy some ice cream on the way home from work. The store is about to close and if I am to keep my promise, I must go there directly. As it happens, I am passing a building about to be demolished. Out of the corner of my eye, I think I see a figure inside the building. I am probably wrong: most likely it was just the shadow of a passing bird. I judge it slightly more likely than not that there is no one in the building. I could stop and tell the wrecking crew what I thought I saw and suggest another check of the building, but then I would be unable to buy the ice cream tonight. Armed with ... [PR2] ... I pass on without stopping. After all, the course of action most likely to be morally right (once the uncertainty is resolved) is hurrying to the store to get the ice cream. . . . [T]his is the wrong answer.[9]

In this example, if my objective moral obligation depends on whether there really is someone in the building and if PR2 is construed as a principle of subjective morality, then it follows that my subjective moral obligation is to continue to the store without stopping. Clearly, however, it is my subjective obligation to stop and notify the wrecking crew. I must consider not only the probability that someone is in the building but also the harm that will be done if this is the case and the wrecking crew is not notified. Therefore, PR2 is deficient as a principle of subjective moral obligation.

But is PR2 also inadequate as a principle of *rationality?* Does the preceding example expose its insufficiency as a principle for decision-making under moral uncertainty? The answer, I believe, is "No" for the following reasons: *Subjective* morality is, for a particular conception of *objective* morality, the "best that we can do" given the information available to us in the decision situation. What kind of information is relevant depends, of course, on which conception of objective morality we have in mind. For example, if our theory of objective morality directs us to maximize utility, the corresponding subjective theory prescribes maximizing expected utility. Since our information is often incomplete, actions that are objectively right are often not subjectively right, and conversely. But I never actually have to choose between alternatives that I know *with certainty* to be objectively right and others that I know *with certainty* to be subjectively right. An alternative that I know *with certainty* to be objectively right must be subjectively right as well. For example, if I know *with certainty* that a particular alternative would maximize actual utility, then I must also know (or at least be capable of knowing) that it would maximize expected utility. Usually, however, I do not know *with certainty* of any alternative that it would be objectively right. Therefore, in most cases I seek to identify and select some alternative that is subjectively right. Whether it turns out to be objectively right can only be determined after the fact if at all.

But what if I am in a situation in which I am uncertain which alternative(s) are *subjectively* right? This might happen, for example, if I was uncertain which theory of objective morality is the true theory and thus was unsure which theory of subjective morality is correct. Under these conditions, I would have to choose among alternatives none of which I know with certainty to be subjectively right. However, this does not mean that I would know nothing about their subjective rightness. My information may tell me that some alternatives are more likely to be subjectively right than others. I may know, for instance, that the true theory of subjective morality is on a relatively short list of such theories. Alternatives that accord with one or more of the theories on the list would be more likely to be subjectively right than alternatives that do not. In this event, PR2 would advise me to choose some alternative such that its probability of being subjectively right is at least as great as that of any other alternative. Ex hypothesi, I would not be certain that the alternative I chose was subjectively right. Therefore, the alternatives that PR2 recommends need not be subjectively right and thus PR2 would not serve as a principle of subjective morality.

In the story about the daughter, the ice cream, and the building demolition, it is clear which alternative is subjectively right—namely, stopping to inform the wrecking crew. Thus it is clear also that that alternative is the more *likely* to be subjectively right. Hence, if we interpret PR2 as a principle of decision-making under uncertainty about *subjective* rightness, it produces the right answer. However, we have seen that if the kind of moral rightness we have in mind is objective rightness, then PR2 gives us the wrong conclusion.[10] Therefore, we should interpret PR2 as applying to uncertainty about subjective moral rightness. And this makes sense, because by doing what we are certain is subjectively right we respond rationally to our uncertainty about what is objectively right. But when we are uncertain which of our alternatives are subjectively right, the best that we can do is follow PR2. PR2 thus serves a very different purpose from that of principles of subjective morality.

Another objection to PR2 is that just as moral agents are sometimes uncertain which moral principles are true, they may also have doubts about PR2's adequacy as a principle of rationality. There may be some other approach to rational decision-making under moral uncertainty, formulated in some principle PR2', that we cannot completely rule out as an alternative to PR2. If so, then we must contend not only with moral uncertainty but also with uncertainty about which principle for decision-making under moral uncertainty we should follow. Then there would be some principle PR3 that would advise us to maximize the expected *rationality* of our actions by taking into account our degrees of confidence in PR2 and PR2' and in their implications for our moral decisions. But why stop here? For we may have doubts about PR3 and see fit to entertain a rival principle PR3'.

This would force us to resort to an even higher order principle of rationality PR4—and so on ad infinitum. The best way to escape this jungle, one might argue, is not to enter it in the first place. It was a mistake to try to outflank our initial moral uncertainties by resorting to PR2. Therefore, in making moral decisions we should nip the problem in the bud by contenting ourselves with simply following whatever moral theories, principles, or arguments appear to us to be the most reasonable.

This infinite regress problem is not peculiar to PR2, however. It crops up, for example, in the MEU approach to ordinary decision-making under risk. The reason is that we who make nonmoral decisions under ordinary factual uncertainty may have serious doubts about the MEU principle.[11] Therefore, if the infinite regress problem is a serious problem for moral decision-making, then it may be a serious problem for nonmoral decision-making as well.

Even if we have doubts about PR2, we may have no alternative principle in mind to replace it with. In that event, we would have no idea what an unknown principle would say about a particular decision and thus we would have no way of taking it into account. Of course, our choice of decision strategy will depend on whether we classify our situation as one of *decision-making under risk* or *decision-making under ignorance*. The difference is that for decisions under risk the agent is assumed to know the pertinent probabilities, while for decisions under ignorance the probabilities are unknown. For decisions of the latter sort, the available decision rules include the maximin principle, the minimax-regret principle, the optimism-pessimism rule, and the principle of insufficient reason. For decision-making under risk, however, maximizing expected utility is by far the predominant approach, although there continues to be much discussion about many of the technical details.[12]

We have assumed in all of our examples thus far that the probabilities are known. PR2, of course, does not prescribe maximizing expected utility, since our agenda is to do what is morally right rather than to maximize utility. However, as we saw earlier, in effect what we want to do is maximize expected moral rightness, which, if we assume the binary hypothesis, amounts to maximizing the probability that our actions will be morally right. PR2 borrows the form, but not the substance, of the expected utility principle. PR2 uses all pertinent information available to the decision-maker, including probability measurements that are as precise as possible. It makes little sense not to use that information if it is available. Hence, for the sorts of decisions we have considered so far, it seems much more sensible to take our cue from expected utility theory than from the theory of decision-making under ignorance.

For these reasons, the objection that PR2 is just one of a number of plausible principles for decision-making under moral uncertainty does not appear to be a damaging one. However, the reader may wonder how realistic it is to assume that the typical decision-maker knows the exact values of the probabilities. This is a reasonable concern that we shall have to address. In the following chapters, I shall consider decisions where I make much weaker, and more realistic, assumptions about the decision-maker's knowledge of the pertinent probabilities

It may appear to some readers that PR2 illicitly devalues questions about right and wrong in the following respect: If, as I have argued, what we should ultimately do is act rationally and if acting rationally means simply maximizing the probability that our actions are (subjectively) morally right, then why should we ever worry about the accuracy of our moral beliefs? PR2 tells us to take whatever moral beliefs we happen to have and choose some alternative that, with respect to those beliefs, has the greatest likelihood of being morally right. Nothing in this procedure requires us to try to resolve our moral uncertainties or to confirm our moral beliefs before deciding what to do. However, surely it is a mistake to think that rational decision-making never requires us to try to resolve pertinent moral issues. Therefore, PR2 must be rejected.

The error in this argument is closely related to the defect in one of the decision principles that we considered and discarded earlier. It is to assume that attempting to resolve one's moral uncertainties or to confirm one's moral beliefs cannot be the way in which she maximizes the probability that her actions will be morally right. This assumption is false. Decision-makers may sometimes have good reasons for thinking that attempting to resolve pertinent moral uncertainties will succeed in reducing or even removing some of them and that in this way they will maximize the probabilities that their actions will be morally right. In such cases, PR2 recommends investigating the moral rightness or wrongness of one's alternatives further. However, in cases in which there is not enough time to try to resolve pertinent moral issues or in which there is strong reason to believe that such attempts would be unsuccessful, PR2 would direct moral agents not to engage in protracted moral reflection. But this is the correct conclusion. One who persisted in moral reflection even after it became clear that doing so was interfering with her ability to perform some action with maximum likelihood of being morally right would be acting irrationally. It is a *virtue* of PR2 that it recognizes and sets reasonable limits to moral inquiry.

There is, however, a variation on this criticism of PR2 that is not so easily deflected. We study moral philosophy not only to determine how to make the next moral decision but also to try to resolve moral issues that we expect to encounter in future decisions. There is no reason to believe that our decisions to devote time and energy to the study of ethics are never themselves moral decisions. As I observed in the first paragraph of chapter 1, instead of spending time writing an essay on moral decision-making, I could be collecting donations for a Third World relief organization or teaching an illiterate person to read. In this light, it appears that my decision raises moral questions. Perhaps my conducting the inquiry in which I am currently engaged is itself morally defensible. However, my current purpose is not really to do what is morally right or even to achieve maximum probable moral rightness, but rather to acquire knowledge that will have some important moral bearing on a broad range of future action choices.

What then justifies my current activities? Is there any *rational* justification for them? Ex hypothesi, I cannot appeal to PR2 to defend my action choices. Therefore, if they are rational they must be so with respect to some principle of rationality other than PR2. This conclusion means that PR2 is not the final word on the problem of rational decision-making under moral uncertainty.

These observations raise questions that we are not yet ready to answer. We shall return to them in chapter 8 when we consider *courses of action* and principles of rationality appropriate to them. For the moment, let us set these issues aside and confine our attention to decisions confronted by agents whose overriding purpose is to do what is morally right but who are hindered in this endeavor by their uncertainties about which of their alternatives would best serve that purpose.

Another possible criticism of PR2 is that adopting the policy of always maximizing the probability that our action will be morally right is incompatible with the possibility of *moral dilemmas*. A moral dilemma, according to philosophers' current understanding of the phrase, is a situation in which an agent is morally obliged to perform each of two or more actions but cannot perform both. Moral dilemmas appear to present a problem for PR2 because if an agent A is morally *obliged* to perform each of two different actions x and y, then each is morally wrong for A to perform since each constitutes A's failure to perform a morally obligatory act. Since no action is morally right for A to perform, it is pointless for A to seek to maximize the probability that her action will be morally right.[13]

I strongly doubt that there can be moral decisions for which all the agent's alternatives are morally wrong. In my estimation, the best argument for the existence of moral dilemmas is given by Walter Sinnott-Armstrong, who characterizes moral dilemmas as situations in which there are conflicts between nonoverridden moral requirements.[14] However, if we conceive moral dilemmas in this way, then nothing prevents us from regarding all the alternatives sponsored by one or more of the nonoverridden requirements as morally right. An action is morally wrong only if it violates an *overriding* moral requirement—-that is, a requirement that outweighs all competing moral requirements. In a situation in which no such requirement exists, two or more moral requirements must have equal, maximum "strength." To say that two requirements conflict in a situation is to say that no alternative satisfies both. Therefore, if two or more moral requirements are equally and maximally "strong," then any alternative that satisfies one or more of them is morally right.

However, even if two or more *overriding* moral requirements can somehow conflict, the problem for PR2 is more technical than substantive. Moral agents who find themselves in such dilemmas still must act and therefore must decide what to do. And even if none of one's alternatives are morally right, it will often be the case that some are *better*, morally speaking, than others. For example, in William Styron's novel *Sophie's Choice*, a Nazi guard demands that Sophie choose one of her two children for extermination. If she refuses to choose, both will be killed. One who believes in the possibility of conflicts among overriding moral requirements may view all of Sophie's alternatives as wrong. Each would result in the death of at least one of her children, and there will be a "moral residue" of regret and self-blame whatever she decides to do. However, Sophie's refusing to choose either child seems the worst, morally speaking, of her options. It seems better, morally speaking, for her to save one of her children than to allow both to be killed. Thus the case can be made that, *on moral grounds*, Sophie should sacrifice one of her children in order to save the other. Of course, one might argue that by choosing either child to be killed Sophie would be participating in the Nazi guard's morally reprehensible game, which would be worse, morally, than not preventing the death of either child. But even in this light we see a moral difference among the alternatives that she may take into consideration.

It seems reasonable to say that an agent who finds herself in a moral dilemma in which some alternatives are worse, morally speaking, than others should choose an alternative that is no worse than any other alternative. In such a situation, even if all of the alternatives are morally wrong, there may be moral differences among them that the decision-maker should heed. Of course, since ex hypothesi all the alternatives are morally wrong, the concepts of *right* and *wrong* will not capture those differences. Therefore, we shall have to find terms besides "right" and "wrong" to signify the relevant moral distinction. We might, for example, coin "morally acceptable" and "morally unacceptable" to serve that purpose. In a situation that is not a moral dilemma, the morally right alternatives and the morally acceptable ones would be the same set of alternatives, as would the morally wrong and the morally unacceptable alternatives. However, for moral dilemmas of the kind we are discussing, this would not be true, since all alternatives, including the morally acceptable ones, would be morally wrong. Since we want a moral standard that enables decision-makers to tell which alternatives morality recommends and which it disapproves of, we would identify that standard as the standard of *morally acceptable* action rather than of morally right action. Makers of moral decisions would be interested primarily in which of their alternatives are morally acceptable, since an alternative's being morally wrong would not necessarily mean that it should not, *on moral grounds*, be chosen. In short, the work done by the concepts of *right* and *wrong* in a conceptual framework in which moral dilemmas are disclaimed would be done by the concepts of *morally acceptable* action and *morally unacceptable* action in a framework in which moral dilemmas are allowed.

What if a moral dilemma occurred in which none of the agent's alternatives were better, morally speaking, than any other? Here it seems that we should view such situations as special cases in which morality values and devalues all of the alternatives equally. Morally speaking, the agent may choose any of the alternatives, even if all of them are wrong. Such a decision would be like one in which all the agent's alternatives are morally *right* and where it does not matter, morally speaking, which she chooses to perform.

Henceforth, for simplicity of exposition, I shall assume that moral dilemmas do not occur and that the concepts of right and wrong are adequate to capture the distinction between action alternatives that is of primary concern to makers of moral decisions. Readers who wish to include moral dilemmas in their conceptual schemes may adopt appropriate terminology to signify the corresponding distinction.

A final argument against PR2 is based on supererogation. It observes that for some, and probably most, moral decisions the alternative(s) that have the maximum likelihood of being morally right will turn out to be supererogatory. It is not difficult to see why. Supererogatory actions are presumed to go beyond the bare minimum that moral rightness requires. In exceeding the moral minimum by a healthy margin, they take on increased probabilities of not falling below it. By choosing a supererogatory action, we in effect take out insurance against the possibility of acting wrongly. This is analogous to a student's preparing for an examination by studying twice as many hours as she believes to be necessary in order to pass it. By studying enough to get an A on the exam, the student maximizes the likelihood that she will get at least a D on it. Similarly, it will sometimes be true that a moral agent maximizes the probability that her action is morally right by choosing a supererogatory alternative.[15] However, PR2 *prescribes* maximizing the likelihood that one's action will be morally right. Consequently, PR2 appears to *prescribe* supererogatory actions whenever, as will often happen, they are maximally likely to be morally right. But supererogatory actions are necessarily *not* morally required. One who acts supererogatorily is entitled to our praise, but we are not *entitled to demand* or expect supererogatory action of anyone. Since PR2 on occasion demands precisely that, it is too stringent as a principle of moral decision-making.

In evaluating this argument against PR2, we must pay careful attention to the sense in which PR2 is claimed sometimes to "require" or "demand" supererogatory action. PR2 does *not* imply that actions are sometimes "required" to be supererogatory *in order to be morally right*. But this is the only kind of "requirement" that would be inconsistent with the concept of supererogatory action. Therefore, PR2 is not guilty of the inconsistency that the preceding argument accuses it of. PR2 is a principle of *rational* action—of what we should do, *all things considered*. However, it does follow from PR2 that we may find ourselves in situations in which we should, *all things considered*, act supererogatorily. In such a case, our failure to act supererogatorily will be *irrational*. And some readers may find this sort of stringency unacceptable.

I grant that there is a tension here between PR2 and the notion that some actions are supererogatory. However, I believe that the correct way to resolve it is to give up the idea of supererogation rather than to reject PR2. In chapter 5, I shall take up this question in detail. I shall explain there why I believe that the category of supererogatory actions is one that moral philosophy would be better off without.

Applying PR2

One crucial test of PR2 is whether or not we can use it to solve difficult problems of moral decision-making. Later we shall focus on some of those problems, particularly those that pertain to abortion. However, it will be helpful first to identify some of the forms that moral uncertainty often takes to see how PR2 would apply to each. This will enable us to appreciate the approach to moral decision-making that PR2 represents as well as how that approach differs from the strategies that ethicists usually employ.

One kind of moral uncertainty that sometimes occurs, at least among philosophers, is uncertainty about which theory of moral rightness is *the* true theory. Let us imagine a moral agent named Gary who knows that one of two moral theories, T_1 and T_2, is the "true" theory but who is uncertain which one it is. Let us suppose that Gary somehow assigns .6 to the probability that T_1 is the true theory and assigns .4 to T_2's probability of being the true theory. If Gary were sure that exactly one alternative would accord with T_1, the theory more likely to be the true theory, then PR2 would imply that choosing that alternative would be rational. However, moral theories are often difficult to apply to actual decisions, and decision-makers sometimes are uncertain which actions in a situation would

Table 2.2   Decision Table for Example 2.3

	T_1 is the true theory. ($p = .6$)		T_2 is the true theory. ($p = .4$)	probability that act is morally right
	T_1 implies that x would be right and y would be wrong. ($p = .7$)	T_1 implies that y would be right and x would be wrong. ($p = .3$)		
do x	1	0	0	.42
do y	0	1	1	.58

satisfy a particular theory. For example, a moral theory that requires us to weigh various prima facie duties to determine which actions are morally right may offer little or no practical advice about how to determine which duties outweigh others in actual situations. We may be left in the dark about which alternative(s) would satisfy the theory in a particular case.

Let us consider the following example:

Example 2.3
Gary must choose between two alternatives, x and y. If Gary were certain that T_1 is the true moral theory, then he would be 70% sure that x would be morally right in that situation and y would be morally wrong and 30% sure that the opposite is true. If Gary were sure that T_2 is the true theory, then he would be 100% certain that y would be morally right for him to do and that x would be morally wrong. However, Gary believes that there is a .6 probability that T_1 is the true theory and a .4 probability that T_2 is the true theory.

Gary's decision in Example 2.3 is represented in Table 2.2. Here we continue to use the numerals 1 and 0 to signify moral rightness and moral wrongness, respectively. According to PR2, which action choice would be rational for Gary? To answer, we must determine which alternative, x or y, is more likely to be morally right. It is a simple matter to show that for the information in the table, the probability that x would be morally right for Gary to choose is .42 and the probability that y would be morally right for him is .58. Therefore, according to PR2, Gary should choose y.[16]

This example nicely shows what is wrong with the my-favorite-theory approach that philosophers often employ when they apply moral theories to specific moral problems. The my-favorite-theory approach sanctions the choice of any action that conforms to whatever theory one subscribes to. Of course, controversy continues to rage in ethics about which moral theory is the true theory and about what implications various theories have for specific moral problems. It is likely, therefore, that the vast majority of ethicists are uncertain whether the moral theories to which they subscribe are true as well as what their theories imply about specific moral choices. Hence, the moral decision represented by Table 2.2 may accurately capture a particular ethicist's beliefs about T_1 and T_2 and about what they imply about the moral rightness of the alternatives. That is, the ethicist may be only 60% sure that the moral theory T_1 to which she subscribes is the true theory and only 70% sure that it prescribes alternative x for Gary in the situation of Example 2.3. The my-favorite-theory approach recommends x for the decision-maker, but x has a lower probability of being morally right than the alternative y according to the table. If doing what is morally right is the agent's highest aspiration, then it would make no sense for him to choose x over y. Thus if Gary follows PR2 instead of the ethicist's favorite theory, T_1, it will make a difference in what he decides to do.

Another shortcoming of the my-favorite-theory approach is that it is sometimes silent about what to do when the decision-maker subscribes to no single moral theory. For example, someone who has studied moral theory extensively may regard three or more moral theories as plausible candidates but yet not have enough confidence in any one of them to accept it as the true theory. It is difficult to say in general how strongly one must believe something in order to believe that it is true. However, it is safe to say that if one assesses the probability that p is true to be less than .5, then she does not believe that p.

We might try to get around this problem by revising the my-favorite-theory approach so that it tells us to follow the (or a) moral theory in which we have the greatest confidence, even if our degree of confidence is insufficient to constitute belief. But the following example shows why this would not work:

Example 2.4
There are three theories, T_1, T_2, and T_3, whose probabilities of being true I assess to be .4, .45, and .15 respectively. I must decide, in a particular situation, between x and y where the pertinent information is given in decision Table 2.3.

For this situation, the modified my-favorite-theory approach would prescribe y, since y is the alternative that is in accordance with the theory (T_2) in which I have the greatest confidence (.45). However, this is the wrong result. Alternative x has a .55 probability of being morally right, whereas y has only a .45 probability of being morally right. PR2 shows that the rational choice for me is x. Thus maximizing the probability that one's action is morally right does not always mean following the most probable moral theory.[17]

One interesting feature of PR2 is that it would sometimes enable agents to break ties among actions sanctioned by a particular moral theory.

Example 2.5
A decision-maker must choose among x, y, and z, where the pertinent facts are given in decision Table 2.4.

Table 2.3   Decision Table for Example 2.4

	T_1 is true. ($p = .4$)	T_2 is true. ($p = .45$)	T_3 is true. ($p = .15$)	probability that act is morally right
do x	1	0	1	.55
do y	0	1	0	.45

Table 2.4 Decision Table for Example 2.5

	T_1 is true. ($p = .48$)	T_2 is true. ($p = .30$)	T_3 is true. ($p = .22$)	probability that act is morally right
do x	1	0	1	.48
do y	0	1	0	.70
do z	0	1	1	.52

T_1 sanctions both x and y, although when T_2 and T_3 are considered y has the greater likelihood of being morally right. According to PR2, y would be the rational choice.

Uncertainty about which moral theory is true is, of course, not the only source of moral uncertainty, and the application of PR2 is not limited to such decisions. Consider the following kind of situation:

Example 2.6

Irene has previously stated, "I shall do x," and now must decide whether to do x or to do y instead. She is uncertain whether her statement that she will do x constituted a promise in the first place. She is unsure whether her statement was the making of a promise to do x or was merely her stating her intentions to do x. Or perhaps it was nothing more than a simple prediction that she will do x in the situation that now occurs. (We are not always sure in our own minds which moral categories apply to our utterances, and we shall suppose this to be the case here.) Also, Irene is uncertain whether the promise that she may have made by her previous statement is morally binding in the current situation. (Perhaps Irene's now doing x would seriously disadvantage her in ways that she could not have foreseen when she made the original statement.) In this example, the moral rightness or wrongness of Irene's doing x and of her doing y depends in her mind on whether she has made a promise to do x and on whether her having done so would morally oblige her to do x.

Let us suppose in Example 2.6 that Irene is completely sure that she is morally right to do x if and only if she made a promise to do x and her having made such a promise means that she now is morally obligated to do x. Let us suppose further that she is certain that it would be morally right for her to do y just in case it would be morally wrong for her to do x. These conditions are represented in decision Table 2.5.

As shown in Table 2.5, p_1 is the probability that Irene has promised to do x and p_2 is the conditional probability that, assuming that Irene has promised to do x, she is therefore morally obliged to do x. We can then express $p(x)$, the probability that it would be morally right for Irene to do x, as follows: $p(x) = p_1 p_2$. Similarly $p(y)$, the probability that it would be morally right for Irene to do y, is given by $p(y) = p_1(1-p_2)+(1-p_1) = 1-p_1 p_2$. If Irene knows the magnitudes of p_1 and p_2, then she can determine which of $p(x)$ or $p(y)$ is the greater. PR2 advises her to choose the action with the greater probability of being morally right. This example thus shows how PR2 is applicable to decisions in which the relevant uncertainties are not about which moral principle is true.

The examples we have considered so far illustrate why a Rawlsian maximin decision principle would not work for decisions under moral uncertainty. For all of our examples and for most real-world moral decisions, every alternative has the same minimum—0. This is so because in every case to this point, for each alternative there is a possible state of affairs in which that alternative would be morally wrong. Since all alternatives have the same moral minimum, all of them would end in a tie if a maximin strategy was followed. A maximin strategy would discriminate among alternatives only in situations in which there is at least one alternative that would be morally right under all possible conditions. Although this may occasionally occur, such a happy set of circumstances is undoubtedly very rare. In the vast majority of situations, a maximin strategy would offer no reason for choosing any alternative over any other.

As I argued earlier, to accept PR2 as our principle for rational decision-making requires us to distinguish morality from rationality in action, since there is no guarantee that an action that has the maximum likelihood of being morally right will actually turn out to be morally right. As we have seen, this means that we must abandon the thesis that we should always, *all things considered*, do what is morally right, even if we limit its application to situations in which only moral considerations are relevant. One who wishes to hold onto the thesis might try to argue that although PR2 will not in general enable a decision-maker to overcome her moral uncertainty, in principle it could do so because any action sanctioned by PR2 is ipso facto morally right. According to this view, rational action is never really morally wrong even though we may sometimes act rationally without realizing that we are also acting morally.

However, this maneuver is untenable for the following reasons. If the actions sanctioned by PR2 were always morally right, then PR2 could be used as a *moral* principle:

It is always morally right to act so as to maximize the probability that your action will be morally right.

This is so because, even if a person were ignorant of the alleged connection between morality and rationality, she could be taught that the two are related in this way. If so, she would accept the preceding moral principle. Therefore, she would infer the moral rightness of any action that has maximum probability of being morally right. But this would resolve her initial moral uncertainty. Thus if

Table 2.5 Decision Table for Example 2.6

	Irene has promised to do x. (p_1)		Irene has not promised to do x. ($1 - p_2$)
	Irene ought (morally) to keep her promise to do x. (p_2)	Irene is not (morally) obligated to keep her promise to do x. ($1 - p_2$)	
do x	1	0	0
do y	0	1	1

the preceding moral principle were true, moral agents would in effect be infallible in judging that actions that satisfy the principle are morally right. However, this is not plausible. Moral agents can be mistaken in their moral judgments even if the actions they judge to be morally right have maximum probability of being morally right. Someone who sincerely believes that it is morally right for him to torture small children for his personal amusement believes falsely, regardless of how strongly he believes it. Therefore, we must reject the preceding moral principle and, with it, any identification of moral rightness with rationality in action.

Moral Luck

If we sometimes must make moral decisions without having any option the moral rightness of which we are certain, then sometimes we shall be lucky and choose actions that are in fact morally right while at other times we shall be unlucky in that same respect.[18] This sort of moral luck, which we might call *epistemic* moral luck, relates to our moral beliefs and how much confidence we have in them. For those of us who accept the possibilities both of accuracy and of error in those beliefs, the notion of epistemic moral luck seems unproblematic. However, another concept of moral luck, to which Bernard Williams has called attention, has been enlisted in a recent effort to discredit the traditional view of morality's importance for our action choices. If it succeeds, then it raises serious doubts about the wisdom of any project to develop rational strategies for decision-making under moral uncertainty.

In his essay "Moral Luck," Williams challenges what he contends "may be a basic motive for using . . . [the concept of the moral] . . . at all"—namely, "the motive of establishing a dimension of decision and assessment which can hope to transcend luck."[19] His target is what he takes to be the prevailing, Kantian conception of morality according to which "for the agent's reflective assessment of his own actions . . . at the ultimate and most important level, it cannot be a matter of luck whether he was justified in doing what he did."[20] Williams argues that in our *retrospective* assessments of our actions and of ourselves what is primarily important is whether our projects succeeded rather than whether our deliberations were rational. This is indicated, he thinks, by the facts that what we mainly regret are the failures of our major projects and that we assign those failures to ourselves, whether or not our actions in carrying them out were morally or rationally proper. Moreover, we do not regret successful outcomes, even if our actions violated norms of morality or rationality. Since well-chosen actions often do not guarantee successful lives and poorly chosen actions do not always spell failure, luck determines the final verdict. And since such verdicts judge *us* and the projects we pursue, they are ultimately the ones that count.

Williams's ideas about moral luck are important for our discussion of rational decision-making under moral uncertainty in the following way: If Williams is right and the importance of morality hinges on the impossibility of moral luck, then, it would seem, so does the importance of the problem of rational decision-making under moral uncertainty. So if moral luck, in Williams's sense, is possible, it follows that developing and employing a rational strategy for decision-making under moral uncertainty is much less important than I have claimed.

First, we should note the opposite effects of Williams's notion of moral luck and my notion of epistemic moral luck. For Williams the possibility of moral luck casts doubt on our "basic motive" for using the "concept" of morality. He concludes that skepticism about the "freedom of morality from luck" will make us skeptical also about the importance of morality. However, my notion of epistemic moral luck presupposes nothing about the importance of morality. On the contrary, in my view it is mainly because we recognize both the extreme importance of acting morally and our susceptibility to (epistemic) moral luck that we should adopt PR2 and its recommendation that we maximize the probabilities that our actions are morally right.

Williams would no doubt point out that even if one goes through life applying PR2 to her action choices, whether she will retrospectively judge herself to have been justified in living her life in that way is also a matter of luck. There is no assurance that she will not see herself as having failed even though she has "done the best she can" (according to PR2) at every stage. And, for Williams, it is this retrospective judgment that primarily counts. Her retrospective estimation that she did her best under the circumstances will be at most a consolation prize.

One is tempted to protest that even if we can never ensure that we shall succeed in the projects we embark upon, still we must act. And unless we embrace the implausible view that it never really matters, all things considered, what we do, some choices of action are better than others. PR2 is intended to help us determine which actions are worthy of being chosen. Williams does not deny that for some decisions our retrospective evaluations are properly based on the quality of our deliberations rather than on the successes or failures of the projects to which our actions were intended to contribute.[21] But, he believes, there are other, larger decisions, such as those about what sort of lives we shall lead or what overarching goals we shall strive to reach, for which the ultimate success or failure of our efforts determines whether we and our choices were justified.[22] And since rational decision-making, which is essentially *prospective* in its outlook, cannot guarantee this kind of success, there can be conflict between rationality, which assesses action alternatives *prospectively*, and Williamsian justification, which can only be assessed *retrospectively*.

Does Williams's notion of justification have any *practical* significance for decision-makers? Should it in any way influence what decision-makers decide to do? If not, then whatever conflict exists between our notion of rationality in action and Williamsian justification is, for practical purposes, irrelevant. If Williams's main message is that life is sometimes tragic and that we cannot always expect doing our best to lead to ultimate success, then this is no argument for not doing our best. But perhaps he does think that his views have practical implications in the following respect: If we always act in conformity with principles of rational decision-making, then we may never embark upon risky but worthwhile projects the successful completion of which would afford us the most significant kind of success in life. By slavishly following the directives of rationality, we may lose the only opportunities we have of achieving this sort of success. And by the same token, one who forsakes rationality in pursuit of a perilous project that she successfully completes is justified in a more important respect than one who, though leading a life of perfect rationality, fails to accomplish her chosen mission. There is thus a choice to be made between two lifestyles, which I shall refer to as the life of the *rational agent* and the life of the *romantic*. Perhaps Williams is urging us to take the choice seriously and not automatically assume the superiority of the rational agent. If this is his point, then it does appear to have a kind of practical, decision-making significance.

This interpretation of Williams's position raises the following question: how do I choose among possible life styles, including that of the rational agent and that of the romantic? We shall explore this question in some depth in chapter 8. For the moment, let us note that I may choose either the life of the rational agent, that of the romantic, or neither. And clearly not all lifestyles are equal. A life that aims at no worthwhile goal and that abysmally fails to meet rational requirements is inferior in all relevant respects. Also, among possible romantic lifestyles there are significant differences. The projects I undertake must be at least minimally worthwhile. I may eliminate from consideration the project of becoming the world's greatest con artist, for example.

Should it matter, for the romantic, how likely it is that she would successfully complete the projects that she contemplates? Williams does not address this question specifically.[23] However, it is implausible to say that an individual need not consider the likelihood of realizing her goals. Even if the goal were worthwhile, my launching a training program for the purpose of my becoming a starting center in the National Basketball Association would be absurd if I were 5' 6" tall and had little athletic ability. Therefore, although the choice of a romantic lifestyle may entail accepting relatively large chances of failure, there are limits on the magnitudes of the risks that even the romantic may defensibly accept.

We may ask other questions about the romantic's choices of projects. We may inquire whether the merit of a person's chosen project varies directly with the worthiness of the purpose(s) that the project is intended to serve. But we have said enough at this point to conclude that even for the romantic, justification is prospective as well as retrospective. Romanticism does not mean that "anything goes" as far as choices of projects are concerned. There is a norm, the particulars of which we have not yet identified, that applies prospectively to the romantic's action choices. Of course, prospective justification will not always agree with Williamsiam retrospective justification. But for purposes of action choice, an inherently prospective activity, such incongruity need not concern us. Perhaps it is reasonable for us to wish that we had done things differently even when we view our deliberations that led to action as rationally impeccable. Such a wish may amount to regret, and we might prefer never having regrets to always acting rationally. However, we rarely, if ever, know enough about present and future circumstances to be able to remove all possibility of regret-producing failure. And even if we had it within our power to avert all future regrets, it is doubtful that this should be the only consideration.

If we view matters in this light, we may wonder why we should not regard the norm that would govern choices among possible romantic lifestyles as a criterion for *moral* choices, of the same genus as utilitarian criteria, Kantian criteria, social contract criteria, and other such contenders. Perhaps the factors that a criterion based on Williams's insights into moral luck would appeal to would be moral considerations of a radically new kind.[24] But there is no reason to suppose that we may not handle uncertainty about their authenticity and about their proper application to decision situations in much the same way that we would manage uncertainty about other moral criteria. We need not abandon PR2 on account of them. Perhaps there is no way to immunize ourselves against "moral luck," good or bad, but this does not mean that we should not get on with the job of making decisions in the best way we can.

We are now at the point at which we can fruitfully discuss specific kinds of moral decisions. We shall begin that discussion in the following chapter, where we shall start with PR2 as our principle of rationality for decision-making under moral uncertainty. Although we shall later find reasons to revise and refine that principle, it will be helpful to see what practical implications about moral decision-making follow from PR2 when we apply it to controversial moral issues. The issue of abortion will be a good test for PR2, to test whether it provides any clear direction for moral agents who must make decisions about abortion and also whether PR2's implications for those decisions make sense to us.

Three

Abortion and Moral Uncertainty

As we observed in the preceding chapter, our principle for decision-making under moral uncertainty, PR2, is a dramatic departure from the ways in which ethicists tacitly advise us to manage moral uncertainty in choosing our actions. One reason is that PR2 advises us to *maximize* the probability that our actions will be morally right. In situations in which we have good reason to accept more than one alternative as morally justified, maximizing probable moral rightness will sometimes lead us to decline alternatives that we justifiably believe to be morally right. Moral philosophy has so far failed to recognize such optimization as important for moral decision-making. However, if the discussion in chapter 2 is sound, we should make our moral decisions on the basis of this criterion.

We can find no better example of the impact that PR2 would have on our moral decision-making than by seeing its implications for decisions about abortion. There are few moral issues that are more controversial or that engender uncertainties that are more difficult to resolve. Those who must decide whether to have abortions are highly likely to be at least somewhat unsure of the moral rightness of abortion. And the more those decision-makers know about what contemporary moral philosophy has to say on the subject, the more profound their uncertainty is likely to be. Nevertheless, they must decide what to do. Obviously they cannot postpone their decisions until philosophers have reached a consensus on abortion.

Given the world as it is, these decision-makers will act under moral uncertainty. How best to do so is our main concern in this chapter.

Despite the difficulties we encounter in attempting to discern when it is morally right for someone to seek an abortion, determining whether it is *rational* to do so is, for many decisions, relatively straightforward. The ease with which we can apply PR2 to those decisions contrasts sharply with the notorious difficulty of applying general moral principles to the abortion issue. In applying PR2 we shall identify some, but not all, of the unresolved moral issues that pertain to abortion. But instead of making futile attempts to achieve certainty about those issues, we shall bypass them by addressing the question of rationality instead. Fortunately, this latter question, we shall find, is generally much easier to answer. Furthermore, answering it allows agents to proceed with their decision-making in the best, most reasonable way available.

Some abortion decisions, however, present difficulties in the application of PR2 that will require us to employ a second-order decision principle. We shall consider such decisions later in this chapter. PR2 thus represents work-in-progress. We shall not finish our project of developing a satisfactory account of moral decision-making until the end of this book.

Making Decisions about Abortion

The abortion issue is fraught with uncertainty. Despite philosophers' best efforts at resolving it, the question of the moral rightness of abortion remains extremely contentious. No general agreement has been reached on such underlying issues as whether, or which, fetuses are persons and whether fetal persons would have a right to life that is violated when they are aborted. The arguments on opposite sides of those issues have become extremely intricate, and no consensus is likely to be reached in the foreseeable future—if ever. Virtually no one who has carefully considered questions that relate to the moral rightness of abortion is 100% certain that fetuses are, or are not, full-fledged persons who possess a right to life that is violated whenever they are aborted. In the contemporary debate about abortion, certainty about the moral rightness or wrongness of abortion is a sign of gross ignorance or fanaticism.

There is, however, one aspect of the abortion issue that appears to generate little, if any, disagreement or uncertainty. Although they rarely assert it, the vast majority of moral agents tacitly accept the proposition that in most situations *not* having an abortion is morally right and therefore justified *all things considered*. Almost everyone agrees that, except perhaps for special cases like deformed fetuses or serious threats to the lives of pregnant women, it is morally right *not* to have an abortion. No one has noticed that, in almost every case, decision-makers who choose between having an abortion and not doing so are choosing between alternatives the moral rightness of which are of definitely unequal degrees of certainty. Since the problem is ultimately one of rational decision-making under moral uncertainty, this difference in degree of certainty is critically important.

The following argument shows why this difference is important:

1. In situations in which decision-makers are uncertain about the moral rightness of some of the alternative actions, the *rational* strategy is to choose an action that has maximum probability of being morally right. (This is PR2 from the preceding chapter.)
2. In the vast majority of situations in which decision-makers decide whether to have abortions, *not* having an abortion has greater probability of being morally right than having an abortion.

   Therefore,

   In the vast majority of situations in which decision-makers decide whether to have abortions, *not* having an abortion is the *reasonable* choice of action.

The significance of this argument is that, if sound, it shows that much of philosophers' discussion of the morality of abortion is for practical (i.e., decision-making) purposes unnecessary. For the most part, ethicists who seek to provide guidance for women who must decide whether to have abortions are concerned with the question of whether, or when having an abortion is morally right. These ethicists assume that women are justified, all things considered, in having abortions if it is morally right for them to do so. The preceding argument shows what is wrong with this assumption.

It is important to contrast this reasoning with what is called the moral safety argument or the argument from uncertainty. The latter argument says that because we cannot be sure that fetuses are not persons, abortion is at risk of killing innocent persons and is therefore *morally* wrong. By contrast, the conclusion of the preceding argument is about the *rationality* of abortion—whatever moral status abortion may have. This argument leaves completely open the question of whether, or when, abortion is morally right and thereby avoids the most potent criticisms of the moral safety argument.[1]

Even ethicists who are the strongest defenders of abortion would hesitate to claim that they are as certain that abortion is morally right in the most common cases as they are that *not* having an abortion is morally right in those cases. It is possible, of course, that further progress will be made on the morality-of-abortion issue. I do not claim that ethicists should not continue to try to remove as much of our doubt as possible. It is even conceivable that we shall eventually eliminate all uncertainty and disagreement on this issue. But given the inconclusiveness of the abortion debate so far, many decision-makers who must decide what to do, both now and in the near future, cannot avoid making their personal abortion decisions in an environment of uncertainty about the moral rightness of abortion.

Because ethicists have been preoccupied with the moral rightness question and have ignored the problem of rational decision-making under *moral* uncertainty, they have provided at best conflicting and misleading advice to moral agents about what they should, in the final analysis, do. However, if the preceding argument is sound, philosophers can speak with a clear voice on the question of how abortion decisions should, *all things considered*, be made, even if there is no consensus on the question of the moral rightness of abortion. For *decision-makers*, the former is the more acute issue.

Abortion Decisions and Moral Uncertainty

Let us consider in greater detail the implications of PR2 for morally problematic decisions, such as those that involve abortion. We must bear in mind that in order for *not* having an abortion to be morally wrong, having an abortion must be morally *obligatory*. That *not* having an abortion under normal circumstances is morally right is accepted by almost everyone, even the strongest proabortion advocates. Doubts about the moral propriety of not having abortions exist, if at all, only for exceptional cases such as those that involve defective fetuses, serious threats to the health of pregnant women, and pregnancies that result from rape or incest. Almost everyone agrees that, ordinarily, women who choose to bring their fetuses to term do not act wrongly. The moral questions are raised only about women who decide to discontinue their pregnancies. Thus only rarely will having an abortion be more likely in the decision-maker's mind to be morally obligatory than to be morally wrong.

Recent philosophical discussion of the morality of abortion has concentrated on two underlying issues: (1) Are fetuses persons (or, more precisely, which fetuses, if any, are persons)? and (2) would a fetus's being a person make aborting it morally wrong? Some philosophers who take a generally proabortion point of view, Judith Jarvis Thomson notably, contend that the personhood issue is not always critical and that pregnant women often may exercise their rights by removing an unwanted fetus without violating the fetus's right to life.[2] Other philosophers, such as Mary Anne Warren and Michael Tooley, believe that the moral justification of abortion requires the nonpersonhood of the fetus, and they propose criteria for personhood that, in their view, fetuses do not satisfy.[3] The debate on these two issues has been extremely difficult to resolve, and no clear-cut resolution is in sight. For our purposes here it is sufficient simply to note that significant uncertainty exists about whether, or which, fetuses are persons and whether fetal personhood implies the moral wrongness of having an abortion.[4]

Table 3.1 represents one kind of abortion decision in which these uncertainties arise. Here the decision-maker is uncertain whether *her* fetus is a person and whether *her* fetus's being a person would make *her* having an abortion morally wrong. Consequently, she is uncertain whether having an abortion would be morally right. However, she has no doubt that continuing her pregnancy would be morally right. The "no abortion" alternative is the moral analogue of what decision theorists call a dominant strategy—that is, an action that in every eventuality produces a result at least as desirable as any other option would produce and,

Table 3.1   Decision Table for One Kind of Abortion Decision

	This fetus is a person.		This fetus is not a person.
	Personhood implies that abortion is wrong.	Personhood does not imply that abortion is wrong.	
abortion	0	1	1
no abortion	1	1	1

under at least one set of circumstances, produces a more desirable result. Clearly, only this "dominant strategy" would satisfy PR2 in the preceding situation.[5]

Does recent philosophical discussion of the morality of abortion alter the picture painted here? The answer appears to be "No." Virtually all of that discussion continues to be concerned with the moral rightness of having abortions. It is extremely difficult to find any ethicist willing to argue that seeking an abortion, except in unusual or pathological situations, is morally obligatory.[6] Thus there appears to be general agreement that in ordinary situations not having an abortion has the greater likelihood of being morally right. Therefore, according to PR2 the former is the rational choice of action. This means that in light of PR2 ethicists should recommend the "no abortion" alternative for the vast majority of women who must decide whether to have abortions.

But do we ever really know *with certainty* that not having an abortion is morally right? Can we ordinarily be completely sure that there is no moral obligation to have an abortion? The preceding results may prompt us to reconsider our answer to this question. One's certainty about the moral rightness of the "no abortion" option may erode when she notices that it makes not having an abortion a *dominant* strategy. Of course, changing one's beliefs or pretending to change them in an ad hoc way for the sole purpose of maintaining some preconceived notion is, logically speaking, bad faith. But we are not talking here about changing one's beliefs in the sense of going from believing p to believing not-p, or conversely. Rather, we are talking about going from being certain that p to being less than certain that p. And the shift occurs as a result of seeing that believing p with certainty leads to conclusions that the moral agent is indisposed to accept. This is not unusual. It is reasonable for us to question our beliefs if we find that they do not cohere. Questioning our beliefs does not mean that we abandon them, although that may sometimes be the result. Nor does it always mean that we are intellectually dishonest. A weakening of one's prior beliefs about the morality of abortion may be a reasonable reaction to the kind of consideration we are discussing here.

It would be unreasonable, however, to weaken one's beliefs without having grounds for doing so. For Table 3.1, if the agent were no longer 100% certain that the "no abortion" option is morally right, then that option would no longer dominate and the table would have to be revised. But how could not having an abortion be morally wrong, except possibly under such dire circumstances as mortal danger to the woman of continuing her pregnancy, strong evidence that the fetus is seriously defective, or pregnancy that resulted from rape or incest? And even these extreme cases are problematic. For what would we say of a woman who, though pregnant as a result of rape, chose not to have an abortion in order not to blame the fetus for the actions of the rapist? Would we claim that she acted wrongly? Or would we believe instead that her action was supererogatory?[7] If the latter, then unless supererogatory actions can somehow be morally wrong we must conclude that she acted rightly in not having an abortion.[8]

However, the following objection to this reasoning might be raised: Criticizing someone's choosing to have an abortion on the grounds that not having an abortion would be supererogatory would be like condemning someone's swatting mosquitoes or houseflies on the basis of an extreme but not totally improbable "reverence for life" principle. Our admiration of famously humane individuals, like Albert Schweitzer, appears to betray at least a little doubt in our minds about the morality of killing sentient beings. Are the actions of someone who, out of reverence for sentient life, refuses to kill insects any less supererogatory than those of one who abstains from abortion in the situation described earlier? And if not, why do our observations about the supererogatory rape victim not also apply to someone who, for similar reasons, refrains from killing insect pests? Since the latter policy is obviously absurd (it would be claimed by the critic of PR2), something must be seriously wrong with the argument about the rape victim.

One reply to this criticism is that there is a very slender boundary between supererogation on the one hand and foolish or pointless self-sacrifice on the other. While the actions of someone who endures personal hardship in order to preserve the life of a human fetus may perhaps be deemed supererogatory, the actions of another who on principle refuses to swat mosquitoes might more accurately be described as pathological. We need not be sure exactly where to draw the line between supererogation and morally illicit self-denial. If there is doubt in a particular case, like the "swatting mosquitoes" illustration, that alone is sufficient to disqualify the act as a morally dominant alternative.

Nevertheless, for some abortion decisions it may be difficult to say whether refraining from abortion would be supererogatory or morally wrong. Consider (1) a situation in which continuing a pregnancy would, with virtual certainty, cause the deaths both of the woman and of the fetus and (2) a situation in which the fetus is known to be so terribly defective that its life after birth would be one of unremitting suffering. Would refraining from having abortions in these two cases be supererogatory—by expressing the decision-maker's reverence for human life? Or would it be morally wrong because it fails to give sufficient weight to the decision-maker's own interests and, in the second case, those of the fetus as well? If one had doubts about the answers to these questions, she would also have doubts about the moral rightness of not having an abortion in those situations. Therefore, it behooves us to consider abortion decisions in which the "no abortion" alternative is not dominant.

This brings us back to the question, How can it be morally obligatory for someone to have an abortion? One plausible answer is that having an abortion would be morally obligatory if the consequences of not having an abortion were worse than those of ending the pregnancy. This answer, of course, assumes a consequentialist morality that is fundamentally different from the moral perspective presupposed in the preceding decision table, which casts the moral issues in terms of the moral status of the fetus. Let us call the latter the nonconsequentialist perspective.

Would the consequentialist perspective really support the view that not having an abortion in the situation we are imagining would be morally wrong? The answer is not obvious. One would have to infer somehow that the overall consequences of not having the abortion would be worse than those of having the abortion. And this would depend on the agent's expectations about the effects of each of her alternatives on those whose welfare will be affected by her decision. But who are these people whose welfare will be affected? This is impossible to say with any precision, since there is no way to tell what sort of person will enter the world if the agent decides to continue her pregnancy. Will the child grow up to be a great medical researcher? a violent criminal? a prominent engineer? a corrupt politician?

Of course, one person whose welfare will definitely be affected by the agent's decision is the agent herself. And we can suppose that she has at least some reason to doubt that it is in her interest to continue her pregnancy because it is she who is contemplating abortion. Perhaps she is single and will suffer the stigma that attaches to young, unwed mothers in some sectors of society. Or having a child at this stage of her life may seriously disrupt her plans for college or a career. To make the case interesting, let us suppose that the agent has good reason to believe that it would be in her interest to have the abortion. Let us also assume that, from a consequentialist perspective, her welfare is a major consideration because she expects her interests to be affected by her decision far more than the interests of others, including the (potential) father, her other children, other members of her family, and society at large.

Is there anyone else whose interests need be considered? How about the fetus's interests? Here the personhood issue reappears. The reason is that, from one kind of consequentialist perspective, the only interests we are obligated to weigh are those of persons. Let us hypothesize that this is the form of consequentialism that the agent is using. On this view, whether the fetus's interests are morally relevant depends entirely on whether the fetus is a person. And this is one of the questions, we are assuming, about which the decision-maker is uncertain. Therefore, whether not having the abortion would be morally right according to this consequentialist criterion depends in part on whether this particular fetus is a person.[9]

If this fetus is a person, does it have an interest in not being aborted? In some cases, it may be possible to argue that a fetus's interests would best be served by being aborted. This might be true if the fetus were seriously deformed or defective. It might also be true if the child that the fetus would become would have to endure great poverty, suffering, or abuse because of the social environment that it would inherit. However, for most of us our lives are rewarding and worth living. Being aborted would have deprived us of the joys, accomplishments, friendships, and other benefits that, despite the disappointments, failures, and losses we all experience, make our lives valuable to ourselves. It was in our interest, as fetal persons, not to be aborted. Unless the agent has special reason to believe otherwise, she should make similar judgments about other fetuses. Let us suppose that this is her judgment.

If we assume that the consequentialist criterion is the "true" moral theory and that the agent cannot even estimate the effects of her decision on anyone other than the fetus and herself, then her decision may be represented by Table 3.2. Here p_1 is the probability that this fetus is a person (i.e., has a right not to be killed), and p_2 is the conditional probability that, given that this fetus is a person, its interests outweigh the agent's interests. Ex hypothesi, only the agent's and fetus's interests can affect the moral outcome. Therefore, in the event that the fetus's interests need be taken into consideration (i.e., in the event that the fetus is a person), whether an alternative is right or wrong depends entirely on whose interests have the greater weight. This is so because we are assuming that our consequentialist moral criterion regards only persons as having morally relevant

Table 3.2   Abortion, Consequentialism, and Moral Uncertainty

| | This fetus is a person. (p_1) | | This fetus is not a person. ($1 - p_1$) |
	This fetus's interests outweigh the agent's interests. (p_2)	The agent's interests outweigh this fetus's interests. ($1 - p_2$)	
abortion	0	1	1
no abortion	1	0	0

interests. In the third column of the table, where the fetus is not a person, the only interests that matter are the agent's interests, which we have assumed are best served by her choosing the abortion alternative. We must remember that our consequentialist criterion obliges the agent to choose the alternative that would have the better overall consequences. If either the agent's interests outweigh the fetus's or the fetus's interests are irrelevant, she is morally obligated to have the abortion. Hence, the 1s and 0s in the second and third columns. Here, unlike Table 3.1, neither of the agent's alternatives dominates the other. Therefore, in order to apply PR2, we would have to consider the magnitudes of the probabilities involved.

It may be helpful to contrast Table 3.2, which we would construct in order to apply PR2 to the agent's decision, with the sort of decision table we might use if we were applying an MEU decision principle. For the latter, the numbers in the table would measure the utilities of various possible outcomes rather than the moral rightness or wrongness of the alternatives under the various combinations of conditions. Let us suppose, for the moment, that underlying the uncertainty associated with p_2 is the agent's uncertainty about whether the fetus, if brought to term, would live an exceptionally happy and interesting future life or would live a relatively unhappy and unrewarding life. Let us also make the unlikely assumption that in the agent's mind these are the only two possibilities—no moderately happy and successful life for the fetal person need be considered—and that she has precise utility measurements for all possible outcomes. Then we might have something like Table 3.3. The 100s in the first row represent the fact that, if the fetus is aborted, its contribution to the total utility is 0. In that case (let us suppose), the utility for the agent is the total utility and is not affected by the conditions associated with p_1 and p_2. The 50 in the table is the agent's diminished utility if she chooses the "no abortion" alternative. Ex hypothesi, because the third

Table 3.3   Abortion and the MEU Decision Principle

| | This fetus is a person. (p_1) | | This fetus is not a person. ($1 - p_1$) |
	This fetus's interests outweigh the agent's interests. (p_2)	The agent's interests outweigh this fetus's interests. ($1 - p_2$)	
abortion	100	100	100
no abortion	150	80	50

column represents the condition of the fetus's nonpersonhood, the utility of its future life does not affect the total. However, under the conditions of the first and second columns, the fetus's utility does enter into the total utility. The two remaining utilities, 150 and 80, reflect the agent's uncertainty about which of the two possible future lives the fetus would live if it were not aborted.

If we apply the expected utility formula to Table 3.3, we get EU(abortion) = 100, and EU(no abortion) = $150p_1p_2 + 80p_1(1-p_2) + 50(1-p_1) = 70p_1p_2 + 30p_1 + 50$. If $p_1 = .8$ and $p_2 = .6$, then it turns out that EU(no abortion) = 107.6, which is greater than EU(abortion). Hence, the MEU decision principle prescribes the "no abortion" alternative. This disagrees with PR2. From Table 3.2, EMR(abortion) = $1 - p_1p_2$, and EMR(no abortion) = p_1p_2. For $p_1 = .8$ and $p_2 = .6$, EMR(abortion)=.52, which exceeds EMR(no abortion)=.48. One reason we get different results is that the consequentialist moral criterion employed by Table 3.2 directs the agent to *achieve* the best outcome. By using PR2 as her decision principle, she gives herself the greatest possible chance of doing so. However, for Table 3.3 the alternative that has the greater probability of achieving the best outcome is not the alternative that has maximum *expected* utility. Thus, PR2 produces a different prescription from the MEU decision principle.

But what if an MEU principle were the agent's *moral* principle rather than her decision principle? And what if that MEU moral principle required the agent to include the utility of all affected persons in her expected-utility calculations? Then the *correct* application of the MEU principle would depend on whether the fetus is a person, and the agent would be unsure whether to include the fetus's utility in the total. Under these conditions, the agent might resort to PR2 to deal with her *moral* uncertainty about the true implications of the MEU principle for her decision. She could use the following reasoning: If the fetus is a person, then EU(abortion) = 100, and EU(no abortion) = $150p_2 + 80(1-p_2) = 70p_2 + 80$. However, if the fetus is not a person, then EU(abortion) = 100, and EU (no abortion) = 50. In the latter case, the MEU moral principle prescribes the "abortion" alternative. In the former case, which alternative the MEU principle prescribes depends on the magnitude of p_2. Table 3.4 summarizes the pertinent information. Table 3.4 is like Table 3.2 in that what PR2 prescribes depends on p_1 and p_2. For $p_1=.8$ and $p_2=.6$, EMR(abortion) = $(.8)(0)+(.2)(1) = .2$, and EMR(no abortion) = $(.8)(1)+(.2)(0) = .8$. Since EMR(no abortion) > EMR(abortion), PR2 prescribes the "no abortion" alternative.

Let us now return to Table 3.2 and assume that it describes the agent's situation and, moreover, that the consequentialist moral principle we have in mind is a maximize-utility principle. In the decision represented by Table 3.2, the agent is uncertain (1) whether this fetus is a person who possesses a right not to be killed and (2) whether, in the event that this fetus is a person, its interests outweigh those of the agent. In concord with the consequentialist moral perspective outlined earlier, the agent is morally *obligated* to have an abortion except when the fetus's interests outweigh her own, in which case she is obligated not to have an abortion. This situation is more difficult to analyze than that of Table 3.1 because there is no morally dominant strategy. Which of the two alternatives is more likely to be morally right depends on two "component probabilities"—(1)

the probability that *this* fetus is a person and (2) the conditional probability that, provided that *this* fetus is a person, its interests outweigh the agent's interests.

Let us adopt the following abbreviations:

$p(A)$: the probability that having the abortion is morally right

$p(\text{not-}A)$: the probability that not having the abortion is morally right

In order to apply PR2, we must determine which of the two alternatives has the greater probability of being morally right—that is, whether $p(A) \geq p(\text{not-}A)$ or conversely. It is easy to show that $p(A) \geq p(\text{not-}A)$ if and only if $p_1 p_2 \geq .5$. It is quite possible that the decision-maker will have no difficulty deciding which alternative has the greater likelihood of being morally right.[10] If, for example, $p_1 \geq .5$, then $p_1 p_2 \geq .5$ regardless of the size of p_2. This means that if there is no more than an even chance that *this* fetus is a person, then PR2 sanctions the "abortion" alternative. Moreover, if $p_2 \geq .5$, the same conclusion applies. Thus, according to PR2 and Table 3.2, in order for the "no abortion" option to be a rational choice, both p_1 and p_2 must be no less than .5.

What if the decision-maker is not sure that both p_1 and p_2 are at least .5? Then she may wish to assess their magnitudes more precisely in order to determine which of the two "resultant probabilities," $p(A)$ and $p(\text{not-}A)$, is greater. Let us consider how she might analyze her decision to produce such a probability comparison.

The direct approach to testing the inequality $p_1 p_2 \geq .5$ would be to measure each of the probabilities p_1 and p_2 and then check to see whether the inequality holds. And how she should go about measuring them depends on what kind of probabilities she considers them to be. The standard method of measuring *subjective* probabilities involves agents' making hypothetical choices between receiving certain sums of money outright and taking gambles in which the probability to be measured determines the odds of winning some monetary prize. The sums are varied until a point of indifference is found, and then the probability being measured is evaluated on the assumption that the decision-maker's choices are directed toward maximizing her expected utility.[11] One complication is that it is necessary first to measure the utilities associated with the various sums of money.

The drawbacks to this method of measuring subjective probabilities are well-known. Decision-makers may have little confidence that their hypothetical choices accurately predict what their actual choices would be if they were actually to make those choices. Moreover, for complicated situations one's choices may vio-

Table 3.4 Abortion and Uncertainty about Application of the MEU Moral Principle

	The fetus is a person. (p_1)			The fetus is not a person. ($1 - p_1$)
	$p_2 < 2/7$	$p_2 = 2/7$	$p_2 > 2/7$	
abortion	1	1	0	1
no abortion	0	1	1	0

late the probability calculus and may be affected by the manner and order in which the agent entertains the various options. Also, decision-makers may be averse to risk itself, which may distort the utility and probability measurements.[12]

What if we conceive p_1 and p_2 as *objective* probabilities rather than as subjective probabilities? Then it may not be possible to obtain exact single-number measurements. The agent may have to settle for estimating the values of p_1 and p_2. One method would try only to locate the probabilities within ranges or intervals of possible values. For example, a decision-maker may be unable to say with assurance that the probability that a certain fetus is a person is exactly .5 but may be confident that p_1 is somewhere between .4 and .6. This sort of information about component probabilities may be enough to allow the decision-maker to apply PR2.[13]

To illustrate, let us consider again the preceding situation and suppose that the decision-maker assesses the probabilities as follows: $.5 \leq p_1 \leq .7$ and $.4 \leq p_2 \leq .6$. The situation may be represented graphically as in Figure 3.1, where the small square in the graph contains all the points that satisfy the constraints on p_1 and p_2. The curve, labeled $p_1p_2 = .5$, represents that relationship between p_1 and p_2. The region below and/or to the left of the curve represents the values of p_1 and p_2 for which the "abortion" alternative would satisfy PR2. The small square in the graph, labeled "region of uncertainty," represents the values of p_1 and p_2 that satisfy the constraints on the two probabilities. The graph shows that the region of uncertainty is entirely contained within the region where the "abortion" alternative would be a rational choice. This means that for the consequentialist moral perspective and the preceding assessments of p_1 and p_2 the "abortion" option would be the rational choice according to PR2. The opposite would be the case if the region of uncertainty were wholly outside the area where the "abortion" option is the rational choice.

What if the region of uncertainty had been partly inside and partly outside the region where the "abortion" alternative would be the rational choice? Let us

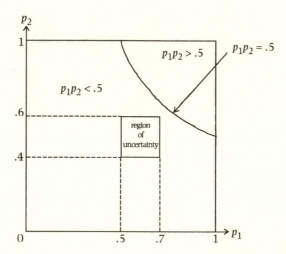

Figure 3.1   Application of PR2 to Decision of
Table 3.2—I

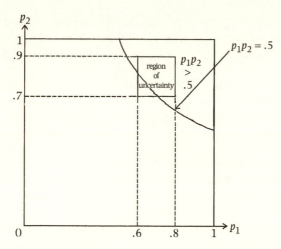

Figure 3.2   Application of PR2 to Decision of
Table 3.2—II

modify our example by supposing that $.6 \leq p_1 \leq .8$ and $.7 \leq p_2 \leq .9$. This situation is represented in Figure 3.2. Here the region of uncertainty is partly inside the region where the "abortion" option would be the rational choice according to PR2. Since the decision-maker is not sure of the true values of p_1 and p_2, it is impossible to say with certainty whether $p_1 p_2 \leq .5$. However, if we assume that p_1 and p_2 are as likely to have one value as another within their respective ranges, then it seems reasonable to suppose that the *likelihood* that the "abortion" alternative would be the rational choice according to PR2 would be the ratio of the size of the region of uncertainty that is inside the area where the "abortion" option would be the rational choice to the total size of the region of uncertainty. For this example, this ratio can be shown to be approximately .18.[14] It follows that the *likelihood* that PR2 prescribes the "no abortion" alternative is approximately .82.[15]

We should note here that in treating the magnitudes of p_1 and p_2 as unknown and considering which alternative is more likely to accord with PR2, we are appealing to a second-order probability—namely, the probability that the "abortion" option has a greater probability of being morally right than the "no abortion" option. We must use second-order probabilities, since there is not enough information to say with certainty which alternative has the greater probability of being morally right. All we can say is that one or the other is more likely to have the greater probability of being morally right.[16]

What then should the decision-maker do in this situation of uncertainty? We cannot answer on the basis of PR2 alone, since we cannot say with certainty which alternative has the maximum probability of being morally right. However, we can say what PR2 *probably* would approve if we had more precise information about the probabilities p_1 and p_2. Therefore, it seems reasonable to employ the following rule:

PR3

Whenever there is uncertainty about which actions are approved by PR2, act so as to maximize the probability that your action is approved by PR2.

PR3 is a second-order principle of rationality that is useful whenever one does not have enough information to apply PR2 directly. It is helpful to decision-makers who are uncertain about moral theories, rules, and principles and their implications for their particular decisions and also about the magnitudes of the pertinent first-order probabilities.

The reader may wonder how we can have two principles of rationality, PR2 and PR3, that are not equivalent to each other. They are not equivalent because maximizing the probability that one's action satisfies PR2 need not actually satisfy PR2. Therefore, the potential for conflict between PR2 and PR3 exists and thus rationality seems potentially to be at war with itself. However, this is a problem that, for practical decision-making purposes, moral agents need not worry about. Whenever agents are certain what PR2 prescribes, there will be no conflict between the two principles. And whenever they are uncertain what PR2 calls for, they will not have to choose between doing what *they believe* PR2 advises and doing what *they believe* PR3 recommends. Therefore, decision-makers will never have to resolve conflicts between the two principles in order to make decisions.

Still we may wonder which actions *really* are rational in cases in which PR2 and PR3 conflict. If we wish to say that the agent who correctly follows PR3 acts rationally, then we may either (1) identify PR3 as *the* true rational criterion that we follow ipso facto whenever we act in accordance with PR2 or (2) view rationality as a genus with two species, rationality$_1$ and rationality$_2$, embodied in PR2 and PR3, respectively. If we follow the second route, then there may be instances in which we act rationally$_2$ but not rationally$_1$. In that event, there will be no simple unitary answer to the question of whether we are acting rationally. But, again, these are matters that, for practical purposes, we need not concern ourselves with.

There are several potential drawbacks to the sort of analysis employed here. One is that the assumption that all values of the component probabilities within their respective ranges are equally likely to be the true values of those probabilities may not be valid. For example, decision-makers may consider values near the midpoints of the intervals to be more plausible than those near the end points. Another problem is that the final result may depend on somewhat arbitrary choices of the ranges of the values of the component probabilities. For example, a decision-maker may be certain that p_1 is between .3 and .7 and only slightly less confident that p_1 is between .5 and .6. Which interval then should the decision-maker take as the range of possible values of p_1? The final result may depend on the selection. It seems plausible that smaller intervals will give more significant results, since they will more closely envelop the true values. However, as the intervals get smaller, decision-makers may become unsure whether the true values of the probabilities are contained in them. Therefore, decision-makers may find it difficult to decide which ranges of values to use.[17]

A different method of analysis, and one that makes weaker assumptions about decision-makers' abilities to measure probabilities, is based on the use of ordinal measurements of the component probabilities. Instead of assigning a single number or interval of numbers as the magnitude of a particular probability, the decision-maker simply judges which probabilities are larger than others. For example, for the preceding abortion decision in which neither action is dominant, the decision-maker may be certain only that, say, $0 \leq p_1 \leq p_2 \leq 1$. If this was the only information available about p_1 and p_2, it would not be possible to say with assurance whether $p(A) > p(\text{not-}A)$. Hence, PR2 would not be directly applicable. However, PR3 would be applicable. To see how, let us consider the following analogous decision:

You are to play the following game. There are two urns, A and B. Each urn contains 100 balls. In A all the balls are either black or white, and in B all the balls are either red or blue. To play the game, you do nothing other than choose between two gambles, X and Y. The game proceeds by first selecting a ball at random from urn A. If the ball turns out to be black, the game ends. If it turns out to be white, a ball is then selected at random from urn B. The game then ends. At the end of the game, you collect either $1,000 or $0 in accordance with Table 3.5. The object of the game is to win $1,000.

Which gamble, X or Y, should you make in order to maximize your expected winnings? We may think of the numbers of balls of each color in the two urns in terms of probabilities. For example, we may associate the number of white balls in urn A with the probability p_1 that a ball drawn at random from urn A would be white. Similarly, we may let the probability p_2 that a ball drawn at random from urn B would be red be the number of red balls in urn B divided by 100. If you knew how many balls of each color were in the two urns, it would be relatively easy to determine which option, X or Y, would have the greater expected value. For example, if you knew that there were 60 white balls in urn A and 70 red balls in urn B, then $p_1 = .60$ and $p_2 = .70$ and the expected values of X and Y are $E(X) = p_1 (1 - p_2)(\$1,000) + (1 - p_1)(\$1,000) = \$580$, and $E(Y) = p_1 p_2(\$1,000) = \$420$. Thus X would be the rational choice.

Let us suppose, however, that it is not revealed how many balls of each color are in each urn. You are told only that the number of red balls in urn B is greater than the number of white balls in urn A. It follows, of course, that the number of black balls in urn A is greater than the number of blue balls in urn B. If this is the only information you are given, which option, X or Y, should you choose in order to maximize your chances of winning the $1,000?

We can capture what is known about the numbers of balls of each color in the two urns by asserting the inequality $0 \leq p_1 \leq p_2 \leq 1$. We should note that the probabilities p_1 and p_2 are unknown *objective* probabilities. Since they are not subjective probabilities, their magnitudes cannot be assessed introspectively. It will

Table 3.5 Decision-making under Uncertainty about Probabilities

	white ball from urn A (p_1)		black ball from urn A ($1 - p_1$)
	red ball from urn B (p_2)	blue ball from urn B ($1 - p_2$)	
gamble X	0	$1,000	$1,000
gamble Y	$1,000	0	0

do you, the decision-maker, no good to conduct thought experiments involving hypothetical gambles in order to decide which gamble, X or Y, to take.

The important question is, given only the information provided, which choice, X or Y, is the more likely to win you $1,000? One way to proceed, and I believe the most reasonable way, is to consider all possible states of the two urns compatible with the constraint that $p_1 < p_2$, calculate the expected winnings of the two options, X and Y, for each state, calculate the mean of the expected winnings over all the states, and choose the option that has the greater average of expected winnings. Actually implementing this procedure would be enormously tedious if the expected winnings of the two options were calculated for each state, since there are 5,050 states compatible with the constraint. However, we get a sufficiently close approximation if we assume that in each urn the number of balls of a certain color that it is possible to have ranges continuously from 0 to 100. This shortens the computations considerably.

It turns out that the average of the expected winnings if X is chosen is approximately $62.50 greater than the average if Y is chosen.[18] This means that it is more *likely* that you will maximize your expected winnings if you choose X than if you choose Y. (Note the difference between this assertion and the assertion that choosing X maximizes your expected winnings.) By a rationale that is analogous to that expressed by PR3 (where we substitute for the goal of maximizing the probability that your action will be morally right the goal of maximizing the probability that you will win the $1,000 prize), we have determined that your more reasonable choice is X.

The similarity between Table 3.2 and Table 3.5 is obvious. The two decisions are completely analogous. Hence, we can use PR3 to choose between the "abortion" and the "no abortion" options in the following manner: In the absence of additional information, we may assume that all couples $< p_1, p_2 >$ that accord with the $p_1 < p_2$ constraint are equally likely to contain the true values of p_1 and p_2. We should recall that we are interested in whether $p(A) > p(\text{not-}A)$—that is, whether $p_1 p_2 \leq .5$. If we take the average of the values of $.5 - p_1 p_2$ for all the couples $<p_1, p_2>$ that satisfy the constraint on p_1 and p_2, we shall be able to say whether $p(A)$ is *probably* greater than $p(\text{not-}A)$. If the computations are performed for the case we are now considering—that is, $0 < p_1 < p_2 < 1$—it turns out that the average value of $p(A) - p(\text{not-}A)$ is $1/16$.[19] Since this number is greater than 0, we conclude that *probably* $p(A) > p(\text{not-}A)$ and thus, by PR3, the "abortion" option would be the rational choice.

Does this settle the issue? May we say at this point that the agent should (rationally) choose the "abortion" option? The answer is "Yes" if we suppose that the agent is 100% committed to the consequentialist moral perspective assumed in Table 3.2. However, it is unlikely that the agent would have no doubts whatsoever about this way of looking at her decision. A more realistic hypothesis is that she is uncertain between the moral perspectives represented by Tables 3.1 and 3.2. If so, then we need a decision table that represents this higher order uncertainty, Table 3.6.

In Table 3.6, p_1 and p_2 are the same as in Table 3.2—namely, the probabilities that this fetus is a person and that the fetus's interests outweigh the agent's interests, respectively. However, since there is no dominant strategy, we have to

Table 3.6   Abortion and Uncertainty about Moral Perspective

	Nonconsequentialist moral perspective is correct. (p_4)			Consequentialist moral perspective is correct. ($1-p_4$)		
	This fetus is a person. (p_1)		This fetus is not a person. ($1-p_1$)	This fetus is a person. (p_1)		This fetus is not a person. ($1-p_1$)
	Personhood implies that abortion is wrong. (p_3)	Personhood does not imply that abortion is wrong. ($1-p_3$)		Fetus's interests outweigh agent's interests. (p_2)	Agent's interests outweigh fetus's interests. ($1-p_2$)	
abortion	0	1	1	0	1	1
no abortion	1	1	1	1	0	0

consider the probabilities associated with the two moral perspectives. We must also consider the probability that, on the condition that the nonconsequentialist perspective is correct, the fetus's being a person would mean that it would be morally wrong for the agent to have an abortion. Therefore, we shall adopt

p_3: the conditional probability that, provided that the nonconsequentialist moral perspective is correct, the fetus's being a person would mean that the agent's having an abortion would be morally wrong

p_4: the probability that the nonconsequentialist moral perspective is correct

It is easy to show that $p(A) = p_1p_2p_4 - p_1p_3p_4 - p_1p_2 + 1$ and $p(not\text{-}A) = p_4 - p_1p_2p_4 + p_1p_2$. It follows that $p(A) - p(not\text{-}A) = 2p_1p_2p_4 - p_1p_3p_4 - 2p_1p_2 - p_4 + 1$. Therefore, $p(A) \leq p(not\text{-}A)$ if and only if $2p_1p_2p_4 + 1 \geq p_1p_3p_4 + 2p_1p_2 + p_4$.

As before, the agent may regard p_1, p_2, p_3, and p_4 as subjective probabilities or as objective probabilities. If they are subjective probabilities, then the agent may attempt to measure them either by assigning each of them a cardinal value or by locating each of them in an interval of cardinal numbers within [0, 1]. To determine whether $p(A) \geq p(not\text{-}A)$, or whether *probably* $p(A) \geq p(not\text{-}A)$, she would use the same techniques as in the previous case. She would then interpret the results in light of PR2 or PR3 to ascertain which alternative is rational. However, if we regard p_1, p_2, p_3, and p_4 as unknown objective probabilities, then cardinal number measurements may be dubious and the agent may have more confidence in ordinal number values. Let us suppose that the second approach is adopted and that the agent ranks the probabilities as follows: $p_1 \leq p_4 \leq p_3 \leq p_2$. If this is the only information about the magnitudes of the probabilities that is available, then we would use the same method as before in order to apply PR3 to the decision. We consider all 4-tuples $<p_1, p_2, p_3, p_4>$ that satisfy the ordinal ranking and calculate the mean of $p(A) - p(not\text{-}A)$ for all of those 4-tuples. If the mean is positive, then PR3 implies that the "abortion" alternative is the rational one. If the mean is negative, then PR3 recommends the "no abortion" option.

It turns out that the mean value of $p(A) - p(not\text{-}A)$ over the set of 4-tuples that satisfy the ordinal ranking is 11/30, which is greater than 0.[20] This means that *probably* $p(A) > p(\text{not-}A)$, which by PR3 identifies the "abortion" option as the rational one. However, this result looks suspicious. It says that, on average, $p(A)$ exceeds $p(\text{not-}A)$ by more than .36—a very large difference. It can be shown that the mean value of p_1 among the 4-tuples that satisfy the constraints $p_1 \leq p_4 \leq p_3 \leq p_2$ is .2. This means that our assumptions about p_1, p_2, p_3, and p_4 are *imposing* an average value of .2 on the probability that the fetus is a person. The decision-maker may believe that this number is much too low, although she may not be willing to place another constraint on p_1, such as $p_1 \geq .4$. One way of fixing the problem is to consider p_4, the next smallest among the four probabilities. The agent may believe that the nonconsequentialist perspective is the more plausible of the two moral perspectives and may be confident that $p_4 \geq .5$. By imposing this as a constraint on p_4, the mean value of p_1 among the 4-tuples $<p_1, p_2, p_3, p_4>$ will increase to .32,[21] which to the agent may be a more plausible value. If the $p_4 \geq .5$ constraint is added, $p(A) - p(\text{not-}A)$ turns out to be 1/300.[22] This means that the "abortion" option will still be the more likely to have the maximum probability of being morally right, but the margin by which the mean value of $p(A)$ exceeds that of $p(\text{not-}A)$ will be much smaller than before. This close contest between the two options may better reflect the agent's moral quandary.

Am I seriously suggesting that decision-makers who contemplate having abortions should make their decisions on the basis of mathematical computations? Such a suggestion will likely strike many readers as misplaced or even ludicrous. Many who consider it perfectly normal to use sophisticated mathematics and supercomputers to assist them in making decisions where the weather or the economy is a factor will balk at the suggestion that such devices should be used to make moral decisions. Yet it is unclear (at least to me) why this should be so. Some ethicists believe that any attempt to find moral algorithms or to "reduce" moral problems to mathematical ones is wrongheaded. The process of moral *judgment*, it will be said, is properly personal or subjective in a way that is fundamentally incompatible with the calculating attitude I am recommending.[23]

In reply, two points may be made: First, some moral theories, such as versions of utilitarianism based on the notion of expected utility, require relatively sophisticated mathematical reasoning when applied to concrete cases.[24] Consequently, mathematical methods should not be ruled out unless one is willing to reject certain prominent moral theories on those grounds. Second, and more important, the sort of procedure illustrated earlier is intended to be used for determining which course(s) of action are *rational*—not which are *morally right*. While it can be plausibly argued that moral deliberation must be more than just calculating and comparing expected utilities (although this is controversial), the same cannot be credibly maintained of rational decision-making. Mathematical analysis may be appropriate for determining how, under moral uncertainty, to choose one's actions in a rational way even if it is inappropriate for judging which actions are morally acceptable.

For the overwhelming majority of situations, however, no sophisticated mathematical methods would be needed to apply our principles of rational decision-making. In many instances, determining which alternative is most probably morally right will require no more than the decision-maker's unmediated comparing of the magnitudes of the resultant probabilities, the assessment of which may sometimes not require that of the component probabilities. In many situations, even if no alternative is a dominant strategy, decision-makers will have little doubt about which alternative is more likely to be morally right. Most decisions whether to seek abortions will be of this type. No computations will be needed in such cases. Only when there is significant uncertainty about which resultant probability is larger will mathematical analysis be needed. Even after calculations have been performed, a decision-maker may choose to reconsider her probability assessments. She may find that revisions in her estimates of the component probabilities are called for if she is strongly reluctant to accept the results of the analysis. Preanalysis estimates of the resultant probabilities may be compared with the results of the analysis, and adjustments may be made until "reflective equilibria" among decision-makers' considered probability assessments are reached. One would use mathematical analyses mainly to check the consistency of decision-makers' probability assessments rather than to generate, in some algorithmic fashion, final conclusions about what choices are rational.

Of course, moral agents who must decide immediately or in the very near future cannot be expected to undertake the sort of decision-theoretic analysis that we have illustrated in the preceding discussion. And some may not be suited either intellectually or temperamentally to do so under any circumstances. However, even if individual decision-makers are not expected to perform mathematical computations as part of their deliberations, this is no reason for professional ethicists, from whom decision-makers may expect to receive some useful information, to eschew such methods. Such procedures appear inevitable if we are to take seriously the problem of rational decision-making under moral uncertainty. Taking uncertainty into account often means taking probabilities into account, and reasoning cogently about probability cannot always avoid mathematical considerations and methods.

It should be clear from the preceding discussion that rational decisions about having abortions, or anything else, will depend on decision-makers' beliefs and particular circumstances. For example, the probability that a 6-week fetus is a person will be judged to be smaller than the probability that a 24-week fetus is a person, and decision-makers' probability measurements will ordinarily reflect this. The procedure recommended here recognizes this dependence and consequently accepts the proposition that for some decision-makers abortion will be the rational course of action while for others the opposite will be true. Similarly, in extraordinary situations, such as those in which the fetus is known to be seriously deformed, one may have considerable doubt whether *not* having an abortion would be morally right, while under usual circumstances one may be virtually certain of the moral rightness of *not* having an abortion. Therefore, the results of applying PR2 and PR3 will reflect these differences among situations.

Other Morally Problematic Abortion Decisions

Let us now consider other problematic abortion cases. These include abortion decisions for which there are reasons to doubt the moral rightness of *not* having an abortion. We shall assume here that, as in the preceding section, there is uncertainty about the personhood of the fetus and about the moral implications of personhood. We shall again consider situations in which decision-makers are uncertain whether *not* having an abortion in a particular situation would be morally right. However, we shall not identify the specific reasons that having an abortion might be obligatory, such as those based on consequentialist moral principles. Instead, for simplicity we shall limit our attention to decision-makers who are sure that having an abortion can be morally obligatory only if the fetus lacks personhood status. Therefore, let us assume that the decision-maker is uncertain about the truth of the statement "if *this* fetus is not a person, then aborting it is morally obligatory."

The sort of situation we have in mind is represented by Table 3.7. Again we have a decision table that has no morally dominant strategy. Which of the two alternatives is more likely to be morally right depends on three component probabilities: the probabilities that *this* fetus is a person, that fetal personhood implies that having an abortion is morally wrong, and that fetal nonpersonhood implies that having an abortion is morally obligatory.

It is quite possible that, as before, the decision-maker will have no difficulty deciding which alternative has the greater likelihood of being morally right. I suspect that many decision-makers who do not rule out the possibility that having an abortion may be morally obligatory are nevertheless quite confident that not having an abortion has the greater likelihood of being morally right. This would happen if the probability that having an abortion is morally obligatory, though greater than 0, were much less than the probability that having an abortion is morally wrong. However, some decision-makers in some situations may be unsure which probability is greater. They may wish therefore to consider the magnitudes of each of the component probabilities in order to determine which of the two resultant probabilities—(1) that having an abortion would be morally right and (2) that not having an abortion would be morally right—is greater. Let us consider then how the situation might be analyzed to produce such a probability comparison.

We shall label the probabilities as follows:

> p_1: the probability that *this* fetus is a person
> p_2: the probability that the statement "if *this* fetus is person, then having an abortion is morally wrong" is true
> p_3: the probability that the statement "if *this* fetus is not a person, then having an abortion is morally obligatory" is true
> $p(A)$: the probability that having an abortion is morally right
> $p(\text{not-}A)$: the probability that not having an abortion is morally right

In order to apply PR2, we must determine which of the two alternatives has the greater probability of being morally right—that is, whether $p(A) \geq p(\text{not-}A)$ or conversely. It is easy to show that $p(A) \geq p(\text{not-}A)$ if and only if $p_1 p_2 \leq p_3(1 - p_1)$. As before, the direct approach to testing this inequality would be to measure each of the probabilities p_1, p_2, and p_3 and then check to see whether the inequality holds. As in the preceding example, there are serious difficulties in performing reliable single-number cardinal measurements of probabilities of this sort. It would

Table 3.7 Decision-making under Uncertainty about the Obligatoriness of Abortion

	This fetus is a person (p_1)		This fetus is not a person ($1 - p_1$)	
	Personhood implies that having an abortion is morally wrong. (p_2)	Personhood does not imply that having an abortion is morally wrong. ($1 - p_2$)	Non-personhood implies that having an abortion is morally obligatory (p_3)	Non-personhood does not imply that having an abortion is morally obligatory ($1 - p_3$)
abortion	0	1	1	1
no abortion	1	1	0	1

be easier and more credible to locate the probabilities within ranges or intervals of possible values. For example, a decision-maker may be unable to say with assurance that the probability that her fetus is a person is exactly .5 but may be confident that p_1 is somewhere between .4 and .6. This sort of information about the component probabilities may be enough to enable one to determine which course(s) of action would be rational.

Let us consider again this situation and suppose that the decision-maker assesses the probabilities as follows: $.4 \leq p_1 \leq .6$, $.5 \leq p_2 \leq .7$, and $.1 \leq p_3 \leq .3$. The situation is represented graphically in Figure 3.3 where the small square contains all the points that satisfy the constraints on p_2 and p_3. The two slanted lines, labeled $p_1 = .4$ and $p_1 = .6$, represent the constraints on p_1. For each value of p_1 there is a slanted line that passes through the intersection of the two axes. The region above and to the left of each line will represent the values of p_2 and p_3 for which the "abortion" alternative would be a rational choice for that value of p_1. Similarly, the region below and to the right of each line will represent the values of p_2 and p_3 for which the "no abortion" option would be a rational choice. The graph clearly shows that the region of uncertainty is entirely outside the region where the "abortion" alternative would be a rational choice, regardless of which value of p_1 between .4 and .6 is the true value. Hence, we may conclude that *not* having an abortion would be the rational course of action in the situation depicted earlier. We would draw the opposite conclusion if the region of uncertainty were wholly contained within the region where the "abortion" option is a rational choice for all values of p_1 between .4 and .6.

What about situations in which the region of uncertainty is partly inside and partly outside the region between the two slanted lines? Let us modify the preceding example by supposing that $.4 \leq p_2 \leq .6$ and $.2 \leq p_3 \leq .4$. This situation may be represented as in Figure 3.4. Here the region of uncertainty is partly inside the region where the "have abortion" option would be a rational choice for some values of p_1 between .4 and .6 and completely outside it for other values of p_1. Since the decision-maker is not sure which is the true value of p_1, it is impossible to say with certainty whether the region of uncertainty is completely outside the region where the "have abortion" alternative would be the rational choice. If she were certain that $p_1 = .6$, for example, then she would know that the region of uncertainty is completely outside the region where the "have abortion" option would be a rational choice. However, if she were certain that $p_1 = .4$, then she would know that part of the region of uncertainty is inside the area where the "have abortion" choice would be a rational one and part of it is outside. If we assume that p_2 and p_3 are as likely to have one value within their respective intervals as another, then we may infer that the likelihood that having an abortion would be the rational choice according to PR2 would be the ratio of the size of the region of uncertainty that is inside the area where the "have abortion" option is a rational choice to the total size of the region of uncertainty. For $p_1 = .4$ this ratio can be shown to be ⅓.[25]

As in the previous case, in treating the magnitudes of p_1, p_2, and p_3 as unknown and considering which alternative is made more likely to accord with PR2 by possible variations in those magnitudes, we are positing a second-order probability—namely, the probability that having an abortion has a greater probability of being morally right than not having an abortion. As before, we cannot apply PR2 directly, since there is not enough information to say with certainty whether having an abortion or not having an abortion would maximize the probability that the agent's action is morally right. All we can say is that one or the other is more likely to have the greater probability of being morally right.[26]

But what about our uncertainty about the value of p_1? So far we have considered only two values of p_1—.4 and .6. What about values between these two extremes? For each value of p_1 there will be an associated ratio of the size of the portion of the region of uncertainty where, according to PR2, the "have abortion" option is a rational choice to the size of the entire region of uncertainty. If we assume that one value of p_1 within its interval is as likely as another, then it seems reasonable to take the average of these ratios as the probability that having an abortion would be in accordance with PR2. This would mean taking the average of an infinite number of ratios, since there are an infinite number of points between

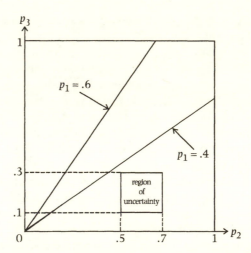

Figure 3.3   Application of PR3 to Decision
of Table 3.7—I

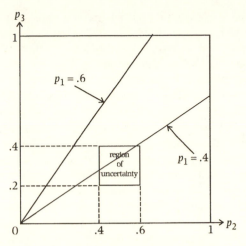

Figure 3.4 Application of PR3 to Decision of Table 3.7—II

.4 and .6, but this can readily be done using calculus. It can be shown that in our example the average probability that having an abortion would accord with PR2 is approximately .055.[27] Hence, the average probability that *not* having an abortion would accord with PR2 is approximately $1 - .055 = .945$.[28] Thus it can be seen for the preceding situation that the probability that PR2 would prescribe *not* having an abortion is much greater than the probability that PR2 would sanction having an abortion. This means that, according to PR3, which we must employ in lieu of PR2, the agent's rational choice is not to have the abortion.

We have the same problems here, however, that we had before with respect to choosing the ranges of values for the probabilities. If we choose large intervals, we lose precision; if we choose small intervals, we lose confidence that the true values of the probabilities are contained in those intervals. Thus our choices of intervals require us to judge how to balance the competing demands of precision and reliability, and there appear to be no rules for making such judgments. Unfortunately, the results that we obtain will sometimes depend on how we make them. For these reasons, some may find this approach to moral decision-making unsatisfactory.

As in the preceding example, the alternative to choosing specific ranges of values of the probabilities is resorting to ordinal measurement. For the decision represented by Table 3.7, the decision-maker may be certain only that, say, $0 \leq p_1 \leq p_2 \leq p_3 \leq 1$. If this were the only information available about p_1, p_2, and p_3, it would not be possible to say with assurance whether $p(A) > p(\text{not-}A)$, since for some values of p_1, p_2, and p_3 that satisfy the constraints, $p(A) > p(\text{not-}A)$, while for others the opposite is true. Hence, PR2 would not be directly applicable. However, PR3 can be applied by calculating the average value of $p(A) - p(\text{not-}A)$ for all triples $<p_1, p_2, p_3>$ that accord with the inequality constraints. This means calculating the average value of $p_3(1 - p_1) - p_1 p_2$ for all the triples $<p_1, p_2, p_3>$ that satisfy the constraints. If the average is positive, then we can say that $p(A)$ is *probably* greater than $p(\text{not-}A)$. If the average is negative, then it follows that $p(A)$ is *probably* less than $p(\text{not-}A)$. If the computations are performed for the case we are now considering—that is, $p_1 < p_2 < p_3$—it turns out that the average value of $p(A) - p(\text{not-}A)$ is .4,[29] which is greater than 0. Therefore, we conclude that *probably* $p(A) > p(\text{not-}A)$ and thus, by PR3, having the abortion would be the rational choice of action.

Let us now consider a different situation, one in which the decision-maker believes that $p_3 < p_1 < p_2$. If there is no additional information about p_1, p_2, and p_3, the expected value of $p(A) - p(\text{not-}A)$ for all triples that satisfy the inequality turns out to be $-.3$.[30] Hence, PR3 implies that *not* having an abortion would be the rational choice in the situation. Generally speaking, the higher p_1 and p_2 are in the ordinal ranking, the more likely it is that not having an abortion will have maximal probability of being morally right. However, the higher p_3 is in the ranking, the more likely it is that having an abortion will be prescribed by PR3. An interesting case occurs when p_3 is in the middle of the ordinal ranking—for example, when $p_1 < p_3 < p_2$. Here it turns out that the expected value of $p(A) - p(\text{not-}A)$ is .15,[31] which is greater than 0. Therefore, in such a situation, having an abortion would be the rational choice according to PR3.

Perhaps we are being too cautious by assuming that ordinal measurements of the component probabilities are the only sources of information about their magnitudes. A stronger set of assumptions, weaker still than assuming that cardinal measurements of the component probabilities can be obtained, would be that ordinal comparisons among *differences* in the magnitudes of the component probabilities, as well as ordinal comparisons among the magnitudes of the probabilities themselves, are available. For example, our decision-maker might know both that $0 < p_1 < p_2 < p_3 < 1$ and that $p_3 - p_1 < 1 - p_3$. The latter inequality means that the likelihood that having an abortion is obligatory if the fetus is not a person is closer to the likelihood that the fetus is a person than it is to perfect certainty. How does this new information affect the result? It turns out in this case that $p(A) - p(\text{not-}A)$ can be calculated to be .1625,[32] which is greater than 0. Therefore, by PR3, the "abortion" option would, by a slender margin, be the rational choice. This result is particularly interesting because it comes somewhat as a revelation. Ranking p_3 as the largest pushes in the "abortion" direction, while imposing the $p_3 - p_1 < 1 - p_3$ constraint pulls in the opposite direction. It is not apparent until after the calculations have been performed which effect is stronger.

Conclusions

I have proposed the following *practical* resolution of the abortion issue: In the vast majority of situations—that is, those in which there is greater certainty about the moral rightness of *not* having an abortion than about the moral rightness of having an abortion—the rational choice is *not* to have an abortion. If I am right, then much of the debate that rages in public discourse and in philosophical discourse on abortion—that is, whether or when it is morally right to have an abortion—is for practical (decision-making) purposes irrelevant.

It may appear that my analyses oversimplify the abortion decision situation. What about the extenuating circumstances that complicate moral appraisals of such decisions, for example, whether the woman is single or married, whether she is rich or poor, what her social standing is, whether she has supportive friends and family or must go it alone, whether having a child at this time would jeopardize her plans for getting an education and having a career, and so on? However, while such considerations may be pertinent when the question is whether having an abortion would be morally right, they affect our conclusions about *rational* decision-making only if they have a significant bearing on whether having an abortion would be morally obligatory. If a pregnant woman in dire straits has doubts about the moral rightness of her having an abortion that are clearly greater than her doubts about the moral rightness of her *not* having an abortion, then by PR2 she should *not* seek an abortion. She need not agonize over every detail of her individual situation. However, if it is unclear whether having or *not* having an abortion has the greater likelihood of being morally right, then an analysis to determine which alternative is better supported by the available assessments of the component probabilities may be warranted. Such an analysis would be similar to the preceding analyses of situations in which no morally dominant option exists.

My conclusions will perhaps appear to support the antiabortion or "prolife" position, but there are important qualifications to this impression that should be noted. First, the "prolife" position is usually understood as entailing a moral judgment about abortion, whereas the views defended in this chapter entail no such judgment. Second, "prolife" points of view often include the belief that fetuses are persons from the moments that they are conceived. My analysis takes no stand either way on the personhood issue. Third, the "prolife" position is usually interpreted as involving not only a moral judgment about having abortions but also a normative judgment about whether the state should prohibit abortions. This last item raises the issue that divides the "prolife" and the "prochoice" positions. Those who subscribe to the latter often do so not on grounds that having an abortion is morally right in all or most instances, but rather because in their view whether a woman shall have an abortion should ultimately be left for her to decide without interference by the state. One may consistently advocate this position without taking any particular stand regarding the moral rightness of someone's having an abortion. Thus our earlier conclusions have important implications for "prochoice" advocates who must themselves decide whether to have abortions but do not necessarily support the "prolife" doctrine that abortions should be legally proscribed. For the latter issue, which we shall come to in chapter 7, different considerations are relevant and the conclusion may turn out differently.

The preceding analyses show how it is possible to bypass difficult or intractable moral problems by addressing oneself to the question of which choices of action are rational responses to moral uncertainty. It is possible because we can sometimes discern rational courses of action without establishing the moral rightness of any of our alternatives. If rational action may proceed without the prior resolution of moral issues, then for practical purposes there is a way to steer clear of those issues. We steer clear not by ignoring moral considerations, but rather by intelligently taking into account the available information regarding moral rightness, incomplete though it may be, in choosing our actions.

Four

Degrees of Moral Rightness

In his article, "Subjectivization in Ethics,"[1] James L. Hudson argues, convincingly in my view, that subjective moral theories are more satisfactory than objective theories as sources of guidance for our action choices. By "subjective theory," Hudson means a moral theory that "guarantees the agent's ability to use . . . [it] . . . to guide her actions."[2] An example of a subjective theory is subjective (act) utilitarianism, which tells us to maximize expected utility. An "objective theory," by contrast, does not guarantee the agent's ability to apply the theory. An example is objective (act) utilitarianism, which says simply, "Maximize utility." The subjective theory is more useful, Hudson claims, because, although we often do not know which action(s) would actually maximize utility, we always know which action(s) we would expect to maximize utility if they were chosen.[3] When one uses a subjective theory to decide on a course of action, she "hedges for her uncertainty about the . . . [nonmoral] . . . facts"[4] by taking her uncertainties about the "facts" into account. Objective theories provide for no such hedging, and this, according to Hudson, is their major shortcoming.

Although Hudson advocates hedging within moral theories for agents' uncertainties about nonmoral facts, he denies that it is possible to hedge either for "axiological uncertainty" (i.e., uncertainty about intrinsic value) or for "ethical uncertainty" about which moral theory is true. I shall summarize and discuss his arguments for these claims later in this chapter. If Hudson is right in claiming that it is impossible to hedge for moral uncertainty, then it means that the approach to decision-making under moral uncertainty that I have developed and illustrated in the previous chapters must be fatally flawed, since that approach, embodied in PR2 and PR3, amounts to a kind of hedging for moral uncertainty. It is important therefore that we examine Hudson's argument to see whether it exposes a defect in my proposals.

In this chapter, I shall dispute Hudson's claims about the impossibility of hedging for axiological and ethical uncertainty and show why they do not discredit our inquiry into rational decision-making under moral uncertainty. We shall find, however, that there is an aspect of the problem we have not yet considered that will behoove us to amend our principles of rationality. The amendment that I shall adopt will include a modified concept of moral rightness according to which actions come in varying degrees of moral rightness between "right" and "wrong." Therefore, we shall end up abandoning the binary hypothesis about moral rightness in favor of a many-valued conception. This will cause us to revise our principles for decision-making under moral uncertainty in order to take degrees of moral rightness into account. This development will be important throughout the remainder of our investigations.

The Need for Moral Hedging

Hudson argues not only that moral hedging (i.e., hedging for axiological and ethical uncertainty) is impossible but also that it is unnecessary. Let us consider the latter first. Hudson grants that just as we moral agents are often unsure of the consequences of our actions, we are frequently uncertain which moral theory to follow. However, he says, we need not take the latter uncertainty into account:

> The purpose of a moral theory (subjective utilitarianism, for example) is to tell the agent how she should use whatever information she has available at the moment of decision. . . . Any moral theory, in telling the agent what to do, will ignore the agent's possible commitment to other moral theories. And while it should be considered a defect in a theory that it issues instructions that the agent does not know how to follow, it is not similarly a defect if it issues instructions that the agent decides not to follow because she does not believe the theory. If subjective utilitarianism's imperatives are such that in every case the agent who wants to follow them will follow them, it will be to that extent an improvement over objective utilitarianism.[5]

In this passage, Hudson is concerned with moral theories and their role in moral deliberation. As we have already noted, moral deliberation need not always involve moral theories. Nevertheless, let us focus for the moment on deliberation that does involve moral theories. Hudson is certainly correct in saying that a moral theory is not defective simply because some moral agent disbelieves the theory or is uncertain about its truth. But the fact remains that moral agents must often decide without having a theory in which they have complete confidence. How then should those agents decide what to do?

Perhaps Hudson is saying in the preceding passage that the ethicist's concern is properly with moral theories and whether they are "user-friendly." A theory that is not "user-friendly" fails as a moral theory. Only subjective theories are "user-friendly"; therefore, ethicists should limit their inquiries to subjective theories. And once a reasonable, appropriately useful theory has been identified, the ethicist's job is finished. It is then up to the moral agent to use that theory in choosing her actions. If she fails to do so, then it is not the fault of the ethicist or of the moral theory that the ethicist has recommended. Furthermore, moral hedging is unnecessary because a reasonable subjective moral theory is available—namely, subjective act utilitarianism.

Hudson assumes apparently that the only way to accommodate moral uncertainty is within some moral theory. It does not occur to him that there might be other ways in which moral uncertainty could be accommodated. In the previous chapters, I have proposed an intertheoretic approach to decision-making under moral uncertainty, based on PR2 and PR3. If my approach is cogent (whether or not it is the correct approach), it means that Hudson's assumption is mistaken. There can be ways of dealing not only with our uncertainties about how to apply moral theories to concrete situations but also with our uncertainties about which theories to apply.

If one violates the true subjective ethical theory as a result of not knowing that it is the true theory, then on Hudson's view, and on mine, one acts wrongly. However, even if one is unsure which theory is true, some courses of action may make more sense to choose than others. For example, it would make far more sense, ethically speaking, to follow a theory that has at least some chance of being true than to follow one that is totally implausible—for example, a theory that requires us to maximize pain and suffering. Clearly, some policies for decision-making under moral uncertainty will be more unreasonable to adopt than others. But unreasonableness (at least in this context) cannot exist without its opposite. If some policies are unreasonable, then some must be reasonable.

What then would be the "best" or most reasonable policy to follow in situations of moral uncertainty? We are inclined to say that in such instances an agent should do the best that she can, morally speaking. But what does "doing the best that one can under moral uncertainty" amount to? It does not mean simply acting morally, since ex hypothesi one may not know which is the true (subjective) ethical theory. I believe that we should construe "doing the best that one can under moral uncertainty" as acting rationally under moral uncertainty. Acting rationally under moral uncertainty means taking into account all pertinent available information, including whatever information about moral theories may be available. In the next two sections, I shall argue that Hudson's caveats about moral hedging need not apply to the problem conceived in this way.

The Possibility of Moral Hedging

Hudson constructs two examples to show why hedging for ethical uncertainty and hedging for axiological uncertainty are both impossible. Let us consider the axiological uncertainty example first:

> Even mere axiological uncertainty within an unquestioned subjective consequentialist framework is unhedgeable. Suppose the agent assigns probability 0.6

to the view that pleasure-minus-pain is the only intrinsic good, and 0.4 to the view that the good is self-realization. And suppose she must choose between an act that produces ten hedons and two reals and one that produces nine hedons and thirty reals. ("Reals" are the units in which self-realization is measured.) Which act should she do?

The two axiological theories lead to different answers. Since the hedonic theory is more probable, perhaps she should accept its answer. But the self-realization theory seems to find more of a difference between the two actions, and perhaps this should outweigh its slightly lesser probability. But wait—is a difference of twenty-eight reals really greater than a difference of one hedon? What is the common measure between hedons and reals? Note that the agent, for all her uncertainty, believes with complete confidence that there is no common measure: she is sure that one or the other—pleasure or self-realization— is intrinsically worthless. Under the circumstances, the two units must be incomparable by the agent, and so there can be no way for her uncertainty to be taken into account in a reasonable decision procedure.[6]

The problem with axiological hedging, as Hudson sees it, is incommensurability between quantities of intrinsic value measured on different scales and according to different conceptions of intrinsic value. Hedons and reals are incommensurable because they measure intrinsic value according to entirely different conceptions of intrinsic value. One who believes that only pleasure has intrinsic value cannot consistently believe that self-realization is intrinsically valuable or believe that there is a common scale on which both pleasure and self-realization can be measured.

However, Hudson's argument that hedons and reals are incommensurable is not entirely convincing. The problem with comparing hedons and reals is not, as he suggests, that the agent believes that either pleasure or self-realization is intrinsically worthless. For it would be possible to compare hedons and reals if one could somehow confirm a counterfactual of the following form: If pleasure were intrinsically valuable, then one hedon would measure the same amount of intrinsic value as X reals would measure if self-realization were intrinsically valuable. Such a statement would be consistent with the view that either pleasure or self-realization is intrinsically worthless. Analogously, we can compare the value of real money with the value that counterfeit money would have if it were real money. A counterfeit $10 bill would be worth the same as a noncounterfeit $10 bill if if the former were a real $10 bill. The truth of this counterfactual conditional is all that is required in order to compare the value of real and counterfeit money. The same may be true of different conceptions of intrinsic value.

However, even if we can make sense of these kinds of counterfactuals, we may still be at a loss as to how to solve the practical problem of determining how many reals a hedon is actually "worth." I shall later suggest a way in which we might compare quantities across different moral theories that, I believe, we could adapt to compare hedons and reals if we so desired. However, for the moment I shall simply concede Hudson's point about the incommensurability of different concepts of intrinsic value because I think that it can be bypassed in the following way: Instead of searching for a common unit of measurement among disparate axiological theories, let us simply view the agent as being uncertain which of the associated (subjective) ethical theories is true. For Hudson's example, this would

Table 4.1   Decision-making under Axiological Uncertainty

	Maximize expected utility. $(p = .6)$	Maximize expected self-realization. $(p = .4)$
x	1	0
y	0	1

mean that the agent regards two ethical theories as contenders: one directs her to maximize expected utility, and the other dictates maximizing (expected?) self-realization. Posing the problem in this way avoids the problem of making inter-theoretic comparisons of intrinsic value.

Let us return to the moral agent that Hudson describes in the passage quoted earlier. We represent the agent's situation in Table 4.1. Does Table 4.1 suggest any rational resolution of the decision problem? I think that it does. If the agent's overriding objective is to act morally (and I shall assume that it is; otherwise, why bother about moral hedging at all?), then it would make sense for her to choose the action more likely to achieve that objective. In this case, that means selecting x, since x is more likely to be morally right in the situation than is y. Thus we need not worry about comparing hedons and reals. At least in this situation, moral hedging seems to be possible.

I have implicitly appealed to PR2 in this analysis. Since we are assuming that the agent's moral uncertainty consists entirely of her uncertainty about which of the two moral theories is the "true" theory and that there is no question about how the theories are correctly applied to her decision, PR2 recommends following the theory that is more likely to be "true"—namely, the one that prescribes maximizing expected utility. Thus it appears that we have shown that, notwithstanding Hudson's claims to the contrary, moral hedging is possible for the moral agent in the situation that he describes.

Would Hudson accept our analysis as showing that hedging is possible after all? And if not, where would he say it has gone wrong? Let us recall that he is concerned about the disparity in the example between the difference of the 28 reals and that of the single hedon. But how could this be significant for an agent whose overriding objective is to act morally? Wouldn't such an agent seek to maximize the probability that her action is morally right? Wouldn't it be irrational to do otherwise?

The most plausible way I can think of for Hudson to criticize our reasoning would be to challenge PR2 and, particularly, the binary hypothesis which it presupposes. Let us recall how we arrived at PR2. We drew an analogy between decision-making under moral uncertainty and decision-making under ordinary factual uncertainty. For the latter, the well-established principle for decisions in which information about the magnitudes of the pertinent probabilities is available is the MEU principle. The analogous principle for decision-making under moral uncertainty directed us to maximize expected moral rightness. Expected moral rightness, if analogous to expected utility, is a probability-weighted sum of the degrees of moral rightness that would come about under the various possible "states of the world," where the probabilities are the probabilities that those "states of the world" actually obtain. This left "degrees of moral rightness" to be explained. And on the basis of the binary hypothesis, according to which moral rightness comes in only two sizes (right and wrong), we determined that maximizing expected moral rightness amounted to maximizing the probability that one's action is morally right. Of course, this reasoning leans heavily on the binary hypothesis. If the latter is rejected, then maximizing expected moral rightness is not the same as maximizing the probability that one's action is morally right and PR2 will not be the principle that we end up with.

It is difficult to see any weakness in the argument for PR2 other than, possibly, its reliance on the binary hypothesis. Perhaps Hudson would object that PR2, by considering only the probabilities that actions are morally right, ignores the degrees to which actions are right or wrong. Maybe he would say that moral rightness is not the all-or-nothing condition that we have assumed it to be but instead allows for gradations between total rightness and total wrongness.

Should we reject the binary hypothesis? Is moral rightness something that our actions must either have completely or lack completely, or does it also come in intermediate "sizes"? The binary hypothesis certainly seems to be well established in moral philosophy. Very few philosophers have questioned it or taken seriously the possibility of its being false. There are perhaps two reasons for this. One is that for an action to be morally right is for it to be morally permissible, and the notion of intermediate degrees of permissibility appears incoherent. Either an action is permitted or it isn't. There is no in-between. Actions cannot be partially permissible any more than persons can be partially pregnant. Thus the meaning of "permissible" itself seems to preclude any idea of partial permissibility. Let us call this argument that I have just sketched the *semantic* argument for the binary hypothesis.

Another argument against degrees of moral rightness is that even if we could make sense of a many-valued concept of rightness, such a concept would make no practical difference in our choices of action. It would always be our moral duty, in making any moral decision, to choose some action with the maximum degree of moral rightness. Thus we might as well regard maximally right actions as the only really right actions and regard all actions that have less than maximal moral rightness as morally wrong. A many-valued concept of moral rightness would serve no useful purpose. Let us call this second argument against a many-valued concept of moral rightness the *pragmatic* argument. I shall discuss both the semantic and pragmatic arguments later.

Despite the preponderance of philosophical opinion on the side of the binary hypothesis, philosophers have occasionally been tempted in the direction of a many-valued concept of moral rightness. For example, Mill, in the opening pages of *Utilitarianism*, writes, "The creed which accepts as the foundation of morals 'utility' or the 'greatest happiness principle' holds that actions are right *in proportion as* they tend to promote happiness, wrong *as* they tend to produce the reverse of happiness" (emphasis added).[7] It is natural for those who find teleological moral theories appealing to be attracted to a many-valued concept of moral rightness. Between the best and the worst that we can do in a situation there is often a wide variety of choices that would produce intermediately valued consequences. If actions are morally right because they maximize (expected) value, then why not regard actions as right to the degree to which they approach that maximum?

Even a casual survey of the ethics literature reveals that ethicists often employ language that strongly suggests a many-valued concept of moral rightness. For example, at least one philosopher has written about some actions' being "more seriously wrong" than others.[8] Unless this is intended to convey that some actions may have a greater degree of moral rightness than other actions, it is difficult to see what it does mean or what significance it could have. Of course, we could give up the phrase "has a greater degree of moral rightness than" in favor of "is more seriously wrong than" in order not to offend purists' semantic sensibilities. However, the latter phrase would do the same work as the former.

Even for some deontological theories, we have no great difficulty entertaining a many-valued concept of moral rightness. A prima facie duties theory, for example, may readily regard actions that, ceteris paribus, accord with more prima facie duties than others as having greater moral rightness. Moreover, for some prima facie duties, it seems that we can conform to or violate them to greater or lesser degrees. Examples of such duties in W. D. Ross's theory include beneficence, nonmaleficence, and justice.[9]

In the following, I shall argue that neither the semantic argument nor the pragmatic argument succeeds in discrediting a many-valued concept of moral rightness. In refuting the latter argument, I shall explain why the many-valued concept is important for moral decision-making, and I shall detail with some precision what role that concept should play in the deliberation process.

The Case for Degrees of Moral Rightness

The semantic argument against a many-valued concept of moral rightness contends that we can make no sense of such a concept. Moral rightness, if the same as moral permissibility, is necessarily an all-or-nothing condition according to this view. It is possible, of course, to insist that terms be used in accordance with their generally accepted meanings and that different terms be coined if one wishes to depart from those meanings. Against such insistence we have little recourse unless we can show that amending a term's meaning can be done consistently and in a way that is a natural and useful rendering. I believe that this is the case for "morally right," which in ordinary and philosophical parlance presupposes the binary hypothesis. In fact, I see no harm in retaining both meanings of "right" if the contexts in which they ordinarily occur make clear which meaning is intended.

It is actually quite easy to define a many-valued concept of moral rightness and to do so in a natural way that connects it with the traditional two-valued conception. We need only explain how one action can have a greater degree of moral rightness than another in such a way as to allow three actions, x, y, and z, to be related so that x has a greater degree of moral rightness than y and y has a greater degree of moral rightness than z. If we can satisfactorily define "has a greater degree of moral rightness than" so that actions can be related in this way, then we can show that a relational, many-valued concept of moral rightness is intelligible.

I propose the following analysis:

> x has a greater degree of moral rightness than y in situation S for agent A just in case, if x and y were the only alternatives open to A in S, then x would be morally right for A in S and y would be morally wrong for A in S.

The analysis explains "x has a greater degree of moral rightness than y" in terms of the ordinary two-valued concept of moral rightness. Clearly, nothing in this definition precludes the possibility that decision situations will occur in which three action alternatives, x, y, and z, are related in the manner just described. It is open to a utilitarian, for example, to hold that in a situation S x has a greater degree of moral rightness than y for an agent A if and only if the (expected) intrinsic value of the consequences of A's choosing x in S is greater than the (expected) intrinsic value of the consequences of A's choosing y in S. Similar observations may be made about other moral theories.

So far, I have said nothing, explicitly or implicitly, about measuring degrees of moral rightness or whether exact cardinal-number measurements would be possible. Perhaps ordinal measurements of degrees of moral rightness would be sufficient for our purposes. I shall come back to the topic of measurement later when we have a better idea of the purposes we want our many-valued concept of moral rightness to serve. The important result here is that there is a coherent many-valued concept of moral rightness. So much for the semantic argument.

This brings us to the pragmatic argument, the second and more important of our arguments against degrees of moral rightness. It asserts that even if such a concept is coherent, we have no practical need for it, since we should always choose an alternative that has at least as much moral rightness as any other alternative in the situation. Therefore, it will make no difference if we simply regard all maximally right actions in a situation as the only morally right alternatives in that situation and all other action alternatives as wrong. And if so, we might as well dispense with our many-valued concept of moral rightness, for it serves no useful purpose. The challenge from the pragmatic argument is to show how the many-valued concept of moral rightness can have practical application for decision-makers. We can answer it effectively if we can describe a situation that will show how employing that concept would make a difference in the way a particular decision should be made. And, it turns out, such situations abound among moral decisions made under moral uncertainty.

Let us examine the following case of moral uncertainty: The decision-maker's moral uncertainty is rooted in her uncertainty about which of two moral theories, $T1$ and $T2$, is true. There are three three alternatives under consideration—x, y, and z. Let us hypothesize that the agent, Jean, has somehow determined that the probabilities that $T1$ and $T2$ are true are .6 and .4, respectively. Moreover, Jean has determined that the degrees of moral rightness of x, y, and z according to $T1$ and $T2$ are as given in Table 4.2.

Table 4.2 Decision-making under Moral Uncertainty with Degrees of Moral Rightness

	T1 is true. ($p = .6$)	T2 is true. ($p = .4$)
x	1.0	0
y	0.4	1.0
z	0.7	0.7

If Jean regards moral considerations as the most important considerations in choosing an action, what would be the most reasonable choice of action for her? Unfortunately for Jean, there is no action that she is certain would be morally optimal (i.e., would have a degree of moral rightness = 1). If Jean were certain that T1 is the true moral theory, then she could be sure that x would be morally optimal. If Jean were certain that T2 is the correct theory, then she would also be assured that y would be morally optimal. However, Jean is not certain of either T1 or T2.

What guidance would PR2 provide for Jean's decision? According to the pragmatic argument against the many-valued conception of moral rightness, actions are morally right (in the traditional, binary sense of "morally right") if and only if they are morally optimal. Therefore, according to PR2, Jean should ignore degrees of moral rightness less than 1 and choose some alternative that has maximal probability of being morally optimal. This means that, practically speaking, she should regard the preceding decision table as equivalent to Table 4.3, in which degrees of moral rightness less than 1 have been set to 0. This would, in effect, restore the traditional binary conception of moral rightness. Obviously, PR2 would prescribe that Jean do x in the situation.

Suppose, however, that we wish to take intermediate degrees of moral rightness into account. Then the two decision tables will not necessarily be equivalent for practical decision-making purposes. What decision principle will then apply? We find the answer by recalling the point at which the binary hypothesis entered our argument for PR2. It did so when we explicated "expected moral rightness" and, specifically, "degrees of moral rightness" in the maximize-expected-moral-rightness principle. By assuming that there were only two possible degrees of moral rightness, we were led to the conclusion that maximizing expected moral rightness is tantamount to maximizing the probability that one's action is morally right. That step is no longer legitimate if we abandon the binary hypothesis. However, this does not matter if we have degrees of moral rightness to work with. For then we can, at least in principle, assess degrees of moral rightness and compare them to see which alternatives have the greatest expected degrees of moral rightness. The principle that applies is the following:

PR4

In situations in which moral agents are uncertain of the degrees of moral rightness of some of the alternatives under consideration, a choice of action is rational if and only if the action's expected degree of moral rightness is at least as great as that of any other alternative.

Let us apply PR4 to Jean's decision in Table 4.2. If we calculate the probability-weighted sums indicated, we find that the expected degree of moral rightness of x, EM(x), is .6. Similarly, EM(y) = .64. Thus we find that y receives more general support from T1 and T2 than does x, even though x receives more support from the more probable theory, T1. Hence, y would be the more reasonable choice for Jean.[10] Already we see that PR4 is at variance with PR2 for the case we are examining.

We have not yet considered z, however. Now that we have seen that it is important, in one's deliberations, to include all support that actions receive from all sources, it may turn out that, on the whole, z has greater expected moral rightness than either x or y. And in fact this is the case. Since EM(z) = .70, the rational choice for Jean in our example is z.

This example clearly shows how degrees of moral rightness can make a difference in how decisions should (rationally) be made. We are now ready to return to Hudson's arguments against moral hedging. Would Hudson accept my suggestion that we adopt a many-valued concept of moral rightness in addition to the ordinary two-valued concept? It is difficult to say. However, the example that he uses to show why hedging for "ethical uncertainty," that is, uncertainty about the moral rightness of moral agents' alternatives, is impossible seems to intimate a many-valued conception:

> Hedging will be quite impossible for the ethically uncertain agent. Suppose, for example, that she [the moral agent] has to choose between actions A and B; and she attributes a subjective probability of 0.6 to subjective utilitarianism, 0.4 to some deontological theory. According to subjective utilitarianism, A is slightly better than B; according to the deontological theory A is absolutely forbidden, and B is absolutely required. What should her decision be in this case? Since she regards subjective utilitarianism as more probable, perhaps she should do A: but on the other hand perhaps the greater force with which the deontological theory seems to command B makes up for its slightly lesser subjective probability. (But then why think the deontological theory's command has greater force? Subjective utilitarianism held that she ought to do A—what more could it have said?) In short, no clear decision is forthcoming.[11]

Phrases like "slightly better than," "absolutely forbidden" (as opposed to "relatively forbidden"?), "absolutely required," and "greater force" evoke the notion of degrees of moral rightness. If Hudson would accept such an interpretation, then perhaps PR4 would allay his doubts about the possibility of moral hedging in cases that involve ethical uncertainty.

In order to get a handle on this issue, let us modify the first example that we considered earlier, represented in Table 4.1. Instead of assuming axiological un-

Table 4.3   Modification of Table 4.2 for Binary Hypothesis

	T1 is true. ($p = .6$)	T2 is true. ($p = .4$)
x	1.0	0
y	0.0	1.0
z	0.0	0.0

Table 4.4   Decision Table for Modified Hudson Example

	T1 is true. ($p = .6$)	T2 is true. ($p = .4$)
x	10_1	2_2
y	9_1	30_2

certainty about hedonism and the self-realization theory, let us hypothesize uncertainty about which of two moral theories $T1$ and $T2$ is true. Also, instead of assuming that the numbers in the table report hedons and reals, let us suppose that they represent degrees of moral rightness according to $T1$ and $T2$. Thus we get Table 4.4. The subscripts in the boxes remind us that the units of moral rightness are different for the two theories, since presumably a unit of moral rightness for $T1$ cannot be directly compared with a unit of moral rightness for $T2$. Thus our assessments of the expected degrees of moral rightness of the two acts x and y are complicated by the incommensurability of the two scales. We may not simply plug the numbers into the expected moral rightness formula.

Is there any reasonable way to compare the expected degrees of moral rightness of x with those of y for the preceding decision? Hudson would say not, but I think that there is if we are willing to subscribe to the following principle, which I shall call the Principle of Equity among Moral Theories (PEMT):

PEMT
The maximum degrees of moral rightness of all possible actions in a situation according to competing moral theories should be considered equal. The minimum degrees of moral rightness of possible actions in a situation according to competing moral theories should be considered equal unless all possible actions are equally right according to one of the theories (in which case all of the actions should be considered to be maximally right according to that theory).

"Possible actions" include all actions that the agent would be able to perform in the situation. Ordinarily these will include more than just those that the agent consciously considers in her deliberations.

The PEMT says that no moral theory should be regarded as having an advantage over any other theory with respect to the maximum degrees of moral rightness that possible actions in a situation may have. For example, if an action would be morally right to a certain degree according to an act utilitarian theory, then there must be some action in the situation that would be morally right to at least as great a degree according to, say, a deontological theory. And conversely. The principle says the same thing about moral wrongness (minimum rightness)—that is, no theory is capable of conferring a greater amount of moral wrongness in a situation than another theory, except on those very rare occasions on which, according to the second theory, all possible actions would be equally right. Conceivably, an agent's options would be so limited that there would be no moral differences among them with respect to a particular theory. For example, suppose that a sadistic tyrant demands that I choose which of two perfect strangers, B or

C, is to be tortured to death. I have no information at all about B and C except their names. Refusal to choose will result in B's being selected for torture. The three options—choose B, choose C, refuse to choose—might be equally right according to a consequentialist moral theory. However, a deontological theory might prescribe refusing to participate in the tyrant's malevolent scheme. This would mean that, with respect to the deontological theory, only the third option would be morally optimal in the situation. In this event, each of the three options would be morally optimal according to the consequentialist theory, although according to the deontological theory only one option would be morally optimal. Thus the PEMT does not rule out situations in which one moral theory differs from another with respect to the amount of wrong that can be done.

How would the PEMT allow us to solve the commensurability problem of Table 4.4? Let us assume that x and y maximize moral rightness according to T1 and T2, respectively. This is a plausible assumption, since presumably the agent takes into consideration at least some of the actions that, according to competing (subjective) moral theories, would be morally optimal in the situation. Therefore, according to the PEMT, the degrees of moral rightness represented by 10_1 and 30_2 should be considered equal. We may not, however, assume that either x or y minimizes moral rightness according to either T1 or T2, because ordinarily minimally right (i.e., maximally wrong) acts will already have been eliminated from consideration. Therefore, for the purpose of calibrating the two moral rightness scales, one may have to consider additional acts in order to locate minimal moral rightness with respect to T1 and T2 in the situation. Let us suppose that actions z and w have been identified as minimizing moral rightness according to T1 and T2, respectively. The augmented decision table is, let us suppose, Table 4.5. For each theory, some acts have a greater degree of moral rightness than others. Thus, according to the PEMT, -15_1 and -30_2 represent equal quantities of moral rightness.

How about the intermediate quantities 2_2, 9_1, 12_2, and 6_1? If we suppose that the two moral rightness scales are interval scales,[12] then the distances between points on the scales are proportional to differences between the degrees of moral rightness represented by the points. This enables us to measure the degrees of moral rightness on a common scale. Simple calculations transform the moral rightness measurements of Table 4.5 into measurements on a 0-to-10 scale, given in Table 4.6. For these measurements, it turns out that $EM(x) = 8\ 2/15$ and $EM(y) = 9.76$. Hence, y would have the greater expected degree of moral rightness in the situation.

Table 4.5   Augmentation of Table 4.4

	T1 is true. ($p = .6$)	T2 is true. ($p = .4$)
x	10_1	2_2
y	9_1	30_2
z	-15_1	12_2
w	6_1	-30_2

Table 4.6   Table 4.5 with Transformed Measurements

	T1 is true. ($p = .6$)	T2 is true. ($p = .4$)
x	10	5 1/3
y	9.6	10
z	0	7
w	8.4	0

To obtain this result, I have had to assume that degrees of moral rightness with respect to $T1$ and $T2$ can be measured on interval scales and that minimally right actions with respect to $T1$ and $T2$ can be identified in the situation. It may appear that I have, in an ad hoc manner, concocted the PEMT for the sole purpose of defending the otherwise indefensible claim that moral hedging is possible. Admittedly, it is difficult to see how comparisons among expected degrees of moral rightness can be made without employing something like the PEMT, if we are working with a many-valued concept of moral rightness. Nevertheless, even if one doubts that intertheoretic comparisons of degrees of moral rightness can be made in general, it seems reasonable to regard the maximum degrees of moral rightness that different moral theories confer on actions as being equal.

The PEMT might be thought of as a principle of fair competition among moral theories, analogous to democratic principles that support the equal counting of the votes of all qualified voters in an election regardless of any actual differences in preference intensity among the voters. Of course, an agent might view some of the competing moral theories as more plausible than others and wish to take the more plausible theories more strongly into account. But this is already accounted for in the probabilities assigned to the various theories. Assigning lesser maximum degrees of moral rightness to a theory as well as assigning that theory a lower probability of being true would constitute an unfair sort of "double jeopardy" for the theory.[13] The PEMT does not say that moral theories cannot be different with respect to the intermediate degrees of moral rightness it is possible for actions to have. For example, a Kantian theory might allow only two degrees of moral rightness, while an act utilitarian theory might allow infinite variation between maximum and minimum values.

Still, one might raise the following objection to the PEMT: To say that the maximum possible moral rightness attainable in a situation must be the same according to all moral theories disqualifies any view according to which more moral rightness can be at stake on some occasions than on others. With respect to a consequentialist theory, for example, there will be more utility at stake in some situations than in others. Let us suppose that consequentialist theory C prescribes maximizing utility and that at time t_1 Ken must choose between x and y, where the utility of y is 1 hedon greater than that of x. Furthermore, at time t_2 Ken must choose between z and w, where the utility of w is 10,000 hedons greater than that of z. (Let us pretend that utility can be measured in such a way that a difference of 10,000 hedons is 10,000 $\times$ a difference of 1 hedon.) Thus for Ken at t_1 only 1 hedon is at stake while at t_2 10,000 hedons are at stake. The PEMT implies that, with respect to theory T, Ken's producing a gain of 1 hedon at t_1 would generate the same quantity of moral rightness as his producing 10,000 times as great a utility gain at t_2. However, consequentialism is the doctrine that moral rightness is entirely a matter of the (expected) success of our actions in producing valuable outcomes. And this suggests that Ken's producing a gain of 10,000 hedons at t_2 should count for much more, morally speaking, than his producing a gain of 1 hedon at t_1. The PEMT seems to ignore this intuition.

We can develop the objection further. Let us suppose that, in addition to the consequentialist theory C, Ken finds plausible a deontological theory D. According to D, moral rightness is entirely a matter of conforming to specific duties and has nothing to do with utility. Furthermore, according to D there are no intermediate degrees of moral rightness between "right" and "wrong." If Ken used the PEMT in order to heed both C and D, he would assign the same weight to C in every decision situation, and similarly for D. However, one might argue that C should carry more weight in situations in which more utility is at stake and less weight when less utility is at stake. That is, the relative weights of C and D should vary depending on the salience of the situation with respect to the two theories' moral criteria. The PEMT fails to take this into account.

These arguments against the PEMT rely on the idea that with respect to some moral theories, one moral decision may offer greater opportunities for moral rightness than another. Let us call this view the Varying Potential for Moral Rightness (VPMR) thesis. On this view, in relation to a consequentialist theory, not only is more utility at stake in some situations than in others, but more moral rightness is at stake as well. And the thesis suggests that the weights we assign to competing moral theories for a particular moral decision should reflect how much moral rightness is at stake according to the respective theories. If this suggestion is correct, then the PEMT is inadequate and should be replaced by a principle that takes variations among situations' potentials for moral rightness into consideration. It is very difficult to imagine what such a replacement principle for the PEMT would be or how we might compare the quantities of moral rightness that are at stake according to different moral theories. Take, for instance, theories C and D mentioned earlier. Suppose we were to claim that at t_1 the same amount of moral rightness is at stake with respect to C and D, while at t_2 the amount of moral rightness at stake with respect to C is 10,000 times the amount that is at stake with respect to D. Then a proponent of D would accuse us of giving C an unfair advantage by assigning such disproportionate weights to the two theories. However, if we took things in the opposite order and assumed that the same amount of moral rightness is at stake at t_2 according to the two theories and that at t_1 10,000 times as much moral rightness is at stake according to D as is at stake according to C, we would get a similar complaint from a defender of C. It would appear that any conversion factor we proposed to use to relate utility according to C to degrees of moral rightness according to D would be arbitrary. By contrast, PEMT appears not to play favorites among moral theories or to give some type(s) of moral theories unfair advantages over others.

But can we give any positive reasons to accept the PEMT? If not, should we not abandon the whole idea of comparing degrees of moral rightness according to different moral theories? Let us try to get at these questions by considering the implications of the VPMR thesis for a decision-maker, Leah, who is 100% certain that moral theory T is *the* correct theory. And let us imagine that, like Ken, Leah confronts moral decisions at t_1 and t_2 where there is more moral rightness at stake at t_2 than there is at t_1. If Leah follows a maximize-expected-moral-rightness decision strategy, does it matter, for decision-making purposes, whether she accepts the VPMR thesis? Clearly the answer is "No." In each situation, the same alternative(s) would maximize expected moral rightness regardless of whether she accepts the VPMR thesis.

How then might the VPMR thesis make a *practical* difference for Leah? One way would be this: What if Leah's decision at t_1 were connected to her decision at t_2 in the following way? If she maximizes moral rightness at t_1 then she fails to do so at t_2, and if she fails to maximize moral rightness at t_1 then she succeeds in maximizing utility at t_2. According to the VPMR thesis, more moral rightness is at stake for Leah at t_2 than at t_1. Hence, if she acts to maximize moral rightness for the two decisions *as a set*, she will act differently at t_1 from how she will act if she disregards the connection between the two decisions and maximizes moral rightness at t_1 only. What then should Leah do at t_1? If we say that she should take each decision as it comes and maximize moral rightness on each particular occasion, then we imply that the VPMR thesis has no significance for moral decision-making. If, on the other hand, we say that she should consider the connection between the two decisions and sacrifice moral rightness at t_1 in order to achieve greater moral rightness at t_2, then we imply that the VPMR thesis has considerable practical significance.

The purpose of the thought experiment we have just conducted is not to suggest that moral decisions are related to each other as Leah's decision at t_1 is related to her decision at t_2. (We shall raise the possibility of such connections among moral decisions in chapter 8.) The aim is rather to separate questions about the practical significance of the VPMR thesis from other questions that relate to moral uncertainty. If the VPMR thesis has practical significance for Leah, for whom we have assumed that moral uncertainty about moral theories, principles, or considerations is not a constraint, then it will also have practical significance for Ken, for whom moral uncertainty is a constraint. If the VPMR thesis does not have practical significance for Leah, neither will it have practical significance for Ken. Whether the thesis does have practical significance for our moral decisions is an issue the discussion of which we shall postpone until chapter 8. For the moment, let us note that all of the conclusions we have reached so far disregard the VPMR thesis.[14]

For decision-making under moral uncertainty, what we need is a way of measuring, on a common scale, the degrees of moral rightness that an action would have in a particular situation according to different moral theories. May we assume that moral rightness, as a many-valued quantity, can be measured on an interval scale? I shall not attempt here to say in general how this might be done. For teleological theories like utilitarianism, it seems reasonable to regard acts as right to the degree to which they cover the gap between the minimum and the maximum quantities of intrinsic value that could be produced.[15] For example, if the "worst" action would produce -50 hedons and the "best" action would produce 40 hedons, then an action that produced 22 hedons would have a score of $[22-(-50)]/[40-(-50)] = .8$ on the normalized (i.e., 0 to 1) moral rightness scale. In this instance, measuring degrees of moral rightness would be no more difficult than measuring intrinsic value (which, admittedly, is problematic). Moreover, it seems to be a difficulty that Hudson is not particularly worried about, since the example he uses assumes that hedons and reals have somehow been measured.

A weaker assumption about the meaning of the numerals in Table 4.5 is that the numerals represent ordinal scale measurements of degrees of moral rightness. The numerals would indicate, for moral theories T1 and T2, which quantities are larger/smaller than which other quantities, but they would not tell how much larger/smaller they are. In fact, we can capture all the information contained in the ordinal scale measurements by just ranking the four quantities from smallest (1) to largest (4). Doing so generates Table 4.7, where the brackets indicate that the quantities are ordinal.

With such information, would it be possible to determine which action, x or y, would maximize expected moral rightness? Obviously, it would not be possible to do so with certainty, since there would be no basis for claiming that [3] on one ordinal scale would represent a larger quantity than [2] on the other. The PEMT would allow us to equate the [1]s in the two columns with each other, and the [4]s as well; but we could draw no such conclusions about the [2]s and [3]s. Therefore, it appears that PR4 could not be directly applied to this decision.

What recourse would a decision-maker have in the situation of Table 4.7? There are a couple of possibilities: An agent might use the familiar "rank-order" or "Borda count" method, which would mean here simply treating the ordinal numbers as if they were cardinal numbers and taking the probability-weighted sums across the rows of the table as the degrees of moral rightness for the four alternatives. It is easy to show that this procedure would recommend y as the rational choice. However, one of the main problems with this method is that it violates the well-known "independence condition" in decision theory, which says that which of two acts one chooses should not be affected by adding to the list of alternatives another act that is inferior to the original two.[16] For the situation we are considering here, our choice of y over x might be reversed if we added another act v to our list of alternatives and applied the rank-order procedure. How serious an objection this is depends on how much importance we should attach to the independence condition.

Another approach to the ordinal measurement decision problem adopts a higher order rationality principle, PR5 (precisely stated later), which tells us that in cases in which we lack sufficient information to apply PR4, we should choose an action that, for the available information, has the greatest probability of sat-

Table 4.7   Table 4.5 with Ordinal Measurements

	T1 is true. ($p = .6$)	T2 is true. ($p = .4$)
x	[4]	[2]
y	[3]	[4]
z	[1]	[3]
w	[2]	[1]

isfying PR4. Thus if the agent had some reason to believe that x is more likely to satisfy PR4 than is y and had no other basis for favoring one over the other, PR5 would direct her to choose x in the situation. However, if there were no information on the basis of which one act could be regarded as more likely to satisfy PR4 than the other, then the agent might reasonably infer that the two acts are equally likely to satisfy PR4 and therefore equally rational to choose under the circumstances.

Finally, let us discuss our supposition that agents can identify minimally right alternatives in decision situations. For objective moral theories this would be most implausible. For example, how often can we determine which action(s) of all possible actions would actually lead to the worst consequences in the long run? But we must remember that Hudson regards only subjective moral theories as contenders, and for subjective theories we need not be omniscient about the consequences of our actions. We need only identify some action such that there is no other possible action in the situation that we believe would (probably?) lead to worse consequences than it. That an agent can identify at least one such action does not seem an unreasonable assumption.[17]

We have seen that Hudson's arguments against moral hedging, even under the most favorable interpretations, are not successful. However, in evaluating those arguments, we have gained an important insight—namely, that we should take seriously the possibility that the binary hypothesis is mistaken and that moral rightness occurs in varying degrees. This proposal has practical significance for us because if we adopt it, it will in many cases make a difference in which actions we choose. This is so because maximizing the expected degrees of moral rightness of our actions is not the same as maximizing the probabilities that our actions are morally right, if actions can have varying degrees of moral rightness.

But even if the proposal is one that we should take seriously, do we have positive reason to accept it? It is not enough just to discredit the arguments against it or to say that a doctrine of degrees of moral rightness would make a difference in our action choices if we were to adopt it. If we are going to use the doctrine, then we need rational justification for doing so. How might we obtain such justification? One way is the following: If we can imagine a moral decision for which it is clear that a particular choice of action would be the most reasonable choice and then show that the best explanation of this fact is that the many-valued concept of moral rightness is the correct one, then we shall have good reason to adopt that concept. I believe that one of our previous examples can serve this purpose. The decision of Table 4.6 meets the stated requirements if we construe the two theories $T1$ and $T2$ as consequentialist theories and interpret the numbers in the table as measuring the value of the consequences of the various alternatives according to the two theories. ($T1$ and $T2$ might differ only in the theories of intrinsic value that they assume.) We shall hypothesize also that the two scales of measurement are comparable 0-to-10 interval scales.

Clearly y is the best choice, given the maximum value of its consequences according to $T2$ and their almost maximum value according to $T1$. Even though $T1$ is the more probable theory, the likelihood that $T2$ is the correct theory is great enough that the agent should not ignore it in deciding which alternative to choose. And the fact that x maximizes value according to $T1$ is not enough to compensate for its mediocre performance with respect to $T2$. If the reader is not convinced by the numbers in the table, she need only increase the probability that $T2$ is the "true" theory to, say, .48 and decrease that of $T1$'s being the "true" theory to .52. And we can make the argument even stronger by lowering the value produced by x with respect to $T2$ to, say, 2.

What is the best way to explain the fact that y is the most reasonable choice in the situation we have just described? Obviously, the "my favorite theory" approach to moral decision-making does not work here. But neither does PR2 give us the desired result, since it assumes the binary hypothesis and therefore would prescribe x in this situation. I can think of no plausible explanation other than that moral rightness is a many-valued quantity and that PR4 is the correct principle of rationality. Of course, it is possible to specify a moral theory according to which moral rightness can have only two possible "sizes." Kantians, perhaps, would define their theories as having this feature. But for at least some theories, particularly consequentialist theories, it is natural, in light of situations like the one we have just discussed, to conceive the moral rightness of an alternative as proportional in magnitude to some continuously varying quantity, such as the (expected) value of its consequences. This seems the best way to explain why y would be the rational choice in the situation represented by Table 4.6.

We are, of course, pretending in our reinterpretation of Table 4.6 that we have precise cardinal-number measurements, with respect to both $T1$ and $T2$, of the value of the various possible sets of consequences. This is perhaps an unrealistic assumption for actual moral decisions. However, the purpose of the example is to address the question of whether we should conceive moral rightness as a two-valued quantity or as a many-valued quantity. And in order to answer the conceptual question, we need not worry whether such an assumption is realistic. If accepting the correctness of a many-valued conception of moral rightness is the best way to explain why y is the rational choice in our imaginary situation of perfect information, then we have good reason to adopt that conception for other situations as well.

We could infuse additional realism into the example by abandoning the cardinal-measurement assumption and simply hypothesizing that the agent believes that x would maximize value according to $T1$, that y would maximize value according to $T2$, that x would produce a relatively low amount of value according to $T2$, and that y would produce a relatively large amount of value according to $T1$. Even with these imprecise assessments of the various quantities of value, the same conclusion would follow about which alternative would be the rational choice. And the best explanation would still be that moral rightness is a many-valued rather than a two-valued quantity.

It may occur to some readers that even if my argument for conceiving moral rightness as a many-valued quantity should persuade us to accept that concept, there may remain some doubt in our minds about its correctness. If so, then in making moral decisions we should hedge our bets and take into consideration our uncertainty about which concept of moral rightness is the correct one. And doing so may make a difference, in some instances, in what we should ultimately do. I agree with these observations. Decision-makers who are uncertain about which concept of moral rightness is the correct one may accommodate both concepts by creating columns in their decision tables so that each concept is properly represented. For the two-valued concept, the two possible degrees of moral rightness might continue to be represented by 1 and 0. For the many-valued concept, degrees of moral rightness might be any numbers in the interval [0,1]. The PEMT would remain in effect, of course.

Generally speaking, for the decision situations that I shall examine in the remainder of this book I shall assume the many-valued concept of moral rightness only and not consider agents' uncertainties about which concept of moral rightness is correct. Readers who are curious about how taking such uncertainties into account would affect the final results may modify the decision tables accordingly and redo the analyses. One who wishes to keep an open mind and not foreclose the possibility of a many-valued concept of moral rightness may think of PR2 as a special case of PR4 that applies when the binary hypothesis is assumed. PR4 then becomes our general principle of rationality for decision-making under moral uncertainty.

The examples that we have considered in this chapter thus far have mostly been schematic decisions in which few details have been provided and for which strong, and perhaps unrealistic, assumptions have been made about decision-makers' information (e.g., exact cardinal measurements of "hedons" and "reals"). Nothing is wrong with this if our purpose is to explore general issues about the nature of moral rightness and the structure of decision-making under moral uncertainty. However, one of our objectives is to avail ourselves of practical methods of moral decision-making that we can employ in the real world. Such methods must not assume that we have information that we ordinarily do not have. Therefore, it behooves us to test the decision principles that we have formulated to see whether they are helpful when we confront difficult moral decisions. A good test case is the abortion case that we considered in the preceding chapter in which the agent was uncertain which of two general moral perspectives was correct. One of those perspectives was a consequentialist view that bases moral rightness on the (expected) consequences of one's alternatives. We have now seen how tempting it is for consequentialists to adopt a concept of degrees of moral rightness. It would be interesting to see whether a many-valued conception of moral rightness would make a difference in how rational moral agents would decide in that situation. It would also give us some practice in applying our decision principles for degrees of moral rightness to more realistic moral decisions. Therefore, let us next undertake that reexamination.

Abortion and Degrees of Moral Rightness

In the previous chapter, I arrived at PR2 as a principle for decision-making under moral uncertainty by assuming the binary hypothesis. I then tested PR2 by applying it to several decisions about abortion, including the decision represented by Table 3.6. One consequence of the binary hypothesis is that the rows of decision tables in which the hypothesis is assumed will contain only 1s and 0s, representing "right" and "wrong." If we abandon the binary hypothesis, then the numbers in the table may represent intermediate degrees of moral rightness and may be any

Table 4.8 Abortion and Moral Uncertainty with Degrees of Moral Rightness

	Nonconsequentialist moral perspective is correct. (p_4)			Consequentialist moral perspective is correct. ($1-p_4$)		
	This fetus is a person (p_1)		This fetus is not a person. ($1-p_1$)	This fetus is a person (p_1)		This fetus is not a person. ($1-p_1$)
	Personhood implies that abortion is wrong. (p_3)	Personhood does not imply that abortion is wrong. ($1-p_3$)		Fetus's interests outweigh agent's interests. (p_2)	Agent's interests outweigh fetus's interests. ($1-p_2$)	
abortion	0	1	1	m_1	1	1
no abortion	1	1	1	1	m_2	m_3

numbers from the interval $[0,1]$. If we revise Table 3.6 to take degrees of moral rightness into account, then, generally speaking, there will be at least one 1 in each column of the table. The reason is that decision-makers will ordinarily consider, for each set of conditions or "state of the world," alternatives that are morally optimal. They may also consider some alternatives that are morally optimal under no set of contingencies, since such options will sometimes have the maximum expected degree of moral rightness.

For the decision represented by Table 3.6, the agent must decide between having and not having an abortion. She is presumed to be uncertain about the following: (1) whether the fetus that she carries is a person who possesses a right to life, (2) whether, if her fetus is such a person, that fact means that she morally ought not to have an abortion, (3) whether, on the assumption that her fetus is a person, her interests outweigh those of the fetus, and (4) whether a consequentialist or a nonconsequentialist viewpoint is the correct moral perspective for her decision. Let us assume that the binary hypothesis continues to hold for the nonconsequentialist perspective, which casts the main moral question in terms of a conflict between the rights of the agent herself and the rights that the fetus has if it is a person. Let us also assume that for the consequentialist perspective the binary hypothesis does not hold and that the degrees of moral rightness of the two options from that perspective represent their (normalized) utilities under the various combinations of conditions in the table.

Table 4.8 is identical to Table 3.6 except that the 0s in columns 4, 5, and 6 have been replaced by m_1, m_2, and m_3, representing the degrees of moral rightness of the "abortion" and "no abortion" options under the conditions indicated in the table. The 0 in column 1 remains because we have assumed that the binary hypothesis continues to hold with respect to the nonconsequentialist perspective. It is easy to show that

$$\text{EM}(A) = p_1 + p_4 - p_1 p_2 - p_1 p_4 + p_1 p_2 p_4 - p_1 p_3 p_4 + p_1 p_2 m_1 - p_1 p_2 p_4 m_1$$

and

$$EM(\text{not-}A) = p_1 + p_4 + m_3 + p_1p_2 - p_1m_3 - p_4m_3$$
$$- p_1p_2p_4 - {}_1p_2m_2 - p_1p_4m_2 + p_1p_4m_3 + p_1p_2p_4m_2.$$

It follows that

$$EM(A) - EM(\text{not-}A) = -m_3 - p_1p_4 + p_1m_3 + p_4m_3 - 2p_1p_2 - p_1p_3p_4 + p_1p_2m_1$$
$$+ p_1p_2m_2 + p_1p_4m_2 - p_1p_4m_3 + 2p_1p_2p_4 - p_1p_2p_4m_1 - p_1p_2p_4m_2.$$

Therefore, $EM(A) \geq EM(\text{not-}A)$ if and only if

$$p_1m_3 + p_4m_3 + p_1p_2m_1 + p_1p_2m_2 + p_1p_4m_2 + {}_2p_1p_2p_4 \geq$$
$$m_3 + p_1p_4 + 2p_1p_2 + p_1p_3p_4 + p_1p_4m_3 + p_1p_2p_4m_1 + p_1p_2p_4m_2.$$

As before, the agent may regard p_1, p_2, p_3, and p_4 as subjective probabilities or as objective probabilities. If they are subjective probabilities, then the agent may attempt to measure them either by assigning each of them a cardinal value or by locating each of them in an interval of cardinal numbers within $[0,1]$. If p_1, p_2, p_3, and p_4 are viewed as unknown objective probabilities, then cardinal number measurements may be dubious and the agent may have more confidence in ordinal measurements. Let us suppose that the second approach is adopted and that the agent ranks the probabilities as follows: $p_1 \leq p_4 \leq p_3 \leq p_2$. We shall also impose the constraint $p_4 \geq .5$ for the same reason as in chapter 2—that is, so that the average value of p_1 among the 4-tuples $<p_1, p_2, p_3, p_4>$ that satisfy the constraints will be greater than .2.

How about m_1, m_2, and m_3? How might the decision-maker assess their magnitudes? We should recall that m_1, m_2, and m_3 can be thought of as the normalized magnitudes of the utilities of the two options under the conditions indicated in Table 4.8. The quantities are normalized—measured on a scale from 0 to 1—so that they are commensurable with the numerical representations 1 and 0 (for "right" and "wrong") for the two-valued conception of moral rightness. It is important to remember that 0 on the normalized scale represents the minimum utility for all of the actions that the agent could choose in the situation and not just for the two alternatives given in Table 4.8. The purpose is to calibrate the utility scale so that 0 on that scale corresponds to 0 on other degree-of-moral-rightness scales. 0 means minimum moral rightness on every scale. When the binary hypothesis is assumed, minimum moral rightness simply means "morally wrong."

It might be possible for the decision-maker to obtain single-number cardinal measurements of m_1, m_2, and m_3. To do so, she would have to imagine for each of the three states of affairs that correspond to columns 4, 5, and 6 of Table 4.8 the worst consequences that she would be capable of producing. She might then assign 0 utility to each of the three sets of consequences and then pose hypothetical gambles to determine the values of m_1, m_2, and m_3. There would be difficulties in addition to the usual difficulties of utility measurement. How, for example, does she determine what are the worst consequences that she would be capable of producing in a particular situation?

It seems unlikely that the agent would be able to obtain reliable single-number values of m_1, m_2, and m_3. It also seems unlikely that she would be able to place each of the three quantities within fixed intervals (e.g, [.4, .6]) except perhaps for those that would be too wide to provide much useful information (e.g., [0,1]). Therefore, the best approach might be to perform and use an ordinal ranking of the three quantities, augmented perhaps by constraints that place lower or upper bounds on some of them. This will probably mean that PR4 cannot be applied directly, since the measurements of the probabilities and degrees of moral rightness will not be precise enough for the expected degrees of moral rightness of the two alternatives to be calculated. However, as before, we can ascend to a higher order principle:

PR5

In situations in which one is uncertain of the degrees of moral rightness of some of the alternatives under consideration and in which there is not enough information to determine which alternative(s) have the maximum expected degree of moral rightness directly, one should (rationally) choose some alternative that, with respect to the available information, has an expected degree of moral rightness that is at least as great as that of any other alternative.

PR5 says in effect that when we do not have enough information to apply PR4 directly, we should choose some action that has the greatest likelihood of satisfying PR4.

Let us assume that the decision-maker chooses to follow this approach. What ordinal ranking might she assign to m_1, m_2, and m_3? Different agents may make different assignments. However, she might reason as follows: If her fetus is a person, then its interests must be weighed as well as the interests of the agent herself. Since the abortion decision is a life-or-death decision for the fetus, probably more of its interests are at stake than the agent's interests. To abort is to deprive the fetus of all of life's rewards. Although life is not always rewarding and for some may not be worth living, life's rewards greatly exceed its tribulations, generally speaking. If the agent's interests outweigh the fetus's interests, then the margin is probably quite small—smaller than the margin by which the fetus's interests would outweigh the agent's interests. Therefore, $m_1 < m_2$.

If the fetus is not a person, its interests need not be weighed. Only the agent's interests are relevant. Under this condition, there is no need to subtract the utility that the fetus would lose if it were aborted in order to arrive at a net utility for the "abortion" option. In the other two scenarios, the utilities associated with the fetus's stake in the agent's decision and the agent's stake in her decision are in opposition to each other. Therefore, if the fetus's interests are irrelevant, the agent's loss of utility if she pursues the "no abortion" alternative will probably be greater than the net loss of utility between the agent and the fetus in the other two cases. Therefore, m_3 will be smaller than either m_1 or m_2. Therefore, m_1, m_2, and m_3 should be ranked as follows: $m_3 < m_1 < m_2$.

Should any other constraints on m_1, m_2, and m_3 be observed? As already noted, m_1, m_2, and m_3 are measured on utility scales on which 1 represents the maximum utility and 0 represents the minimum utility (i.e., the utility of the worst state of affairs that the agent could bring about by any action that she could perform). It may be difficult to imagine a situation that corresponds to 0 utility, but it is likely that neither of the two alternatives that she is considering would come close to producing such a state of affairs. Either would probably produce consequences that would be significantly closer to the best that she could produce than to the worst that she could produce. Therefore, it seems conservative to suppose that $m_3 > .5$. Thus the information about the magnitudes of m_1, m_2, and m_3 that we shall use in our analysis may be summarized as follows: $.5 < m_3 < m_1 < m_2$.

In order to apply PR5 to the agent's decision, we compute the mean value of $EM(A) - EM(\text{not-}A)$ over the region defined by the constraints on p_1, p_2, p_3, p_4, m_1, m_2, and m_3. If the mean value is positive, then this shows that $EM(A)$ probably exceeds $EM(\text{not-}A)$ and thus the "abortion" alternative is recommended. If the mean value is negative, then the "no abortion" option is prescribed. Computations reveal that the mean value of $EM(A) - EM(\text{not-}A)$ is approximately $-.383$, a negative number.[18] Hence, for the measurements given, PR5 prescribes the "no abortion" alternative by a relatively wide margin.

The reader may not be satisfied with the result just obtained and may have additional or different constraints in mind for the ps and the ms in our example. And, of course, different results are to be expected when different individuals assess the magnitudes of various nebulous quantities or recognize different moral considerations. However, our analysis has confirmed the practical significance of degrees of moral rightness, since including them has reversed the prescription. When we assumed the binary hypothesis, we concluded that the "abortion" alternative was likelier to have maximum expected moral rightness. However, as we have just seen, assuming a many-valued conception of moral rightness produces the opposite result. Degrees of moral rightness makes a difference in how we should (rationally) make moral decisions.

Conclusions

If the arguments of this chapter are sound, then we have shown that, contrary to Hudson's claims, moral hedging is possible for a variety of ethical decisions. The linchpin of my argument against Hudson is the PEMT, which allows us to make sufficient connections among disparate moral theories to determine which of our decision alternatives have, or are most likely to have, maximum expected moral rightness. However, as we have seen, those connections may be quite loose and do not require of moral agents superhuman powers of moral discrimination.

Except for bolstering the claim that rational decision-making can take place under conditions of profound moral uncertainty, the most important result of this chapter is that we have proposed and justified a conception of degrees of moral rightness. We have shown that such a conception is not only coherent but also essential to rational decision-making. This notion of degrees of moral rightness, while it has been occasionally hinted at by ethicists, has not been systematically developed or supported by argument. More significantly, its importance for moral decision-making has not been recognized, probably because ethicists have not seen moral uncertainty as an important consideration in moral decision-making. I have shown why the concept of degrees of moral rightness is important, and I have illustrated how decision-makers who have in mind a many-valued conception of moral rightness might go about determining which action choices are rational.

It is clear that for some moral theories, especially those that include value maximization as a moral criterion, moral rightness should be conceived as having degrees between "right" and "wrong." While it may be possible to avoid explicit reference to degrees of moral rightness in moral discourse, in order to give an adequate account of rational decision-making it would be necessary to present methods of deliberation that would be equivalent to those that I have illustrated in this chapter—methods that explicitly recognize degrees of moral rightness. Therefore, I see no reason not to adopt such a conception of moral rightness. I shall continue to use it throughout the rest of this book. In PR4 and PR5 we have at our disposal rationales for our choices of action that we may apply to problems that arise in medical ethics, business ethics, and other areas of applied and professional ethics, as well as to the myriad moral decisions that arise in everyday life.

Five

Shall I Act Supererogatorily?

There is an important criticism of my approach to moral decision-making, which is embodied in PR4 and PR5, that I have yet to consider. PR4 and PR5 advise us always to do the best that we can, morally speaking, when we are not sure of the moral rightness of any of our options. Doing the best that we can, I have argued, amounts to maximizing the expected moral rightness of our actions. However, some ethicists contend that morality itself does not require us always to do the best that we can. And some make the same claim about rationality—that it at least sometimes happens that we can act rationally without maximizing intrinsic value (for oneself or others) or anything else.[1] We must draw a distinction, it is argued, between what morality or rationality *requires* of us and what goes beyond those requirements. Acts that go "beyond the call of duty" are said to be *supererogatory*. In order to distinguish between duty and supererogation, it is claimed, we must observe limits on duty and not think of duty as always maximizing or optimizing with respect to some desirable quantity.

The term *satisficing* has been coined to refer to the behavior of an agent who seeks "less than the best."[2] A conception of morality or rationality that emphasizes satisficing behavior contrasts with one, like that expressed by PR4 and PR5, that counsels us always to maximize. For example, a satisficing principle of decision-making under moral uncertainty might advise us to choose actions that achieve at least a certain minimum expected degree of moral rightness but leave up to us whether and how far we go beyond that minimum level. Perhaps we are entitled to praise if we go far above the minimum that is required. However, to require maximization as a necessary condition for moral or rational behavior is to confuse the obligatory with the supererogatory. This distinction is pertinent not only to ethical inquiry but also to investigating decision-making under moral uncertainty.

I believe that the optimization model of rational decision-making is superior to the satisficing model, which is seriously flawed in my view. Of course, even if the "true" moral theory made satisficing (rather than optimizing) the criterion for moral rightness, this would not necessarily mean that the same holds for the "true" theory of rational decision-making under moral uncertainty. Clearly, it is possible that rational behavior must come as close to morally right behavior as possible, even if morally right behavior need not maximize (expected) utility or any other quantity. One who wishes to defend a satisficing conception of rationality on the grounds of a distinction between morally right action and supererogatory action must explain how the latter is supposed to support the former. Nevertheless, we who oppose a satisficing conception of rationality in action must admit that in view of the intimacy of the relationship between morality and rationality, if one of the two standards guides us in the satisficing direction then we have some reason to suspect that the other does so as well.

The safe strategy here for a defender of PR4 and PR5 is to challenge the inference from satisficing morality to satisficing rationality and to argue that it is unjustified. I suspect that that strategy would succeed. However, the topic of supererogation is interesting and important in its own right, and I shall attempt a more thoroughgoing defense by arguing against the distinction between rightness and supererogation *even within morality*. I shall argue that to try to draw that distinction in either context, morality or rationality, is a mistake. If the whole notion of supererogation is, as I shall maintain, unsatisfactory, then it does not really matter whether the inference from satisficing morality to satisficing rationality is justified. One who attempts such an inference will be inferring from a false premise. This is important not only for my main purpose here, which is to defend my views about rational decision-making under moral uncertainty, but also for the purpose of discrediting moral perspectives that attempt to distinguish the supererogatory from the obligatory.

Supererogationism

Supererogationism is the doctrine that some of our actions qualify as acts of supererogation.[3] Although the definition of *supererogatory action* is a matter of some philosophical disagreement, supererogationists agree that, in some sense, such actions go "beyond duty" and that they possess greater moral value than non-supererogatory actions. Furthermore, supererogatory actions are conceived as "optional"—that is, moral agents are not "required" to perform them, although one who does so usually deserves praise. Many philosophers, and perhaps most ordinary people as well, now share this view, first articulated by J. O. Urmson in his essay "Saints and Heroes."[4] To a considerable degree it is the perspective of common sense, and I shall often refer to it as the "commonsense view" in the following discussion. It is the view that I shall examine and criticize in this chapter.

Perhaps the principal motivation for recognizing supererogatory actions as a distinct category is the feeling that morality must not make excessive demands on us. If we should always do what is morally optimal, then we must always, or at least very often, act as saints and heroes, and this would be an unreasonable expectation. Therefore, we need to distinguish between the sort of behavior it is reasonable to expect of ourselves and others and that which is laudable or praiseworthy but not "required."[5]

Many ethicists regard the concept of supererogation as having much significance for moral theory. Some allege that any moral theory that does not recognize supererogatory actions as a moral category is inadequate and should be rejected.[6] Act utilitarians especially have come in for this criticism.[7] Defenders of the criticized theories have responded either by alleging that the critics are mistaken in charging that their theories cannot account for supererogatory actions or by arguing that their particular theories avoid the necessity of such a notion.[8]

Some ethicists, like Peter Singer and Elizabeth M. Pybus, have rejected supererogationism itself and the doctrine that moral theory should recognize a special class of actions that have a higher moral status than merely right actions.[9] Pybus argues that when we praise the actions of others we are really praising the agents who perform those actions and expressing our aspirations to be as virtuous as they. She contends that such an attitude does not require us to recognize their actions as going beyond duty or to demand that others perform similar actions. Her essay has provoked considerable discussion in the literature.[10]

Joseph Raz has noted a difficulty in conceiving of supererogatory actions as praiseworthy but not required:

> If doing a supererogatory act is praiseworthy there must be reasons for doing it, and the reasons must outweigh any conflicting reasons for not doing it. But if there are conclusive reasons for performing the act then not to perform it is to act against the balance of reasons. If reason requires that the act be done then surely one ought to do it, and the "ought" is based on all the reasons which apply to the case; it is a conclusive ought. But this entails that failing to perform the act is failing to do what one ought (conclusively) to do, so why isn't it blameworthy not to perform a supererogatory act?[11]

Raz attempts to solve this problem by appealing to a second-order, "exclusionary permission" that allows one not to do what she has (conclusive) first-order reasons for doing. Unfortunately, Raz does not explain what he means by "conclusive reasons," and as David Heyd has noted, it would seem that "conclusive reasons" that one is permitted to disregard would not really be "conclusive." Also, Robin Attfield observes that Raz's analysis ignores the possibility that some actions are right but not obligatory. Perhaps there are praiseworthy actions the reasons for doing which do not outweigh the reasons for doing other praiseworthy actions.[12]

Although Raz's argument is flawed, I think that his basic idea of considering the strength of the reasons for performing supererogatory actions is on the right track, and I shall exploit it in the following discussion. Heyd denies that we have better reasons for acting supererogatorily than for not doing so, even though supererogatory actions are "morally praiseworthy and meritorious."[13] However, I shall argue that the fact that one action has greater *moral* rightness than another is good reason for choosing the first action over the second.

Although I agree with the critics of supererogationism, I do not think they have been entirely successful in exposing its essential failing. In this discussion, I shall present and attempt to support a more fundamental sort of misgiving about the concept of supererogation. I shall argue that if we bear in mind the overriding importance of moral considerations in action choice, we shall be able to discern an inconsistency in the notion of a category of actions that are of superior moral value and yet optional for moral agents.

Anyone who denies the distinction between supererogatory and nonsupererogatory actions should be prepared to respond to the motivating impulse for supererogationism—namely, that to deny the existence of supererogatory actions allows morality to demand too much of us. In the penultimate section of this chapter, I shall deal with this issue by showing how responding rationally to a kind of moral uncertainty that I think is common among reflective moral agents may call for striking a balance between egoistic and altruistic conceptions of moral obligation while recognizing the plausibility of both conceptions. In particular, I shall illustrate how the deliberations that lead to such action need not involve a distinction between doing what duty calls for and going beyond the call of duty.

Many philosophical discussions of supererogation adopt what we might call a spectator perspective and consider what sort of behavior "we" (the spectators) may "demand" or "expect" of others. From such a perspective, we can easily sympathize with the supererogationist's conviction that while it is fair to expect some minimal level of self-sacrifice, regard for others, commitment to principle, and so forth, we demand too much if we demand that moral agents always act in a laudable manner. It seems inappropriate to brand someone a moral failure simply because we do not find her actions admirable.

Rarely do philosophers in their discussions of supererogation adopt an "actor" perspective and consider what sorts of deliberations "I" might engage in if "I" were to choose between acting supererogatorily and acting rightly but nonsupererogatorily. But this is precisely the kind of choice that moral agents must actually make if supererogationism is true and decision-makers can act rightly without acting supererogatorily. It is from this "actor" perspective that we shall begin our investigation.

A Case Study: How Much Shall I Contribute to International Relief?

I have a decision to make: whether and, if so, how much to contribute to international relief agencies to alleviate starvation and disease in the Third World. For simplicity, let us suppose that I have only three options—contribute $100, contribute $10,000, or contribute $0.[14] I am assured that there are reliable, efficient relief agencies like CARE and Oxfam that would make effective use of my donation. I am also confident that even the $100 contribution would have a significant impact on at least one person who is in desperate need of food, medicine, or other vital goods. But I believe that a $10,000 contribution would benefit many more desperate people. I am not wealthy, at least not by American standards. I cannot afford to spend even $100 frivolously, but I cannot think of a use of my money that would do more good than supporting such a cause. Unfortunately, contributing $10,000 would virtually wipe out much of my financial reserves and place me and my family in some jeopardy should some unforeseen exigency arise. What shall I do?

There are, of course, a variety of norms on which I might base my decision. They include nonmoral norms such as the laws of the state, which permit me to donate any amount I wish, including $0. But what about moral standards? Proponents of the commonsense view would likely say that contributing either $100 or $10,000 would be morally right but that my contributing $0 would be wrong. According to this view, the standard of moral rightness approves my donating either $100 or $10,000. However, it also says that it would be "better," morally speaking, and that my action would be especially meritorious and praiseworthy if I contributed the larger amount. Thus the commonsense view implies a second, more exclusive standard for action choice and appraisal that, for my moral decision about donating to international relief, would choose the $10,000 contribution.

One decision, therefore, that I must make at the outset is which standard of conduct I shall base my choice of action on. Shall I act supererogatorily, or shall I do what is right but not supererogatory? I shall assume here that, in an important sense of the word, morality is not "optional." Although many beginning ethics students and other ethical subjectivists would dissent, it is not entirely "up to me" what sort of standard to base my decision on. Of course, I shall decide what standard my decision *will* be based on, but I cannot by fiat determine what standard is, in the final analysis, the *correct* standard for my decision. In particular, it is not "up to me" to dictate how important moral considerations are. Moral considerations are of extreme importance whether I recognize them as such or not. I cannot, in the final analysis, justify contributing nothing to international relief by declaring that I am simply not interested in acting morally. Someone who does not recognize moral considerations as having this extreme importance is simply ignorant of the weight that they should have. To fail to deliberate on the basis of moral considerations is, in the final analysis, to fail to deliberate *correctly* about what to do.

But what does this thesis about the extreme importance of moral considerations for action choice amount to if there are two moral standards—moral rightness and supererogation? If supererogatory actions are among my alternatives, do I act supererogatorily, or do I settle for a morally right but nonsupererogatory action? The reasons for calling supererogation a *moral* standard should be clear. To say that supererogatory actions go "beyond duty" means that their moral status is intimately related to that of morally right actions. David Heyd puts it the following way: "Not every non-obligatory good act is supererogatory. It has to be *morally* good, its value being of the same *type* that makes obligatory action good and valuable. . . . Supererogation should be characterized as realizing *more* of the same type of value attached to obligatory action."[15] The point here is that with two (or more) moral standards, the unqualified injunction to "act morally" becomes ambiguous. For my decision about how much to contribute to Third World relief, one moral standard, moral rightness, advises me to contribute either $100 or $10,000 while the other, supererogation, tells me to contribute $10,000. If I ask, naively, what morality instructs me to do, I get two answers. And the two standards, while they overlap, also conflict: one sanctions contributing $100 while the other does not. Thus, for the commonsense account, in which supererogation is distinguished from moral rightness, there is a question about how to decide *what to do* that is not adequately answered by the simple admonition to *act morally*.

How then do I approach the bottom-line question of whether to contribute $100 or $10,000? One suggestion is that I contribute $10,000 if I *want* to act supererogatorily or if I *regard* supererogation as the more important standard; otherwise, I contribute $100. But such a policy seems inconsonant with the extreme importance of moral considerations. I must act morally whether or not I recognize moral considerations as the most important considerations for action choice. Why then should my desire about acting supererogatorily or my beliefs about the relative importance of supererogation and moral rightness determine which of the two standards is the one that I should ultimately follow? In the final analysis, I must act morally whether or not I want to do so. Of course, I do not *want* to contribute the $10,000, but there is no reason to suppose that morality never requires us to do what we would rather not do. There is also no reason to believe that my beliefs about which standard is the more important cannot be mistaken. Furthermore, I may have no opinion about which moral standard is the more important in this situation. In that event, the advice to follow the standard that I believe to be the more important would be no advice at all.

Proponents of the commonsense view will respond by reminding us that supererogatory actions are necessarily "optional" and that it is always "enough" for us to do what is morally right. However, upon reflection, how actions can be both optional and superior in moral value is puzzling. Or, more precisely, it is puzzling how it can be optional whether we perform supererogatory actions in situations in which the alternatives include at least one such action.[16] For if the moral value of supererogatory actions exceeds that of nonsupererogatory actions, how may we settle for the lesser value? And what does it mean to say that it is "enough" to act rightly? "Enough" for what? It would, of course, be question-begging to reply that "enough" means sufficient to be morally right. We want to know why moral rightness itself is "enough" if there is another, more exclusive moral standard that we might consult. Why not base our moral decisions on the more exclusive standard?

It would not help matters for the supererogationist to recite the claim that only moral rightness is "required" or "demanded" by morality. For we may ask what it means to say that a certain kind of behavior is "required" or "demanded" by morality. Does it mean that that type of behavior alone satisfies the conditions that are necessary for morally proper behavior? If so, then what sort of moral propriety are we talking about? Is it propriety in the form of moral rightness or in the form of supererogatoriness? And this, of course, sends us back to the question with which we started.

Alternatively, saying that a certain kind of behavior is " 'required' or 'demanded' by morality" means that such behavior is not morally blameworthy. For this interpretation to yield the desired implications, we must assume that all and only morally wrong actions are blameworthy and that not all morally right alternatives in a situation can be supererogatory. Then, according to this analysis, we would not have to act supererogatorily in order to do what is "required" or "demanded" by morality. This version has intuitive appeal when viewed from the "spectator" perspective, for it seems inappropriate to criticize someone who does "well," morally speaking, for not doing "better." When people perform actions of extraordinary moral value they deserve our praise, but we should not expect them always to reach such heights or blame them when they fall short.

However, when we look at the issue from the "actor" perspective—that is, from the point of view of the decision-maker—blameworthiness seems a much less pertinent consideration. For if supererogationism is true, we often have to choose between nonblameworthy actions that are supererogatory and nonblameworthy actions that are not supererogatory. And how do we make such choices? Do we settle for nonsupererogatory actions of lesser moral value? Or do we follow our moral aspirations and choose actions of greater moral value? Even if no one will have reason to blame us and if we shall not have reason to blame ourselves if we do not act supererogatorily, do we not have better reason to choose actions that have greater moral value than not to do so? In the final analysis, whether our actions are blameworthy or not does not really seem to be the relevant issue.

Ethicists sometimes make judgments that morality "requires" this or that kind of action without having a clear, precise idea of what this means. The same is true of their claims about what morality "permits." They seem to suppose that when they make statements that morality "requires" x or that morality "permits" x, those verbs mean different things from what they mean in statements about what the law "permits" or what custom "requires." And because of this difference, it is assumed, the requirements of morality are more "binding" on us than those of nonmoral standards like the law or custom. However, in my view, the meanings are different only with respect to the standard of conduct to which they refer. To say that a certain standard S "requires" that Max do x means only that Max's not doing x violates S. Similarly, to say that standard S "permits" Max to do x says no more than that Max's doing x does not violate S. In this respect, it does not matter whether the standard we have in mind is morality, the laws of a particular state, the customs of a particular society, etiquette, or the rules of baseball. Of course, some standards are more important than others for our action choices. But this is a fact about the standards themselves and not about what the words "requires" and "permits" mean with respect to those standards.

Perhaps some would argue that morality "requires" certain action choices in the sense that it implies *categorical* imperatives that those actions be performed. According to this view, because it has this characteristic of prescriptivity, morality is different from other standards, which do not entail categorical imperatives. However, even if this view is correct, it does not explain why morality "requires" morally obligatory actions but does not "require" supererogatory actions. In view of the *continuity* feature of the conceptual relationship between obligation and supererogation, whatever prescriptivity attaches to judgments about the former would seem to attach at least as securely to judgments about the latter. The burden is on the supererogationist to explain why there is such a dramatic practical difference between obligation and supererogation. And it is highly unlikely that such an explanation will depend entirely on the prescriptivity characteristic of moral judgments.

In a perfectly meaningful sense of "requires," we can make statements about what supererogation "requires" of a certain individual in a particular situation. To say that supererogation "requires" that Max do x means only that Max's not doing x would not be supererogatory. This runs parallel to the assertion that moral rightness "requires" that Max do x, which says no more than that Max's not doing x would not be morally right. Of course, what moral rightness "requires" of us is more important than what other standards, such as custom or etiquette, "require" of us. The point here is only that the way we talk about what morality "requires" is not what gives morality its practical importance. It also does not settle the issue of whether what moral rightness "requires" should, in the final analysis, take precedence over what supererogation "requires" in our deliberations about *what to do*.

One way to dramatize these issues is to imagine someone's adopting the following principle: Whenever I must choose among supererogatory actions and nonsupererogatory but morally right actions, I shall choose the latter. Let us suppose that this person, whom I shall name "Jane," *as a matter of policy* always chooses a right action that involves the least possible self-sacrifice. Jane is glad that there are the Mother Teresas of the world. The world is a much better place because of them. Moreover, Jane is willing to accord them the praise they are due. After all, it would be morally wrong to withhold praise from those who perform praiseworthy actions. However, she has no desire or intention whatsoever to emulate those individuals, and she cheerfully conducts her affairs on the basis of her minimalist moral policy.

It would seem that proponents of the commonsense view should have no criticisms of or reservations about Jane's policy. After all, Jane always does what is morally right. And although she never acts supererogatorily herself, she responds properly to the supererogatory actions of others—that is, by praising them. However, we should be at least a little uneasy about Jane's choice of lifestyle. For Jane somehow seems morally derelict if she eschews *all* supererogatory actions. Supererogatory actions are not just an arbitrary subclass of morally right actions, like those that occur on Tuesdays. Supererogation means going "beyond" moral rightness and following a "higher" standard of conduct.[17] Perhaps metaphors like "beyond" and "higher" are vague and potentially misleading. However, if moral considerations have extreme importance for our action choices, it is difficult to see how such terms could make any sense at all unless supererogation should have greater bearing on our action choices than does moral rightness.

Gregory Mellema has proposed a category of "quasi-supererogatory" actions that he conceives as being praiseworthy to perform but blameworthy to omit.[18] He contends that one who repeatedly fails to perform supererogatory actions that she has an opportunity to perform may reach a point at which continued failure becomes blameworthy. Even if Jane always does what is morally right, sooner or later we are justified in blaming her for her continual omission of supererogatory actions. In this way, Mellema believes, we can capture what is morally derelict about Jane's conduct in a way that preserves the distinction between supererogatory and morally obligatory actions. However, this proliferation of moral categories only complicates the task of moral decision-making. Even if we convince Jane that she will deserve blame if she fails to act quasi-supererogatorily, she must then decide whether to do what is morally right, for which we shall justly blame her, or to do what is quasi-supererogatory, for which she will merit praise. And she may wonder whether it is "enough" for her to do what is right or whether she should, *all things considered*, act so as to avoid blame. Is it ultimately more important not to deserve blame than to do what is right? Should we always act quasi-supererogatorily, even though we are not obligated to do so? How does one tell?

We are tempted to say that if the concept of quasi-supererogation has any practical significance for our action choices, then it must be because we should, *all things considered*, act quasi-supererogatorily. Mellema seems sympathetic to this conclusion, for he writes, "Perhaps it can be agreed that there is a sense in which we ought to perform these [quasi-supererogatory] acts."[19] However, he must avoid, on pain of inconsistency, the conclusion that we are morally obligated to act quasi-supererogatorily. He argues:

> The point I have tried to make is that there is an important middle ground between what is neutral to omit and what is forbidden to omit. The antisupererogationist is determined to remove morally praiseworthy acts from the realm of what is neutral to omit, and the end result is that they are transported wholesale into the realm of what is forbidden to omit. I have argued, on the other hand, that acts of quasi-supererogation are neither neutral nor forbidden to omit. They provide a basis for criticizing those who never go out of their way to perform good works (above and beyond duty) without resorting to the drastic expedient of regarding all praiseworthy acts as obligatory.[20]

It is unclear what Mellema means by "neutral to omit" or how there can be a "middle ground" between acts whose omission is neutral and those whose omission is forbidden. Perhaps the neutrality he has in mind is between acts whose omission is forbidden and those whose omission is obligatory. The omission of such acts would be permitted but not obligatory. But then where would be the "middle ground" between those acts and acts whose omission is forbidden? How can there be acts whose omission is neither permitted nor forbidden? Thus this interpretation of "neutral" does not seem to work. Yet it is difficult to see what else it could mean.

Perhaps Mellema simply means that the omission of quasi-supererogatory actions, although not forbidden, is deserving of blame and in this respect occupies a middle ground between being obligatory and being neutral to omit. However, this does not explain the "sense in which we ought to perform these acts" in a way that will inform Jane whether she should, *all things considered*, perform them. For that to occur, Jane must somehow be able to determine whether she should, *all things considered*, avoid deserving blame for what she does or fails to do. It is important to note that for Mellema's moral taxonomy, actions can be both morally right and blameworthy. Morally right actions that omit quasi-supererogatory alternatives would have that property. And if we are to accept the principle that we should never, *all things considered*, act in a way that is morally blameworthy, we need some argument for it, which Mellema does not provide. We must conclude that Mellema's notion of quasi-supererogation does not rescue supererogationism from the problem of people who, like Jane, follow a policy of avoiding supererogatory action.

The Argument against Supererogationism

The observations made in the preceding section contain the seeds of an argument against the commonsense view and its supererogationism thesis that we can now articulate. The essential characteristics of supererogatory actions are that they possess surplus moral value (in comparison with nonsupererogatory actions) and that they are optional. Let us focus on the surplus moral value aspect. Does it have any practical (i.e., action-guiding) significance? If so, what is it?

If moral considerations always defeat nonmoral considerations, then, it would seem, we necessarily have better reason to choose one action than to choose another if the former is of greater moral value. Moreover, it seems unreasonable not to adopt the policy of choosing one action over another if we have better reason to choose the former than to choose the latter. However, if in a particular situation we have better reason to choose a certain kind of action than to choose any action not of that kind, it is not optional for us whether we perform an action of that kind in that situation. The sense of "optional" in the preceding sentence is the very sense in which we said before that morality is not *optional*. Morality is *not* optional for me, not because I shall be rewarded if I do what is right or suffer some penalty if I do what is wrong, but because moral considerations provide me with better reasons for acting than do nonmoral considerations. And they do so because they determine which of my alternatives have greater moral value than others. From this it follows that supererogatory actions cannot both have greater moral value than nonsupererogatory actions and be optional as well. Since being optional and having surplus moral value are essential characteristics of supererogatory actions, supererogatory actions are a conceptual impossibility.[21]

One possible criticism of this argument would object to the premise that says that supererogatory actions' having surplus moral value is compelling reason for us to choose supererogatory actions over morally right, nonsupererogatory actions. A critic might argue that although the surplus moral value of supererogatory actions is reason for us to *aspire* to act supererogatorily, it is not always enough reason for us to *act* supererogatorily. However, it is difficult to see how one could have reason always to aspire to act supererogatorily and yet *never* have sufficient reason to act supererogatorily. If one genuinely aspires to act supererogatorily, then it would seem that one must at least occasionally act supererogatorily. One's aspiration might not produce a corresponding intention if what she aspires to achieve is beyond her means. For example, one might aspire to becoming president of the United States without actually intending to do so if she believed that her efforts would ultimately fail. However, since supererogatory actions are morally right and since all morally right actions must be within the capacities of their agents to perform, ordinarily nothing would prevent one's intending to act supererogatorily from leading to supererogatory action. Thus one's aspiring to act supererogatorily should ordinarily result in her acting supererogatorily. Therefore, this criticism of our argument fails.[22]

Perhaps a proponent of the commonsense view would argue that it is a mistake for us to characterize supererogatory actions as possessing greater moral value than nonsupererogatory actions. Some other explanation should be given of what it means to say that supererogatory actions go "beyond" moral rightness. One possible rendering of that phrase would be that an action goes "beyond" moral rightness if the degree to which it possesses right-making characteristics is greater than the minimum necessary for moral rightness. For example, if producing a certain amount of utility were a right-making characteristic, actions that produced utility in excess of that amount would be candidates for supererogatory status. However, even if we accept this revision of our concept of supererogatory action, it still seems that, given the extreme importance of moral considerations, one would have better reason to choose one action over another if it possessed right-making characteristics to a greater degree. Therefore, it would still follow that supererogatory actions fail to be optional and, consequently, fail to have their own defining characteristics.

Rational Limits on Altruism

I conclude that a conception of supererogatory actions as actions that possess surplus moral value but yet are optional is not tenable. But if so, does it follow that we are morally obligated always to be saints or heroes? Does morality require everyone to become Mother Teresa? Must we live by Peter Singer's principle that if we can prevent something bad from happening without sacrificing anything of comparable moral significance, we morally ought to do it? Are there no rational limits to demands on our altruism?[23]

I believe that the answer to the questions just raised is a *qualified* "No." The argument I shall offer is based on the fact that most of us are uncertain whether the sort of behavior generally regarded as supererogatory is morally obligatory or even morally right. Whether morality prescribes radical altruism depends, of course, on which actions qualify as morally right. For some theories, act utilitarianism for example, it may be very difficult to avoid the conclusion that altruism is obligatory. For other theories, such as ethical egoism, genuine altruism may never be one's obligation. Suppose that the moral theory that I find most plausible, say act utilitarianism, requires extremely altruistic behavior on my part. If I base my action choices entirely on this theory, then I shall exclude all nonaltruistic alternatives. But suppose also that I am not entirely convinced that act utilitarianism is the correct theory. Perhaps I regard theoretical perspectives that prescribe paying special attention to the welfare of persons to whom we have special relationships—for example, spouses, parents, children, friends, compatriots—as serious candidates. Perhaps I cannot rule out even (impersonal) ethical egoism for consideration as the correct theory.[24]

Given my uncertainty about which moral theory is correct, how do I go about making moral decisions? The answer that most ethicists tacitly accept is that I should follow the theory that I regard as most probably "true." I have called this the my-favorite-theory approach and have argued that there is a better policy for decision-making under moral uncertainty than it. In my view, it makes more sense to take into account *all* of the theories under consideration and their likelihoods of being "true," as well as how much moral value each alternative action would have according to the respective theories. The decision strategy that I proposed in the preceding chapter is stated by PR4 and PR5. It advises us to choose actions that, with respect to the available information, have the maximum expected degrees of moral rightness or are most likely to do so.

To illustrate, let us return to the example with which we began—my decision whether to contribute $0, $100, or $10,000 to Third World relief. Let us suppose that, according to act utilitarianism, I would generate utility in proportion to the monetary size of my contribution. Thus, on a 0-to-1 utility scale, the three utilities would be 0, .01, and 1.0, respectively. From an egoistic perspective, the degree of moral rightness of my contribution is proportional to my personal utility, which *diminishes* as the size of my donation increases. Let us suppose that my personal utility is proportional to how much money I do *not* contribute but keep for myself. Then the degree of moral rightness of my contributing $0, $100, or $10,000 would be 1, .99, or 0, respectively, on a 0-to-1 personal utility scale. Finally, from a moral perspective that recognized special obligations to parents, children, spouses, and others, funds withheld from international relief would be available for fulfilling those obligations. Let us assume that whatever funds are withheld will be used in that way. Then the degrees of moral rightness of my alternatives might be .8, 1.0, and 0, respectively. Contributing $100 would be the optimum, let us suppose, because it would optimally balance my obligations to the world's needy against my special obligations to family, friends, compatriots, and such. The situation is summarized in Table 5.1.

To apply PR4 to my decision, I need one additional kind of information: the respective probabilities that the three moral perspectives represented by the columns of the table are "true." Let us assume that the probabilities have been assessed as follows: act utilitarianism, .45; ethical egoism, .2; "special" obligations, .35. Calculations yield the following assessments of the expected degrees of moral rightness (EMR):

EMR(donate $0) = 0.48

EMR(donate $100) = 0.5525

EMR(donate $10,000) = 0.45

Thus PR4 supports the felicitous conclusion that donating an intermediate amount between the extremes of $0 and $10,000 is a reasonable choice. More-

Table 5.1   Decision Table for Third World Relief Example

	act utilitarianism	ethical egoism	"special" obligations
donate $0	0	1.0	0.8
donate $100	0.01	0.99	1.0
donate $10,000	1.0	0	0

over, we arrive at that conclusion without appealing to a problematic doctrine of supererogationism. Of course, my calculations presuppose abilities to measure probabilities and degrees of moral rightness with greater precision than may exist in actual decisions. However, these are epistemological matters that we need not resolve in order to appreciate the following conceptual point: From a maximize-expected-moral-rightness perspective, even if a normative theory (e.g., act utilitarianism) that, for a particular moral decision, prescribes extremely altruistic action has the greatest likelihood of being the "true" theory, it does not necessarily follow that that sort of action is the most reasonable choice in that situation. And we may reasonably accept such a judgment even when precise cardinal measurements of probabilities and degrees of moral rightness are not available. Of course, in some cases the most altruistic alternative will maximize expected moral rightness and will thus be the prescribed action. I take it to be a virtue of my approach that it does not rule out any particular alternative prior to a consideration of the morally relevant features of the situation and of the state of knowledge of the decision-maker.

Conclusions

I have argued that supererogatory actions cannot be defined consistently as both possessing surplus moral value and being optional for the moral agents for whom they are alternatives. I have also argued that the maximize-expected-moral-rightness approach to decision-making under moral uncertainty embodied in PR4 and PR5 may validate the widespread sentiment that we need not always act in the most altruistic way available. Hence, not only is the notion of supererogation ultimately incoherent, but also, fortunately, we do not need it to serve the purposes for which we thought it necessary. This, I think, is a welcome result, for it supports a simpler ethical taxonomy than is required by the commonsense view, which embraces supererogationism.

With our refutation of supererogationism, we remove the rationale for one criticism of our approach to decision-making under moral uncertainty. We have no reason to think that a certain degree of expected moral rightness is "enough" and that we need not exceed it. Even if we believed that such a threshold level existed, determining how high to set it would be problematic, and whatever level we chose would probably be arbitrary. Moreover, moral agents in situations in which they have very little certainty about the (degree of) moral rightness of their alternatives may not be able to identify any action the expected degree of moral rightness of which reaches even the threshold level.

As a bonus, the conclusions we have reached help us in our search for the "true" moral theory or perspective. We should not impose as a criterion of adequacy the requirement that a moral theory generate a category of supererogatory actions. In fact, to the extent that theories do so, they are in error and should be revised. Theories whose credentials include their compatibility with supererogationism should decline in our estimation, and theories that we have discounted because of their incompatibility may merit greater esteem.

Six

Confidentiality and Moral Uncertainty

The approach to decision-making under moral uncertainty that I have developed thus far is subjective in the following respect: Which action choices are rational depend on what sorts of moral considerations the decision-maker regards as relevant and what beliefs she has about the magnitudes of the pertinent probabilities. This means that the decision table for one agent may be differently configured from that for another agent who must make the same kind of decision. And even if the decision tables have the same form, the probabilities associated with the conditions represented in the table may be of different sizes or have different rankings. Therefore, there is no guarantee that moral agents will be able to resolve their disagreements about what a particular agent should (rationally) do in a particular situation by appealing to PR4 or PR5.

However, in some cases PR4 or PR5 will facilitate resolution of disagreement about which actions are rational for moral agents to choose. Abortion decisions for which it is clear that not having an abortion has the greater expected degree of moral rightness (which, I suspect, include the vast majority of abortion decisions) are decisions for which there would be little difficulty in determining which choice is the more reasonable. In this and the following chapter, I shall illustrate how disagreements about what moral agents should (rationally) do in particular situations can sometimes be settled by employing the methods that I have developed. In this chapter, the disagreement that I shall consider occurs between two

111

ethicists who take opposing sides of a case in medical ethics. The analysis that I shall offer here will be a model for resolving philosophers' disagreements about how certain kinds of moral decisions should be made. In this way, we ethicists may offer some relief to moral agents whose requests for guidance in decision-making are frustrated by disagreements among those who offer the advice.

Professions and Obligations of Confidentiality

Members of professions are generally regarded as having obligations of confidentiality. Lawyers must keep confidential certain information about their clients that if divulged would harm their clients' cases. Engineers are supposed not to reveal their employers' and clients' proprietary information. Journalists are to conceal the identities of their confidential sources of information. And physicians are not to reveal their patients' medical records without their consent. However, clearly there are limits to these obligations.[1] In some situations, for the professional not to reveal confidential information about a client or patient may greatly endanger innocent third parties. For example, in the *Tarasoff* v. *Regents of the University of California* case, a psychiatric patient confided to his therapist his intentions to murder a young woman who had failed to reciprocate his romantic interest in her. The therapist's superior directed that no action be taken to notify the intended victim, and subsequently the threat was carried out. The court ruled that the physician's obligation of confidentiality should have given way to his obligation to prevent harm to his patient's intended victim.[2]

When should professionals maintain client confidentiality, and when is it more important to protect endangered third parties? Two extreme positions can be staked out. One view is that professionals should *never* allow concerns about non-clients to supplant duties of confidentiality owed to their clients. At the other pole is the view that confidentiality should be sacrificed whenever the collective interests of those who will be affected by the professional's actions would best be served by doing so. The truth appears to be somewhere between these extremes, but it is difficult to find rational criteria that seem generally applicable and appropriate.

Here I shall show how our methods for decision-making under moral uncertainty provide a rational way for members of professions to make moral decisions that involve client confidentiality and third-party interests. We shall consider the implications of the thesis that decision makers should maintain confidentiality whenever, based on available information, doing so would maximize the expected degree of moral rightness of one's action. And to illustrate the application of this principle, I shall apply it to a recent *Hastings Center Report* case in medical ethics. The case involves a physician who must decide whether to inform the fiancée of one of his patients that the patient has tested HIV-positive and to do so *against the patient's wishes*. I shall summarize the arguments of two commentators in the *Hastings Center Report*, who reach opposite conclusions on the case, and show how our strategy for moral decision-making might facilitate a resolution of their disagreement.

A Case Study in Medical Ethics

The case that I shall examine appeared in the February 1987 issue of the *Hastings Center Report* and was titled "AIDS and a Duty to Protect."[3] The case concerns a physician's patient who has tested positive for the HIV virus and who is engaged to be married. When the physician advises his patient to inform his fiancée of the results of the test, the patient refuses on the grounds that doing so would disrupt his plans for marriage. The physician must then decide whether to inform the fiancée over the patient's objections.

One of the case commentators, Morton Winston, considers the ethical decision to be a matter of physicians' weighing "carefully their responsibility to protect confidentiality against their duty to protect others who might be placed at risk by their patients' illnesses." He notes the uncertainties that physicians face in treating AIDS patients: Not all HIV-positive persons actually carry the virus. Some HIV-positive persons might not be infectious. The efficiency of male-to-female transmission of the virus is unknown. And not all infected persons will "develop full-blown AIDS." Winston concludes, however, that if the physician "determines that the risk to his patient's fiancée is significant, and if all other means of persuading the patient to accept his moral responsibility have failed, then [the physician] should attempt to contact [the fiancée]." Thus Winston considers the physician's duty to protect the fiancée to outweigh his obligation to preserve confidentiality in this particular situation.[4]

The second commentator, Sheldon H. Landesman, views the issue as being best resolved "by looking at the broad societal problems associated with HIV infection." He observes that "any legally or socially sanctioned act that breaches confidentiality . . . acts as a disincentive to voluntary testing" and that "public knowledge that . . . a physician has violated confidentiality would result . . . in a sharp decline of potentially infected persons seeking counseling and testing." He believes that a consequence of this decline would be that "a growing number of persons would remain ignorant of their infectiousness as would their sex partners."

Landesman does not clearly identify the moral principles on which his conclusions are based, although he says that "the difficult ethical dilemma is one of balancing long-term societal benefits against short-term benefit to an individual." However, his references to "legally or socially sanctioned" acts and to "public knowledge" suggest an appeal to rule utilitarian considerations. I shall assume this interpretation of his position in the current discussion. Landesman is also somewhat vague about his ethical conclusion. His final statement is that "maintaining the patient's confidentiality ought to be the first principle." Perhaps more significant is Landesman's statement that the physician's "discomfort [in not preventing the fiancée from becoming infected] and the woman's infection may be the cost that society pays if it wishes to implement public health measures to minimize the spread of AIDS." This indicates not only that Landesman favors the physician's not informing the fiancée of the patient's condition but also that Landesman accepts the thesis that physicians should adopt whatever measures would minimize the spread of the HIV virus.

Winston and Landesman thus appeal to different ethical principles in arriving at their conclusions about what the physician should do in this case. As a result, they reach opposite conclusions. It is impossible to tell whether they would be able to resolve their *moral* disagreement in a rational way were they to attempt to do so. The common experience of professional ethicists indicates that the chances that one or the other could be converted to the basic ethical presuppositions of the other are not great. Thus it is not likely that Winston and Landesman would be able rationally to resolve their disagreement about ethical principles. Consequently, the physician who must decide whether to maintain confidentiality or inform his patient's fiancée, and who must make that decision without delay, receives conflicting advice from Winston and Landesman. This is just one situation in which practicing professionals must choose among alternatives each of which is supported by some "ethics expert" or other on the basis of a certain ethical theory, set of moral principles, or model of ethical reasoning to which the expert subscribes. There is no apparent way for the practitioner to tell which expert is to be believed without taking on the task of sorting out the philosophical arguments himself. And if the "experts" themselves cannot resolve their philosophical disagreements, how is the nonexpert to settle those issues? This is, unfortunately, the predicament in which many physicians and other professionals often find themselves.

However, even though Winston and Landesman would probably be unable to reach an accord on basic ethical principles, it is likely that each would grant some plausibility to the views of the other. Winston is likely to be somewhat uncertain that his prima facie duties approach is the correct one and that Landesman's rule utilitarian position is wrong, and Landesman would similarly admit some uncertainty about the correctness of his rule utilitarian perspective and the incorrectness of Winston's prima facie duties point of view. I suspect also that each would confess to some uncertainty about what their respective ethical principles imply for the physician's decision about whether to inform the patient's fiancée. Perhaps Winston would confess to some uncertainty about whether the physician has a prima facie duty to protect the fiancée, since some commentators would say that the physician qua physician has moral obligations *only* to this patient and not to any third party.[5] And even if the physician has an obligation to protect the fiancée, questions may arise about whether the risks to her of contracting AIDS are so high that the physician's prima facie duty to protect the fiancée outweighs his prima facie duty to maintain the confidentiality of information about the patient's medical condition.[6] Landesman also can reasonably be expected to have some doubts about his view that the general policy of physicians' maintaining confidentiality about the identities of their HIV patients would have better consequences over the long run than an alternative policy of warning the sex partners of HIV patients. I believe that if these uncertainties are taken into account, the two commentators may be able to agree on which course of action would be most *likely* to be morally acceptable. If I am right, then which of the physician's alternatives is the most *reasonable* for him to adopt *on moral grounds* may be clearly evident.

Let us represent the physician's decision in this case in Table 6.1.

Table 6.1   Decision Table for "AIDS and a Duty to Protect" Case

	prima facie duties perspective (p_1)				rule utilitarian perspective ($1-p_1$)	
	Physician has prima facie duty to protect fiancée. (p_2)			Physician has no prima facie duty to protect fiancée. ($1-p_2$)	Policy of maintaining confidentiality would have better consequences than policy of informing sex partners of HIV patients. (p_5)	Policy of informing sex partners of HIV patients would have better consequences than policy of maintaining confidentiality. ($1-p_5$)
	Risk to fiancée is significant. (p_3)		Risk to fiancée is not significant. ($1-p_3$)			
	Prima facie duty to maintain confidentiality outweighs prima facie duty to protect fiancée. (p_4)	Prima facie duty to protect fiancée outweighs prima facie duty to maintain confidentiality. ($1-p_4$)				
inform fiancée	0	1	0	0	0	1
do not inform fiancée	1	0	1	1	1	0

In order to simplify the analysis and focus on the disagreement resolution aspect of this case, we shall, for the moment, assume the binary hypothesis about moral rightness/wrongness. Thus the numerals 1 and 0 represent "morally right" and "morally wrong," respectively, and the columns in the table signify the conditions that affect whether the physician's alternatives in the situation would be morally right or morally wrong. The quantities p_1, p_2, p_3, p_4, and p_5 are the probabilities of the morally significant states of affairs with which they are respectively identified in the table. The probabilities of the remaining conditions are the respective $1-p$ quantities in the table.

If we apply the laws of probability, we find that the probability $p(I)$ that the physician's informing the fiancée would be morally right is given by $p(I) = p_1p_2p_3(1 - p_4) + (1 - p_1)(1 - p_5)$. Similarly, it can be determined that the probability $p(\text{not-}I)$ that the physician's *not* informing the fiancée would be morally right is given by $p(\text{not-}I) = p_1p_2p_3p_4 + p_1p_2(1 - p_3) + p_1(1 - p_2) + p_5(1 - p_1)$. By subtracting $p(\text{not-}I)$ from $p(I)$ and doing some simple algebra, it can be shown that $p(I) > p(\text{not-}I)$ if and only if $p_1p_2p_3(1 - p_4) - p_1(1 - p_5) - p_5 + 0.5 > 0$. Obversely, $p(\text{not-}I) > p(I)$ if and only if $p_1p_2p_3(1 - p_4) - p_1(1 - p_5) - p_5 + 0.5 < 0$. Thus if we have specific values for p_1, p_2, . . . , p_5, it will be easy to determine which course of action has the greater probability of being morally right.

Let us consider the physician's decision from Winston's point of view. Clearly, the values that Winston would assign to p_1, p_2, . . . , p_5 would be somewhat different from those that Landesman would assign. For example, Winston regards the prima facie duties approach to ethical decision-making as more plausible than the rule utilitarian approach. Therefore, assuming that he regards these two approaches as the only significant contenders, he would assign p_1 a value greater than .5, whereas Landesman would assign it a value less than .5. However, Winston may have significant doubts about his prima facie duties approach and may believe that there is a significant possibility that Landesman's rule utilitarian principle is the correct basis for ethical decisions. Let us suppose, for the moment, that Winston assigns a value of .6 to p_1. Winston probably has more confidence in his opinion that the physician has a prima facie duty to protect the fiancée. Although it is arguable that the primary obligations of physicians are always to their patients, the view that physicians should *never* allow the interests of nonpatients to compromise the physician-patient relationship seems too extreme. Let us hypothesize that Winston assigns a value of .8 to p_2.

Although Winston mentions a number of uncertainties about the accuracy of the test for the HIV virus, the transmissibility of the virus, and similar issues, he may have few doubts that the risks to the fiancée (of contracting AIDS from the patient) are significant. Let us suppose that he assigns a value of .8 to p_3. Furthermore, since Winston believes that the physician has an ethical obligation to inform the fiancée of the patient's condition, he must also believe that the physician's prima facie duty to protect the fiancée outweighs his prima facie duty to maintain confidentiality over the results of the patient's HIV test. This means that he will assign a value to p_4 that is less than .5. Let us assume that he assigns a value of .3 to p_4. Finally, even though Winston rejects Landesman's rule utilitarian ethical perspective, he may agree with Landesman that a general practice of physicians' maintaining confidentiality about the results of HIV tests would encourage individuals to undergo those tests and thus would have better long-term consequences than a policy of informing the sex partners of HIV-positive individuals. Thus Winston may measure p_5 as relatively large—say, .7.[7]

When the values of $p(I)$ and $p(\text{not-}I)$ are calculated with the preceding values of $p_1, p_2, \ldots, p_5$, it turns out that $p(\text{not}-I)$ exceeds $p(I)$ by .1112. This means that the physician's *not* informing the fiancée about the patient's HIV-positive test results would be the choice more likely to be morally right. What is significant about this result is that it is consistent with Winston's views on the case. That is, the conclusion that the physician's *not* informing the fiancée is more likely to be morally right is consistent with Winston's views (1) that the prima facie duties ethical perspective is the correct one, (2) that the physician has a prima facie duty to protect the fiancée, (3) that the risks to the fiancée (of contracting AIDS) are significant, and (4) that the physician's prima facie obligation to protect the fiancée outweighs his prima facie obligation to maintain confidentiality. If Winston were 100% confident that his views were all correct and if he followed his argument to its logical conclusion, then his final judgment that the physician should inform the fiancée would be inescapable. However, if we estimate realistically how much confidence Winston has in the premises of his argument and use that information to determine which alternative is more likely to be morally right, then both he and we may come to the opposite conclusion.

Of course, I may have underestimated how much confidence Winston has in his beliefs. Perhaps he is more convinced than I have supposed that his basic prima facie duties perspective is correct. Also, he may believe more strongly than I have estimated that the physician's prima facie duty to protect the fiancée outweighs his obligation to maintain confidentiality. Moreover, Winston may be less certain than I have presumed that a policy of physicians' maintaining confidentiality about the identities of HIV-positive patients would have better societal consequences than a policy of informing the sex partners of those patients. However, even if p_1 is increased to .8, p_4 is lowered to .2, and p_5 is decreased to .6, p(not-I) is still greater than p(I). This result is significant because it means that even if Winston had considerable confidence in the premises of his argument (more confidence perhaps than is warranted), it may still be true that the physician would be more likely to do the right thing by not informing the fiancée.

For the medical ethics case we are examining, Winston's position is "unstable" in the sense that it is quite sensitive to variations in the probabilities associated with the premises of his argument. Landesman's position, however, is relatively "stable" in that small changes in the probabilities do not affect the comparative magnitudes of p(I) and p(not-I). To see why this is so, consider the following illustration: Since Landesman argues from a rule utilitarian perspective, he obviously regards that view as more credible than Winston's prima facie duties approach. However, like Winston, Landesman may have significant doubts about which theoretical position is the correct one. Let us suppose that he assesses p_1 as .4, which means that he believes that his rule utilitarian perspective has only a .6 probability of being correct. If he accepts Winston's assessments of p_2, p_3, p_4, and p_5, then it turns out that p(not-I) exceeds p(I) by .1408. Suppose Landesman became less convinced that the rule utilitarian position is the correct one and as a result increased his estimation of p_1 to .5. This would mean that he is now neutral between Winston's general moral perspective (i.e., based on prima facie duties) and his own previous (rule utilitarian) perspective. Suppose also that Landesman became less certain about how his previous perspective applied to the physician's decision. Let us imagine that he became less convinced that the rule utilitarian principle prescribes a general policy of physicians' maintaining patient confidentiality in this sort of situation. Let us lower p_5 from .7 to .6. Even with this weakening of Landesman's argument, it turns out that p(not-I) exceeds p(I) by a healthy margin of .076. Thus his advice to the physician in our medical ethics case would need no revision.[8]

My analysis also shows that there may be no need to have precise measurements of the probabilities p_1, p_2, . . . , p_5 to determine whether p(I) > p(not-I). For if one is sure that p_1, p_2, and p_3 do not exceed .8, that p_4 is no less than .2, and that p_5 is no less than .6, then one can be sure that p(I) < p(not-I). This is true because any values assigned to p_1, p_2, p_3, p_4, and p_5 consistent with these constraints guarantee that p(not-I) exceeds p(I).[9] Thus assessing maximum and/or minimum values of the pertinent probabilities may be enough to determine which alternative is more likely to be morally acceptable.

Suppose, however, that we do not wish to rely on either single-number probability measurements or maximum/minimum value estimates. Ordinal comparisons may then be in order. Which comparisons among the values of $p_1, p_2, \ldots, p_5$ would be plausible? From Winston's perspective, the following inequalities appear reasonable:

$$0 < p_4 < 0.5 < p_1 < p_2 < p_3 < 1$$

$$.5 < p_5 < p_2$$

$$1 - p_3 < p_3 - p_2$$

$$1 - p_3 < p_4$$

The first expression says that the probabilities that the prima facie duties approach is the correct approach (p_1), that the physician has a prima facie duty to protect the fiancée (p_2), and that the risk to the fiancée of contracting AIDS is significant (p_3) are all greater than .5. It also says that the probability that the risk to the fiancée is significant is the largest of the three probabilities and that the next largest probability is the probability that the physician has a prima facie duty to protect the fiancée. Finally, the first expression says that there is less than a 50–50 chance that the physician's prima facie duty of confidentiality to his patient outweighs his prima facie duty to protect the fiancée against HIV infection (p_4).

The second expression says that the probability that a general practice of physicians' not revealing the identities of HIV patients would have better long-term consequences than the alternative practice of physicians' informing the sex partners of those patients (p_5) is greater than .5. However, the likelihood that this is the case is less than the probability that the physician has a prima facie duty to protect the fiancée against infection.

The third expression says that p_3 is closer to 1 than it is to p_2. Or, in other words, the probability that the risk to the fiancée is significant is closer to perfect certainty than it is to the next largest probability—namely, the probability that the physician has a prima facie duty to protect the fiancée.

The fourth expression indicates that p_3 is closer to 1 than p_4 is to 0. This means that the probability that the risk to the fiancée is significant is closer to perfect certainty than the probability that the physician's duty of confidentiality outweighs his duty to protect the fiancée is to 0.

It is helpful to visualize the magnitudes of the probabilities by seeing them as points on a 0-to-1 line, where the distances between pairs of points represent differences in the magnitudes of the probabilities represented by the points (Figure 6.1).

If one computes the average values of $p(I)$ and $p(\text{not-}I)$ for all quintuples $< p_1, p_2, \ldots, p_5 >$ that satisfy the previous inequalities, it turns out that the average value of $p(\text{not-}I) - p(I)$ is approximately .037. This indicates that given only

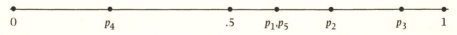

| 0 | p_4 | | .5 | $p_1.p_5$ | p_2 | p_3 | 1 |

Figure 6.1   Graphical Representation of Probabilities for "AIDS and a Duty to Protect" Case

the assessments of the probabilities represented by the previous inequalities, it is more likely that $p(\text{not-}I)$ is greater than $p(I)$ than that the opposite is true. Therefore, based on these assessments, we have further support for the view that it would be reasonable for the physician to choose not to inform the fiancée.[10]

So far our conclusions have been predicated on the binary hypothesis and we have ignored degrees of moral rightness between right (1) and wrong (0). What if we assume a many-valued conception of moral rightness? Then we get Table 6.2, in which m_1, m_2, m_3, m_4, m_5, and m_6 represent intermediate degrees of moral rightness.

What can be said about m_1, m_2, m_3, m_4, m_5, and m_6? It is not likely that decision-makers would be able to obtain reliable single-number measurements. Realistically, an ordinal ranking among m_1, m_2, m_3, m_4, m_5, and m_6 may be the best that one can hope for. From the prima facie duties perspective, the most serious transgression would occur if the physician informed the fiancée even though he had no prima facie duty to protect her. In that case, there would be no moral consideration that would favor the "inform fiancée" option. This means that m_3 is the smallest of m_1, m_2, m_3, and m_5. The least serious transgression from a prima facie duties perspective would occur if the physician informed the fiancée under the conditions represented by the first column of the decision table. In this case, even though the prima facie duty to protect the fiancée is outweighed by the prima facie duty to maintain confidentiality, the margin may well be small and the competition between the two duties may be close. Under these conditions, informing the fiancée would be no great wrong. This means that m_1 is the largest of m_1, m_2, m_3, and m_5.

Which of m_2 and m_5 is the larger? The quantity m_2 is the degree of moral rightness that the "inform fiancée" option has if, although the physician has a prima facie obligation to protect the fiancée, her risks of becoming HIV-infected are not significant. The case for the physician's informing her under those conditions would seem to be relatively weak. The quantity m_5 is the degree of moral rightness that the "do not inform the fiancée" alternative has if the physician's prima facie duty to protect the fiancée outweighs the physician's prima facie duty to maintain confidentiality. Again, the competition between these two duties is likely to be relatively close if both apply and if the risks to the fiancée are significant. Therefore, not informing the fiancée would be a relatively benign transgression. These considerations thus indicate that we should judge that $m_2 < m_5$. Summarizing our results thus far, $m_3 < m_2 < m_5 < m_1$.

The quantities m_4 and m_6 are degrees of moral rightness with respect to a rule utilitarian moral perspective. From that perspective, degrees of moral rightness would reflect the (expected) utilities of the two policies associated with the last two columns of the decision table—namely, the policy of physicians' maintaining confidentiality of medical information about their HIV-infected patients and that of informing the sex partners of their HIV-infected patients. The questions are (1) which policy would better prevent the transmission of the HIV virus and the eventual suffering and death of those who develop AIDS? and (2) how significant are the differences in the effects of the two policies? The two possible answers to the first question are represented by the last two columns of

Table 6.2 Modification of Table 6.1 for Many-valued Conception of Moral Rightness

	prima facie duties perspective (p_1)				rule utilitarian perspective ($1-p_1$)	
	Physician has prima facie duty to protect fiancée. (p_2)			Physician has no prima facie duty to protect fiancée. ($1-p_2$)	Policy of maintaining confidentiality would have better consequences than policy of informing sex sex partners of HIV patients. (p_5)	Policy of informing sex partners of HIV patients would have better consequences than policy of maintaining confidentiality. ($1-p_5$)
	Risk to fiancée is significant. (p_3)		Risk to fiancée is not significant. ($1-p_3$)			
	Prima facie duty to maintain confidentiality outweighs prima facie duty to protect fiancée. (p_4)	Prima facie duty to protect fiancée outweighs prima facie duty to maintain confidentiality. ($1-p_4$)				
inform fiancée	m_1	1	m_2	m_3	m_4	1
do not inform fiancée	1	m_5	1	1	1	m_6

Table 6.2. In effect, m_4 and m_6 represent the possible answers to the second question.

It might seem that there is no reason to rank one quantity as larger than the other. Since m_4 and m_6 are in different columns of the table and in each column we are assuming that one policy would have better consequences than the other, all we can say about m_4 and m_6 is that they are both less than 1. However, even if the two columns represent different hypotheses about which policy would have better consequences, the margin by which one policy would have better consequences than the other might be greater than the margin if the reverse were true. If that were so or if one believed that to be so, then there would be reason to rank m_4 or m_6 as larger than the other.

Is this the case? Is there reason to believe that there would be a difference between the margins by which one policy would have better consequences than the other? I believe that the answer is "Yes." We should recall that in our discussion of the probabilities we concluded that $p_5 > .5$. This means that it is more likely that the policy of physicians' maintaining the confidentiality of information about the medical condition of HIV-infected patients would have better consequences than the policy of physicians' informing the sex partners of those patients than that the reverse is true. If so, then it seems reasonable to suppose that even if the policy of informing the sex partners of HIV patients had the better consequences, the margin by which those consequences would be better would be less than the margin would be if the other policy had the better consequences. This means that the difference between the utilities of the two policies would be greater under the conditions represented by the fifth column of Table 6.2 than it would be under the conditions represented by the sixth column of the table. Therefore, we may judge that $m_4 < m_6$ since informing the fiancée would violate the more clearly superior policy.

It may appear that by assuming that $p_5 > .5$ and $m_4 > m_6$ I am *unfairly* subjecting the policy of informing the sex partners of HIV patients to "double jeopardy," since I am assuming *both* that physicians' adopting that policy probably would not have consequences as good as the alternative policy *and* that even if it did have better consequences, the margin by which its consequences would be better would be less than the margin if the opposite were true. However, the two inequalities say different things and neither is reducible to the other. One concerns the probability that it would have better consequences than the opposite policy, while the other concerns the margin by which its consequences would be better in the unlikely event that they are better. Compare this to a football game between a strong team, Notre Dame, and a weaker team, Northwestern. Clearly, it would be reasonable to predict both that Notre Dame will win the game and that, in the unlikely event that Northwestern wins, it will win by a smaller margin than Notre Dame would win by. From a gambler's perspective, it would be reasonable to place the following bets: (1) Notre Dame will win, (2) conditional on Notre Dame's winning, its victory margin will be at least 14 points, and (3) conditional on Northwestern's winning, its victory margin will be 3 points or less. Thus there is nothing illicit in separating the question of whether one object is better than another from the question of how much better the second object would be if it were better than the first.

So far, we have rankings among m_1, m_2, m_3, and m_5 and between m_4 and m_6. Should we combine the two rankings by comparing quantities in the first set against those in the second? The difficulty is that the first set includes degrees of moral rightness with respect to a prima facie duties perspective, while the second set measures degrees of moral rightness with respect to a rule utilitarian perspective. We should not, of course, forswear all intertheoretic comparisons between degrees of moral rightness, but in the case we are examining here any such comparisons would appear to be quite tenuous. Therefore, let us assume here that the decision-maker in our example chooses not to measure m_1, m_2, m_3, or m_5 against m_4 or m_6.

From Table 6.2, it can be shown that the expected degree of moral rightness of the "inform fiancée" option is given by

$$\text{EMR}(I) = p_1 p_2 p_3 p_4 m_1 + p_1 p_2 p_3 (1 - p_4) + p_1 p_2 (1 - p_3) m_2 \\ + p_1 (1 - p_2) m_3 + (1 - p_1) p_5 m_4 + (1 - p_1)(1 - p_5)$$

and the expected degree of moral rightness of the "do not inform fiancée" option is given by

$$\text{EMR}(\text{not-}I) = p_1 p_2 p_3 p_4 + p_1 p_2 p_3 (1 - p_4) m_5 + p_1 p_2 (1 - p_3) \\ + p_1 (1 - p_2) + (1 - p_1) p_5 + (1 - p_1)(1 - p_5) m_6$$

Doing some algebra shows that

$$\text{EMR}(I) - \text{EMR}(\text{not-}I) = p_1p_2p_3p_4m_1 + p_1p_2(1 - p_3)m_2 + p_1(1 - p_2)m_3$$
$$+ (1 - p_1)p_5m_4 - p_1p_2p_3(1 - p_4)m_5$$
$$- (1 - p_1(1 - p_5)m_6$$
$$+ 2p_1[p_2p_3(1 - p_4) + p_5 - 1] - 2p_5 + 1$$

We want to know whether $\text{EMR}(I) > \text{EMR}(\text{not-}I)$ or, equivalently, whether $\text{EMR}(I) - \text{EMR}(\text{not-}I) > 0$.

There is not enough information about the magnitudes of the ps and the ms to say with certainty whether this is the case. Therefore, PR4 is not applicable. However, we can apply PR5 if we assume that each 11-tuple $<p_1, p_2, p_3, p_4, p_5, m_1, m_2, m_3, m_4, m_5, m_6>$ that satisfies the preceding constraints on those 11 quantities is as likely to contain the true values of the ps and ms as any other 11-tuple that satisfies those constraints. We need only calculate the mean value of $\text{EMR}(I) - \text{EMR}(\text{not-}I)$ over the region determined by the constraints on the ps and the ms. If it is positive, then $\text{EMR}(I)$ is probably greater than $\text{EMR}(\text{not-}I)$; if it is negative, then the opposite is true. It turns out that mean value of $\text{EMR}(I) - \text{EMR}(\text{not-}I)$ is approximately -0.0984.[11] Therefore, the physician's *not* informing the fiancée in the situation we are examining is more likely to maximize expected moral rightness than his informing the fiancée. PR5 thus implies that the physician should (rationally) choose not to inform the patient's fiancée that the patient has tested HIV-positive.

The result just obtained accords with the preceding conclusion, which assumed the traditional two-valued concept of moral rightness. Therefore, it appears not to matter which concept of moral rightness we assume for the physician's decision in this case. However, as we have already seen, degrees of moral rightness can make a difference for some decisions. And if we had ranked the ps and ms differently, then PR5 might have produced a different result.

Conclusions

Our study of the medical ethics case in this chapter indicates how compelling the physician's obligation of confidentiality is, even if that obligation is sometimes outweighed by conflicting obligations. There are very few situations in which questions of confidentiality arise where a better argument could be made for *not* maintaining confidentiality than in the medical ethics case we have examined. Of course, we have confined our discussion to the arguments advanced by Winston and Landesman in their commentaries on this case. Possibly our conclusion would have been different if we had considered other arguments.[12] The revelation that confidentiality should be given such high priority will, I suspect, come as a surprise to those of us to whom it appears initially that the physician should inform the fiancée of his patient's medical condition. Surely other surprises are in store if we apply the decision strategy based on PR4 and PR5 to other problems in applied and professional ethics.

Our inquiry has shown how our decision strategy can, for practical purposes, adjudicate between opposing moral arguments even if we cannot decide which argument is sound. It is important to note that we did not settle the debate between Winston and Landesman in the sense that we did not conclude that either's argument was sound or unsound. We judged only that, given the degrees of confidence that they or we are likely to have in the premises of their arguments, Landesman's conclusion is the more likely to be correct. It is unclear how we could have arrived at this determination without assessing probabilities and degrees of moral rightness in some fashion and employing mathematical methods. And while it is probably unrealistic to expect adversaries in moral controversies to resolve their disagreements by formulating and solving calculus problems, nothing precludes applied ethicists, like Winston and Landesman, from using formal mathematical methods in their studies of the practical problems of moral decision-making. If, as I have argued, moral uncertainty often cannot be avoided and should not be ignored, those of us who wish to offer cogent moral guidance may have no choice but to adopt such methods.

Seven

A Decision-Theoretic Reconstruction of
Roe v. Wade

In the preceding chapter, we saw how a disagreement between two ethicists about a case in medical ethics might be resolved by moving the discussion from questions about the moral rightness of the alternatives to questions about their expected moral rightness. The disagreement would be resolved for *practical* purposes in that the disputants would be able to agree about what the decision-maker should, in the final analysis, do. In this chapter, we shall consider another case of decision-making under normative uncertainty—the U. S. Supreme Court's decision in the *Roe v. Wade* abortion case.

Although it has to some extent been superseded by the more recent *Webster v. Reproductive Health Services* (1989) and *Planned Parenthood v. Casey* (1992) decisions, the *Roe v. Wade* decision is still the cornerstone of the American national policy on abortion.[1] In the following discussion, we shall see how factoring into its deliberations the kinds of uncertainties that the Court acknowledged and intimated in its majority opinion might have affected the outcome. We shall also see whether the forms of decision analysis that we have developed to this point might have facilitated a different consensus on the pertinent constitutional questions. In doing so, we shall be offering a new model for judicial reasoning that differs fundamentally from the modes that are currently recognized by the legal profession. This case will be different from the other cases we have discussed in that the pertinent normative issues do not directly concern the moral rightness or wrongness of action alternatives but rather pertain to the standard of excellence to which Supreme Court justices aspire in their professional decision-making. Thus we shall broaden the scope of our inquiry to encompass decision-making under *normative* uncertainty.

The Argument in *Roe v. Wade*

The majority opinion in the *Roe v. Wade* decision, authored by Justice Blackmun, contained two key premises:

1. Fetuses are not persons who deserve protection under the Fourteenth Amendment.
2. Citizens have a constitutional right to privacy that was violated by the Texas abortion statute.

The decision, of course, did much more than just find that the Texas statute, which limited abortion to situations in which women's lives were at stake, was unconstitutional. It set limits on states' regulation of abortion, which have been in force since 1973. Here, however, I shall focus on the finding of unconstitutionality and, particularly, on the ruling that restrictions on abortion may not be based on fetuses' right to life. I shall neither affirm nor deny statements 1 and 2. My purpose is rather to entertain reasonable doubts about them and consider the ramifications of those uncertainties for the eventual decision.

There is evidence that the Supreme Court majority itself harbored such uncertainties. The discussion of fetal personhood in the *Roe v. Wade* majority opinion contains the following curious passage:

> We need not resolve the difficult question of when life begins. When those trained in the respective disciplines of medicine, philosophy, and theology are unable to arrive at any consensus, the judiciary, at this point in the development of man's knowledge, is not in a position to speculate as to the answer.[2]

The "question of when life begins" clearly was the question of fetal personhood, since there is hardly any doubt that fetuses are biologically living entities. The second statement in the quote noted that the fetal personhood issue was unresolved and that its resolution was not imminent. Yet the first statement appeared to claim that this did not matter. How could this be?

Justice Blackmun observed that there had been no prior judicial finding that "a fetus is a person within the meaning of the Fourteenth Amendment" and also that there is and has been "wide divergence of thinking on this most sensitive and difficult question." He concluded, "In view of all this, we do not agree that, by adopting one theory of life, Texas may override the rights of the pregnant woman that are at stake."[3] It is not clear in these remarks why Justice Blackmun thought that prior judicial decisions on Fourteenth Amendment protections for fetuses and the "wide divergence of thinking" on the question of fetal personhood relieved the Court of the burden of resolving "the difficult question of when life begins."

One possible interpretation of Justice Blackmun's position is that he believed there to be two personhood questions about fetuses. The first is whether (or which) fetuses are persons in a broad metaphysical/moral sense of "person." (Let us use "person$_1$" to refer to persons of this sort.) If fetuses are persons$_1$, then they have a natural right to life that should be respected and protected by the state. Such a right would presumably be among the "unalienable" rights to "life, liberty, and the pursuit of happiness" mentioned in the Declaration of Independence. Whether or which fetuses possess such an unalienable right is clearly a difficult philosophical question that has not yet been satisfactorily answered. Probably this philosophical irresolution is what Justice Blackmun had in mind in accusing Texas of having adopted "one theory of life." He appears not to have meant that such a "theory of life" was false but rather that it was not sufficiently confirmed to justify imposing it on pregnant women.

But what exactly did he mean by the statement that it was not *necessary* for the Court to resolve the personhood$_1$ issue? This is where a second concept of personhood may have entered the picture. In the second, narrower sense, "person" refers to individuals who have a certain legal status—that is, persons "within the meaning of the Fourteenth Amendment." Let us use "person$_2$" for this meaning. Perhaps Justice Blackmun meant that since it was unresolved and, for practical purposes, unresolvable whether fetuses are persons$_1$, the Court was justified in basing its decision on the more tractable question of whether fetuses are persons$_2$. This would explain why he believed that the Court "need not resolve the difficult question of when life begins" if that question is understood as a question about personhood$_1$. It "need not" be resolved if the question whether fetuses are persons$_2$ is really the relevant issue. Whether fetuses are persons$_2$ would be entirely a legal question and could be decided straightforwardly by examining legal precedent.

However, this interpretation of the Court's argument raises serious difficulties. It implies, for example, that whether beings of a certain kind should be recognized as possessing a right to life depends entirely on whether they have been so recognized in the past. This would mean that as long as the judiciary is constant in its rulings about personhood and the right to life, it cannot err. But then on what basis could a court determine initially whether or not a particular being was a person$_2$? Would personhood$_2$ status become entirely arbitrary in the hands of a precedent-setting court? Such a view would hardly be plausible. Should not the Supreme Court at some point review lower courts' findings on the meaning of "person" as used in the Fourteenth Amendment? As Baruch Brody has observed, "Whatever force we want to ascribe to precedent in the law, the Court has in the past modified its previous decisions in light of newer information and insights. In a matter as important as the conflict between the fetus's right to life and the rights of the mother, it would have seemed particularly necessary to deal with the issues rather than relying upon precedent."[4] Moreover, if a review of the constitutional concept of personhood is performed by the Court, on what basis should it be conducted? Would not there have to be some appeal to the personhood$_1$ concept to decide how the Constitution *should* be interpreted?

Strict constructionists would argue that the Court should be cautious in interpreting the Constitution and not read more into its amendments than was intended by their authors. If applied to the fetal personhood issue, this precept would recommend attempting to assess the original intentions of the authors of the Fourteenth Amendment, and of any other articles considered pertinent, in order to determine whether personhood$_2$ properly applies to fetuses. I shall not launch such an investigation here. It is sufficient for my purposes simply to note that a strict constructionist judicial philosophy is itself controversial and uncertain and has been rejected by some current and former members of the Court and by many legal scholars. Furthermore, such a conservative view with respect to the fetal personhood issue is inconsonant with the discussion of the right to privacy in the *Roe v. Wade* majority opinion. As we shall see, that discussion adopted a rather liberal interpretation of the Constitution in order to support its view that a right of privacy exists and is broad enough to support abortion rights for women. Thus a judicial philosophy that would support denying fetuses personhood status under the Constitution would appear also to require denying women the very right on which the Court based their right to abortion.

If there is no resemblance between personhood$_1$ and personhood$_2$ and if the latter is the pertinent concept for abortion, then it is unclear why Justice Blackmun devoted so much of his exposition to the former. But if there is a connection between personhood$_1$ and personhood$_2$, what is it, and how can a court determine that something is not a person$_2$ without first determining that it is not a person$_1$? What basis could there be for prior judicial findings that fetuses are not persons$_2$, given the intractability of the personhood$_1$ issue? And what justification could there be for relying on such rulings? These are among the serious problems that would plague any attempt to resolve the fetal personhood issue by distinguishing personhood$_1$ from personhood$_2$.[5]

Perhaps Justice Blackmun did not intend to distinguish two different kinds of personhood. Perhaps he meant to apply "person" only to beings who are persons in the full-fledged metaphysical/moral meaning of the word. How then might we understand his analysis of the fetal personhood issue? In particular, how might we understand his statements, "We need not resolve the difficult question of when life begins" and "In view of all this, we do not agree that, by adopting one theory of life, Texas may override the rights of the pregnant woman that are at stake"?

In my view, the best explanation is that Justice Blackmun attempted to bypass the question of fetal personhood by appealing to the following principle, which I shall term the "Principle of the Rights of Doubtful Persons" (henceforth PRDP):

PRDP
The rights of beings whose personhood is doubtful (e.g., fetuses) may not override the rights of beings whose personhood is not in question (e.g., pregnant women).

Mary B. Mahowald appears to endorse a position very similar to the PRDP in the following passage:

Pregnant women have rights at least equivalent to those of non-pregnant people. Presumably, this claim is uncontroversial because the personhood of pregnant women is generally accepted. The fact of their pregnancy, whether deliberately undertaken or not, does not diminish their personhood. Accordingly, pregnant women ought not to be subjected to coercive treatment that others might effectively refuse, such as blood transfusions, surgery, or even hospitalization. Even if treatment were imposed on an adult for the sake of minor children, further argument is needed to justify its imposition for the sake of fetuses. Minor children are uncontroversially persons, and fetuses are not.[6]

Mary Anne Warren espouses an apparently similar but very different principle—that the right to life of a *potential* person could not outweigh the right of a woman to obtain an abortion.[7] Warren's principle is different from the PRDP because, for her, although fetuses are potential persons, they are actual nonpersons and, presumably, personhood for them in their fetal condition is impossible. It is important to appreciate the difference between "possible personhood," which I am alleging that the Court did not recognize, and "potential personhood," which the Court counted as an important consideration in its decision.

The PRDP would allow the Court to bypass the fetal personhood issue by simply observing that even if fetuses are persons, their personhood is dubious and thus fetal rights are always outweighed by those of women, whose personhood is not in doubt. It would also help us make sense of the claim that Texas was not permitted to override the rights of pregnant women "by adopting one theory of life," even if that theory were true. The fact that the theory was uncertain would, by the PRDP, mean that fetuses' right to life would be outweighed by women's right to privacy.

If Justice Blackmun assumed the PRDP (and I believe it likely that he did), then the principle is essential to his argument. It is also, in my view, highly questionable. It is essential because without it, or something very similar, the Court might have felt compelled to recognize the *possible* personhood of fetuses as a factor that weighs against women's exercise of their right to privacy in seeking abortions. Moreover, without the PRDP the Court might have ruled that since there was no generally accepted "theory of life" to which it could appeal, the matter of when life begins (i.e., when fetuses become persons) should be left to the discretion of the individual states. In fact, this seems to be the position of Justice White in his dissent in a related case:

> The Court apparently values the convenience of the pregnant mother more than the continued existence and development of the life or potential life which she carries. Whether or not I might agree with that marshalling of values, I can in no event join the Court's judgment because I find no constitutional warrant for imposing such an order of priorities on the people and legislatures of the States. In a sensitive area such as this, involving as it does issues over which reasonable men may easily and heatedly differ, I cannot accept the Court's exercise of its clear power of choice by interposing a constitutional barrier to state efforts to protect human life and by investing mothers and doctors with the constitutionally protected right to exterminate it. This issue, for the most part, should be left with the people and to the political processes the people have devised to govern their affairs.[8]

The PRDP is questionable because it implies that even if the degree of uncertainty about fetal personhood were very small, say 1%, a very important right—the right not to be killed—may be ignored in the abortion decision. Let us consider an analogous case. Imagine a hunter testing his new high-powered rifle. He sees a figure off in the distance that has a vaguely human shape and general appearance but is too far away for him to be sure that it really is a person. He judges that there is roughly a 5% chance that it is not human. Since he is 100% sure that he himself is human, he infers, on the basis of the PRDP, that he may use the object as a practice target. Surely, given his 95% assurance that his target is human, he would be wrong in his decision, and a court would reject his reasoning if the target turned out to be an actual person.

It is, of course, true that a court would rule that the target's rights outweighed the hunter's rights only if the target is revealed to be human (or perhaps a member of a protected animal species). If the target is discovered to be an inanimate object, then, in the eyes of a court, it would have no rights and thus the hunter's rights would not be outweighed. Perhaps we would say that the hunter acted foolishly and was lucky that his target turned out not to be a person, since he was insufficiently sure of the nature of his target. But we would not account for the impropriety of the hunter's actions on the basis of his rights' being outweighed by those of his inanimate target. Similarly, we might say that a woman who chose abortion while being 95% sure that in doing so she was destroying a person with a right to life acted improperly. However, this would not necessarily mean that her rights were outweighed by her fetus's or that she should be denied the opportunity for a legal abortion.

But the important point here is that it is the *combination* of the high probability that the target is a person and the importance of the right to life that it has if it is a person that would outweigh the hunter's right to fire his rifle and ought to discourage him from doing so. Whether the state should protect objects of its kind against the assaults of practicing hunters may depend on how plausible the state finds the proposition that such objects possess a right to life. Similarly, whether the state should protect fetuses against abortion may depend on how likely the state regards it as being that fetuses possess a right to life. Hence, the matter of weighing the rights of dubious persons against those whose personhood is unquestionable is not as simple as the PRDP implies.[9]

I submit also that in addition to weighing the personhood status of an alleged bearer of rights, courts should take into account the relative importance of those rights in the situation about which it is adjudicating. Even if there is significant doubt in a certain instance that a particular entity is the sort of entity that may have a right of a given sort, that right may warrant respect over a less compelling right possessed by someone whose personhood is not in doubt. This means that we must consider two factors whenever we weigh conflicting rights: (1) whether or not the alleged bearer of a particular right in fact possesses that right[10] and (2) how important that right is in the situation. For the abortion issue, consideration of the two factors might mean that the importance of the right to life compensates sufficiently for the fetus's questionable personhood to override the woman's right to determine whether her pregnancy will continue.

These considerations show, in my view, that the PRDP is unsatisfactory. Just as there was perhaps no way for the Supreme Court in *Roe v. Wade* to resolve the fetal personhood issue adequately, neither was the Court able to bypass the issue in a satisfactory way. But what then was the Court to do if fetal personhood was crucial and yet unresolvable? This is an inescapable dilemma if judicial reasoning is not allowed to take uncertainties, such as fetal personhood, into account.

Nancy Rhoden maintains that in *Roe v. Wade* the Supreme Court overstated its argument for its recognition of certain stages of fetal development as having special significance.[11] She urges the Court to embrace some arbitrariness as necessary if there is to be a coherent abortion policy:

> If some right to abortion is justified, and if some limits can permissibly be placed on the extent of this right . . . , then the Court had to draw a line somewhere. Given that fetal development is a continuum, no one, no matter how brilliant or analytically inclined, could draw a line in that continuum that has logical or biological significance. The best anyone could do is draw a line that is within a justifiable range. What this range is is a matter of public policy—policy that should take into account the medical, social, and economic status of the women who seek relatively late abortion, the medical constraints surrounding diagnosis of fetal defects, . . . and so on.[12]

Lisa Newton expresses sympathy for the Court's predicament and suggests that fetuses be regarded as persons of a special sort. She offers convicted criminals as examples of beings whose personhood is granted but whose legal rights are nevertheless tightly circumscribed. An abortion, she thinks, might be reasonably conceived as an eviction of an uninvited person from one's property.[13] Such a model would be one kind of compromise between those who consider fetuses to be persons and those who do not.[14] However, as I shall soon argue, acknowledging and taking into account our uncertainty about whether or which fetuses are persons, as well as the other forms of uncertainty we have identified, would be a more reasonable strategy than attempting to find a compromise abortion policy in the absence of rational justification of the terms of such a compromise.[15]

As we have noted, in addition to raising the issue of fetal personhood, the majority opinion in *Roe v. Wade* also considered whether women possess a right to privacy that would be violated by restricting abortion. It acknowledged that "the Constitution does not explicitly mention any right of privacy" but found evidence of such a right in the common law, in interpretations of several amendments to the Constitution, and "in the penumbras of the Bill of Rights."[16] Justice Douglas, in his concurring opinion in *Doe v. Bolton*, liberally locates sources of abortion rights in the Ninth and Fourteenth Amendments:

> The Ninth Amendment obviously does not create federally enforceable rights. It merely says, "The enumeration in the Constitution of certain rights shall not be construed to deny or disparage others retained by the people." But a catalogue of these rights includes customary, traditional, and time-honored rights, amenities, privileges, and immunities that come within the sweep of "the Blessings of Liberty" mentioned in the preamble to the Constitution. Many of them in my view come within the meaning of the term "liberty" as used in the Fourteenth Amendment.[17]

Among the rights Justice Douglas mentions are "the autonomous control over the development and expression of one's intellect, interests, tastes, and personality," "freedom of choice in the basic decisions of one's life respecting marriage, divorce, procreation, contraception, and the education and upbringing of children," and "the freedom to care for one's health and person, freedom from bodily restraint or compulsion, freedom to walk, stroll, or loaf."

However, Blackmun's opinion for the majority in *Roe v. Wade* was considerably less specific and definite about the constitutional source of the right to privacy: "This right of privacy, whether it be founded in the Fourteenth Amendment's concept of personal liberty and restrictions upon state action, as we feel it is, or . . . in the Ninth Amendment's reservation of rights to the people, is broad enough to encompass a woman's decision whether or not to terminate her pregnancy."[18] This statement suggests that except perhaps for Justice Douglas, the Court majority was not completely sure of the constitutional basis for the right to privacy or whether that right implied abortion rights for women. It would appear that the best interpretation is that the Court was hesitant both about whether a constitutional right to privacy existed and also about whether the Texas abortion statute infringed on it.[19]

Even if the Court was not hesitant about these matters, it may be argued that it should have been. For a number of difficulties confront the thesis that the right to abortion is fundamentally a right to privacy. We often speak of "invasions of privacy." One might conceive of a right to privacy as a negative right against intrusion—a right not to be invaded in some respect. How then could limiting abortion be considered an invasion? Perhaps it invades by preventing women from exercising their options. But this is true of most prohibitions—for example, against exceeding the speed limit or abusing one's children. Yet we do not say that traffic laws or laws against child abuse violate privacy. Some might argue that such restrictions violate privacy but in a justifiable way, since their social utility makes up for those infringements. But if that were so, then apparently the right to privacy is routinely overridden by competing considerations. Such a right would hardly seem substantial enough to serve as the foundation of a constitutional right to abortion as sweeping as that established by *Roe v. Wade*.

Some might argue that it is the fetus, not the state, that is the invader in abortion and that the right to privacy is, at least in part, a positive right to protect oneself against that invasion. According to this view, the state must not interfere with women's exercise of that right, except under special circumstances. But can we reasonably regard fetuses as invaders? Invaders invade from the "outside." Therefore, it would seem, an invader must exist "on the outside" *before* the act of invading occurs. It is difficult to see how fetuses could satisfy this condition.

Suppose we view abortion as evicting an intruder from a woman's body. What eviction measures may she use? In general, what eviction measures may we employ in exercising our right to privacy? May we kill intruders immediately or hire professional intruder eradicators to do so? Should the state protect our right to kill intruders? Or may we kill intruders only as a last resort? (It may be noted that courts have sometimes convicted property owners whose booby traps have killed or seriously injured burglars.) What if the trespasser encroached accidentally and innocently and seriously injured himself while on our property? What if for the next seven months he cannot be removed without causing his death? May the property owner insist on immediate eviction in this situation? Of course, she may argue that one's body is a very special sort of personal territory incursions against which call for extreme measures. However, the apparent innocence of the fetus and questions about whether we can properly regard fetuses as intruders seem to weigh against such considerations.

The main point here is not that the restrictions placed on abortion by the Texas statute did not violate women's right to privacy but rather that there are reasons for doubting that it did so. One might also question whether a right to privacy, even if it existed and applied to fetuses' presences in women's bodies, would deserve greater state protection than fetal rights. Consider that even if parents have a right to rear their children as they see fit, such a right does not entitle them to abandon their children without making adequate provision for their survival and well-being. Similarly, a right of privacy might not entitle women to have abortions at the expense of the lives of the fetuses that they carry. Some prolife advocates would contend that since a fetus is an unborn child, aborting it really is child abandonment, which a right to privacy cannot excuse.[20]

If we regard the question of fetal personhood as unsettled and wish to take such uncertainty into account, then obviously the question whether a fetal right to life would outweigh women's right to privacy becomes relevant and important. The majority opinion strongly suggests that the Court majority would have judged fetuses' right to life to outweigh women's right to privacy, if it had recognized fetuses as persons: "Indeed, our decision in *United States* v. *Vuitch*, 402 U.S. 62 (1971), inferentially is to the same effect [i.e., of not regarding fetuses as persons within the meaning of the Fourteenth Amendment], for we there would not have indulged in statutory interpretation favorable to abortion in specified circumstances if the necessary consequence was the termination of life entitled to Fourteenth Amendment protection."[21] However, the argument might be made that the matter is not so simple and that even if fetuses were recognized as persons with a right to life, women's right of privacy may outweigh that right.[22] Let us, therefore, raise the issue of whether the following statement is true:

> If fetuses were persons, their right to life would outweigh women's right of privacy in determining what constitutional restrictions regarding abortion should be recognized.

It is a question that the Court would have to ponder if it were to take seriously, as I have suggested that it should, the possibility of fetal personhood.

Let us summarize the uncertainties that we have identified so far in connection with *Roe v. Wade*. We have detected uncertainty (1) whether fetuses are persons, (2) whether the Texas statute violated women's right to privacy, and (3) whether, if fetuses were persons, their right to life would have more weight than women's right to privacy. Although the Court raised the questions that relate to (1) and (2), it gave a "No" answer to (1) and a "Yes" answer to (2). However, there is no indication that the majority opinion of the Court properly heeded those uncertainties. My main criticism of the *Roe v. Wade* decision is that the Court, by failing to see the logical relevance of those uncertainties and take them into consideration, violated the requirements of rationality.

But my accusations raise the following questions: How should courts treat these sorts of uncertainties? What choice does a court have but to resolve legal uncertainties in the best, most reasonable way available and then follow the argument to its most sensible conclusion? Without some, at least tentative, resolution of pertinent issues, how could the Court have reached any decision at all? In particular, how could the Court have reached a determination in *Roe v. Wade* without adopting some position or other on questions about fetal rights and the rights of pregnant women?

It should come as no surprise that my answer to these questions is that courts should adopt modes of judicial reasoning in which pertinent uncertainties are acknowledged and explicitly taken into account. This means that judicial reasoning should be probabilistic and that courts must be content with decisions whose principal virtue is that their expected degree of "judicial excellence" is at least as great as the alternatives. In the following, I shall demonstrate how the Court might have dealt with uncertainties about fetal personhood, the right to privacy, and other related matters in framing a cogent judicial policy on abortion.

Decision Theory and the Abortion Policy Question

We may recap the *Roe v. Wade* decision in Table 7.1. The vertical dimension of the table represents the pertinent conditions and combinations of conditions that affect the correctness of the Court's decision and about which we have supposed the Court to be uncertain: (1) whether fetuses possess a right to life, (2) whether the limits placed on abortion by the Texas statute violated women's right to privacy, and (3) whether fetuses' right to life would, if it existed, outweigh women's right to privacy. The two rows labeled "uphold limitation" and "disallow limitation" represent the two options that the Court had in *Roe v. Wade*—to uphold the Texas statute's restrictions on abortion or to disallow them by finding the statute unconstitutional.[23] The intersections of the rows and columns represent the "outcomes" of the two choices under the various sets of conditions. Debating whether the Court's decision was correct assumes, of course, that it was possible for the Court to err in its final ruling. In the decision table, the 0s represent outcomes in which the Court would so err; the 1s represent outcomes in which the Court would act correctly.

But what is the notion of "acting correctly" for a court deciding the constitutionality of a law? It is difficult to give a definitive answer here. It is not terribly informative to say that the Court acts correctly if it acts wisely or judiciously.

Table 7.1   Decision Table for the *Roe v. Wade* Decision

	Fetuses are persons. (p_1)			Fetuses are not persons. ($1-p_1$)
	Limiting abortion violates women's right to privacy. (p_2)		Limiting abortion does not violate women's right to privacy. ($1-p_2$)	
	Fetuses' right to life outweighs women's right to privacy. (p_3)	Women's right to privacy outweighs fetuses' right to life. ($1-p_3$)		
uphold limitation	1	0	1	0
disallow limitation	0	1	0	1

However, unless we take the cynical view that the decisions of the Court can really do nothing more than impose the dominant political paradigm on wayward elements of society, there is a standard of excellence in judicial decision-making to which the Court should aspire. We may not know any more about the details of that standard than we know about the standard of moral rightness. However, we may know enough to make some tentative judgments about that standard and the degrees to which specific alternatives conform to it. Let us for convenience say that the Court acts correctly just in case it acts *justly*. Excellence in judicial decision-making I shall refer to as "justice."

We have documented some of the important issues about which the Supreme Court was (or would have been) uncertain in the *Roe v. Wade* case. They include whether or which fetuses are persons with a right to life, whether the Texas abortion statute violated women's right to privacy, and whether women's right to privacy outweighs fetuses' right to life. Since the appropriate norm for evaluating the actions of the Court is justice and not moral rightness, PR4 and PR5 do not apply in their current forms. However, only simple modifications are needed to generate the appropriate rationality principles. The problem for the Supreme Court in the *Roe v. Wade* case was to act rationally under uncertainty about what justice prescribes. This is directly analogous to acting rationally under uncertainty about what moral rightness prescribes. Therefore, our principles of rationality here are analogous as well:

PR4J

In situations in which judges are uncertain of the degrees of justice of some of the alternatives under consideration, a choice of action is rational if and only if the action chosen has the maximum expected degree of justice of any alternative.

PR5J

In situations in which judges are uncertain of the degrees of justice of some of the alternatives under consideration and in which there is not enough information to determine which alternative(s) have the maximum expected degree of justice, the rational choice is to choose some alternative that, with respect to the available information, is most likely to have the maximum expected degree of justice (i.e., is most likely to satisfy PR4J).

In order to use PR4J or PR5J, we must have some conception of the "expected degree of justice" of judges' actions. If it is analogous to expected utility, the expected degree of justice of an act x should be given by $EJ(x) = p(c_1, x) \cdot j(c_1, x) + p(c_2, x) \cdot j(c_2, x) + \ldots + p(c_n, x) \cdot j(c_n, x)$, where $c_1, c_2, \ldots, c_n$ are the possible conditions (e.g., fetal personhood) that could affect how just action x would be in the situation, $p(c_1, x), p(c_2, x), \ldots, p(c_n, x)$ are the probabilities that those respective conditions would obtain if x were chosen, and $j(c_1, x), j(c_2, x), \ldots, j(c_n, x)$ are the degrees of justice that x would produce if $c_1, c_2, \ldots, c_n$, respectively, were to obtain. The maximize-expected-degree-of-justice rule PR4J directs judges to choose some x from their options such that $EJ(x)$ is at least as large as $EJ(y)$ for any other option y.

The next question is what are "degrees of justice"? One view, perhaps the most popular one, is that justice comes in only two sizes—"just" and "unjust." Let 1 and 0 represent "just" and "unjust," respectively. Then all of the js in the expression for $EJ(x)$ are either 1 or 0, and $EJ(x)$ will equal the overall probability that x would lead to justice rather than injustice. This is so because in the expression for $EJ(x)$ all of the terms that involve $j(c_i, x) = 0$ for some i will be 0 and the remaining terms in the indicated sum will be $p(c_k, x)$ where $j(c_k, x) = 1$. Consequently, $EJ(x)$ will equal the sum of the probabilities of the conditions under which x would lead to a just outcome—that is, the overall probability that x would lead to a just outcome.

What about the probabilities $p(c_1, x)$, $p(c_2, x)$, . . . , $p(c_n, x)$? With respect to the *Roe v. Wade* case, it is very unlikely that justices of the Court would have been able to perform precise, single-number measurements of the pertinent probabilities. However, they may have had enough information to be able to make a meaningful choice between the two options. Let us pursue the model a bit further to see whether this is the case.

We adopt the following abbreviations:

p_1: the probability that fetuses are persons and thus possess a right to life

p_2: the probability that prohibiting abortion would violate women's right to privacy

p_3: the probability that fetuses' right to life would outweigh women's right to privacy (if fetuses were persons)

EJ(uphold): the expected justice of upholding the restriction of abortion (i.e., the probability that it would be just to uphold the restriction of abortion)

EJ(disallow): the expected justice of disallowing the restriction of abortion (i.e., the probability that it would be just to disallow a restriction of abortion)

From Table 7.1, it is easy to show that $EJ(\text{uphold}) = p_1 p_2 p_3 + p_1(1 - p_2)$ and $EJ(\text{disallow}) = p_1 p_2 (1 - p_3) + 1 - p_1$. We are interested in whether $EJ(\text{uphold}) > EJ(\text{disallow})$—that is, whether $p_1 p_2 p_3 - p_1 p_2 + p_1 > \frac{1}{2}$. This would, of course, be a simple problem if we knew the exact values of p_1, p_2, and p_3. As in our previous analyses, we might conceive of p_1, p_2, and p_3 as *subjective* probabilities that represent the decision-maker's degrees of belief in the associated propositions. Or we might think of them as *unknown* objective probabilities the magnitudes of which decision-makers can only estimate.[24]

If, as I suspect is the case, justices of the Supreme Court would not rely on single-number measurements or estimates of the probabililties, it may be necessary for them to resort to ordinal measurements. Obviously, such an approach would make much easier demands on decision-makers' probability estimation powers. For *Roe v. Wade*, how should one order the three probabilities? Obviously, different decision-makers may come up with different rankings, but the following considerations seem pertinent: Each probability represents the likelihood that an associated proposition is true. The proposition most likely to be true seems to be that associated with p_2—that restricting abortion would violate women's right to privacy. Although one might have significant doubts about the truth of this claim, it seems less uncertain than the other two. The least likely proposition appears to be that associated with p_3—that in the event that fetuses are persons who possess a right to life, that right outweighs women's right to privacy. We should recall that the majority's opinion in *Roe v. Wade* disregarded the possibility that fetuses' right to life outweighed women's right to privacy because the Court denied fetuses personhood status, even for fetuses at the latest stages of pregnancy. For this analysis, p_3 represents the degree of likelihood that the conditional statement, *if fetuses are persons, their right to life outweighs pregnant women's right to privacy,* is true. Such a statement might have a relatively high probability of being true even if its antecedent had a very low probability.[25] Nevertheless, p_3 appears to be the smallest of the three probabilities.

What about p_1? Why not rank it higher than p_2 or lower than p_3? Despite the aforementioned reasons for questioning the view that women's right to abortion derives from a basic right to privacy, whether or which fetuses are persons seems an even more controversial thesis. Moreover, a considerable portion of recent philosophical discussion of the ethics of abortion has dealt with infanticide and, particularly, whether there are morally significant differences between fetuses and newborn infants that, ethically speaking, distinguish abortion from infanticide. The difficulty of finding such differences gives reason not to rank p_1 as the least of the three probabilities.

The preceding considerations imply that the ordering $0 < p_3 < p_1 < p_2 < 1$ is the correct ranking of the probabilities. We might stop here with probability measurement and go on to see what conclusions would follow about which alternative would maximize expected justice. However, there may be additional information about the magnitudes of the probabilities that we may wish to consider. In addition to ranking the magnitudes of the probabilities themselves, we might be able to compare at least some of the *differences* between their magnitudes. It seems that the magnitudes of the probabilities are all closer to each other than they are to 1 (perfect certainty of being true) or to 0 (perfect certainty of being false). In symbols, $p_2 - p_3 < 1 - p_2$ (which is equivalent to $2p_2 - 1 < p_3$), and $p_2 - p_3 < p_3 - 0$ (which is equivalent to $p_2 < 2p_3$). Let us add these inequalities to our list and allow them to contribute to the ultimate decision.

What conclusions may we draw from the available information about which abortion policy would have maximum expected justice? We cannot say definitively because for some values of p_1, p_2, and p_3 that satisfy the preceding inequalities, EJ(uphold) > EJ(disallow), while for other values that satisfy the inequalities EJ(disallow) > EJ(uphold). Therefore, our PR4J rule cannot be directly applied to the abortion policy decision. However, if we assume that no other information about the magnitudes of the probabilities is available, then we may reasonably suppose that each triple $< p_1, p_2, p_3 >$ that satisfies the inequality constraints is as likely to contain the "true" values of p_1, p_2, and p_3 as any other triple that also satisfies the constraints. We may then calculate the average value of EJ(uphold)−EJ(disallow) for all such triples. If we get a positive number, that will indicate that *probably* EJ(uphold) > EJ(disallow) and thus that upholding the prohibition on abortion would be the rational policy. If we get a negative number, then we shall infer the opposite conclusion. In this way, we shall be applying our second-order rule PR5J that tells us to maximize the probability that our action satisfies PR4J. If we perform the computations, we find that the average value of EJ(uphold)−EJ(disallow) is −19/120—a negative number. This signifies that EJ(disallow) > EJ(uphold) and would support the Court's actions in invalidating the Texas abortion statute.[26]

Would this argument convince prolife advocates that they are wrong to support the prohibition or strict limitation of abortion? They might, of course, disagree with our ordering of the three probabilities, perhaps claiming greater certainty that fetuses are persons or much less certainty that women's right to privacy outweighs fetuses' right to life or would be violated by placing restrictions on abortion. However, it is unlikely that the prolife side would prevail in a debate before the Court about whose appraisals of the pertinent probabilities are more accurate.

However, there is another mode of criticizing the preceding analysis that I think would be much more potent—namely, challenging the assumption that there are only two admissible degrees of justice and, in particular, arguing that it is much more unjust to violate a person's right to life, or for the state to permit it to be violated, than to violate someone's right to privacy. This would mean adopting the position that some unjust judicial decisions are more unjust than others. For a prolife advocate, not preventing the killing of a fetal person whose right to life outweighs the woman's right to privacy would be more unjust than preventing a woman whose right to privacy outweighs the fetus's right to life from obtaining an abortion.

To implement this idea of taking degrees of justice into account, we would replace the 0s in the decision table by different numbers that represent the degrees of justice/injustice of the outcomes. If we let 0 (perfect injustice) and 1 (perfect justice) represent the extremes on the justice measurement scale, then the quantities represented in the table will all range between 0 and 1. Assuming that no one can reasonably be expected to do better than the best that is possible in a situation, we should retain the 1s at their locations in the previous decision table. However, the 0s will now be replaced by the quantities j_1, j_2, j_3, and j_4, which we have assumed to lie between 0 and 1. The modified table is Table 7.2.

How should one measure j_1, j_2, j_3, and j_4? As for the probabilities p_1, p_2, and p_3, ordinal measurements seem most feasible. How then should j_1, j_2, j_3, and j_4 be ranked? We remarked earlier that failures to protect fetuses' right to life are generally more unjust than violations of women's right to privacy. Since j_1 and j_2 pertain to outcomes in which the injustice stems from violations of the right to privacy, they represent lesser degrees of injustice, and thus greater degrees of justice, than j_3 and j_4, both of which represent violations of the right to life. Furthermore, the injustice that results from violating women's right to privacy would be mitigated somewhat if, in the process, fetuses' right to life were protected, even if the former right outweighed the latter. This means that $j_1 > j_2$. Also, the injustice that would result from not protecting fetuses' right to life would be offset somewhat by the justice that would be done to women by respecting their privacy. The quantity j_3 applies to outcomes in which, although fetuses' right to life is not protected, women's right to privacy is respected. The quantity j_4 applies to outcomes in which fetuses' right to life is not protected *and* violations of women's right to privacy are not at issue, since under the conditions to which j_4 refers

Table 7.2 Modification of Table 7.1 for Many-valued Conception of Justice

	Fetuses are persons. (p_1)			Fetuses are not persons. ($1-p_1$)
	Limiting abortion violates women's right to privacy. (p_2)		Limiting abortion does not violate women's right to privacy. ($1-p_2$)	
	Fetuses' right to life outweighs women's right to privacy. (p_3)	Women's right to privacy outweighs fetuses' right to life. ($1-p_3$)		
uphold limitation	1	j_1	1	j_2
disallow limitation	j_3	1	j_4	1

neither alternative would violate the latter right. Hence, j_3 represents a degree of justice/injustice that is the resultant of the violation of one right and the respecting of another, while j_4 represents the violation of the same right as j_3 without j_3's redeeming feature. Consequently, $j_3 > j_4$. Thus j_1, j_2, j_3, and j_4 are ranked, we shall suppose, as follows: $0 < j_4 < j_3 < j_2 < j_1 < 1$.

The reader may object to my assessment of j_1 on the following grounds: j_1 is the degree of justice of the outcome that occurs when the statutory limitation on abortion is upheld under the conditions that the fetus has a right to life, the pregnant woman has a right to privacy (which is left unprotected), and the latter right outweighs the former. And j_3 is the degree of justice of the outcome that occurs when the statutory limitation on abortion is disallowed under the conditions that the fetus has a right to life (which is left unprotected), the pregnant woman has a right to privacy, and the former right outweighs the former. In both cases, the weightier right is left unprotected while the less weighty right is protected. Why then should j_1 and j_3 represent different degrees of justice? In particular, why should j_1 be greater than j_3? I argued earlier that, in general, violations of the right to life are worse injustices than violations of the right to privacy. However, ex hypothesi, the outcome associated with j_3 occurs when the right to privacy outweighs the right to life. Under that condition, how can failing to protect the right to privacy lead to a worse injustice than failing to protect the right to life? And how can I say that, in general, violations of the right to life are worse, with respect to justice, than violations of the right to privacy and then apply that principle to circumstances under which the right to privacy outweighs the right to life? For these reasons, my assessment that $j_1 > j_3$ appears to be flawed.

I believe, however, that the view that violations of the right to life are generally more unjust than violations of the right to privacy may be significant even for conditions under which the right to privacy is weightier than the right to life. Ceteris paribus, the degree of justice/injustice of an outcome depends on which of the rights involved are protected (or not) and by how much each of the various rights outweigh or are outweighed by the others. For example, if two rights R_1 and R_2 are involved and R_1 outweighs R_2 by a small amount w, then it is a lesser injustice not to protect R_1 than it would be if R_1 outweighed R_2 by a greater amount W. Suppose we believe that R_1 outweighs R_2, but we are not certain that this is so. Then we might well believe that, if R_2 happens to outweigh R_1, it does so by a smaller margin than the margin by which R_1 outweighs R_2 if, as we expect, R_1 does outweigh R_2. Let us return to the Notre Dame–Northwestern football illustration of the preceding chapter: Doris believes that Notre Dame will defeat Northwestern in next Saturday's football game by a wide margin, but she does not rule out the possibility that Northwestern will eke out a victory. In Doris's mind, if the unexpected happens and Northwestern wins, the Wildcats will win by no more than a point or two. However, if, as Doris expects, the Fighting Irish win, they will do so by at least three touchdowns. Thus Doris's expectations concern not only which team will win but also what the winning margins would be for the two possible outcomes. In the same way, we might hold that the right to life is weightier than the right to privacy and yet acknowledge a possibility that the opposite is the case. Then we might believe that if the right to life outweighs the right to privacy, it does so by a margin that is greater than that by which the right to privacy outweighs the right to life if it does outweigh it. We would infer that the injustice of failing to protect the right to life if that right outweighs the right to privacy would be greater than the injustice of failing to protect the right to privacy when that right outweighs the right to life. Hence, $j_1 > j_3$. Similar reasoning would support the other inequalities.[27]

If we accept the preceding relationships among the magnitudes of the relevant quantities and assume that each set of values of p_1, p_2, and p_3 and of j_1, j_2, j_3, and j_4 that satisfies the inequalities is as likely to contain the true values of the probabilities and degrees of justice as any other set, we have all the information we need to apply PR5J. Mathematical analysis reveals that the expected value of EJ(uphold)$-$EJ(disallow) is .01—a small positive number.[28] Thus PR5J would, by a very slender margin, prescribe upholding the Texas abortion statute in this instance.

Can we compare *differences* between degrees of justice, as we did for the probabilities? Usually this will be more difficult because, in general, we have clearer ideas about where specific probabilities lie in the spectrum from 0 to 1 than we have about degrees of justice between perfect injustice (degree of justice = 0) to perfect justice (degree of justice = 1). Of course, perfect justice in a situation would correspond to the 1s in its decision table. But it may be difficult even to imagine what a perfectly unjust state of affairs would be like. Hence, any attempt to compare differences between degrees of justice that involve perfectly unjust states of affairs would be extremely tentative. For example, we would find it very difficult to say whether the difference between j_1 and j_4 is less than or is greater than j_4 (i.e., j_4-0). Therefore, we might agree not to attempt comparisons that involve j_i-0 for any i.

For the *Roe v. Wade* decision, Figure 7.1 may help us see which comparisons among differences between degrees of justice we may want to make. As before, injustice that results from failure to protect persons against violations of their right to life will be significantly greater than injustice that results from violation of a person's right to privacy. This explains the relative remoteness of the pair j_1 and j_2 from the pair j_3 and j_4. We should perhaps recognize a distinction between injustice the prevention of which is properly the concern of the state and "private

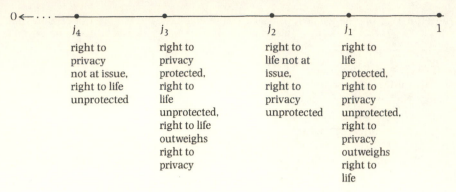

Figure 7.1   Degrees of Justice in the *Roe v. Wade* Decision

injustice" (e.g., the injustice that results from people's not receiving adequate praise from others for their accomplishments), which the state is not concerned with preventing. In our discussion of *Roe v. Wade*, we are assuming that injustice that results from violations of the right to life and the right to privacy is properly the state's concern. Generally speaking, two states of affairs that differ *only* in that in one a particular right is protected while in the other *that* right is not at issue will be relatively close on the justice/injustice scale. This explains the relative closeness of j_1 and j_2 and of j_3 and j_4 on the line. The following inequalities capture the information depicted in Figure 7.1: $j_1-j_2 < j_2-j_3$ and $j_3-j_4 < j_2-j_3$.

As for the previous decision table, we cannot apply the PR4J rule directly, since for some values of the *ps* and *js* that satisfy the inequalities, EJ(uphold) > EJ(disallow), while for others the opposite is true. Hence, we must resort to the PR5J rule and consider which option is more likely to maximize expected justice. If we regard the information given in the decision table and the preceding inequalities as the only information available to the decision-maker, then we may assume that all values of the *ps* and *js* that satisfy the inequalities are equally likely to be the "true" values. The PR5J rule prescribes the option with the greater likelihood of maximizing expected justice. Calculations reveal that the expected value of EJ(uphold)−EJ(disallow) is 467/7200, so once again the "uphold limitation" option is the one prescribed by the maximize-expected-justice approach.[29]

Conclusions

Am I seriously proposing that courts make decisions by performing complex mathematical computations? As in our previous discussion of decision-making under moral uncertainty in chapter 3, such a suggestion may seem inappropriate or preposterous. If asked to explain what is wrong with the approach that I recommend, critics might argue that for important matters of social and political policy, courts and other deliberative bodies should exercise their special, refined powers of *judgment* in weighing the rights and interests that compete for consideration. Such wisdom, it might be claimed, cannot be reduced to calculating out the implications of some artificially quantized and rationalized decision algorithm. We should recall Aristotle's admonition not to expect greater precision in our analyses than the subject matter allows. Those who are called upon to make such important decisions as the *Roe v. Wade* decision, it might be claimed, must adopt a certain attitude, similar to what has been called the *moral point of view*, that is fundamentally incompatible with the sort of detached, calculating posture that the style of deliberation that I recommend would encourage.

Against this objection we must remind ourselves that the methods developed in the preceding discussion are intended to enable decision-makers (e.g., Supreme Court justices) to determine which courses of action are *rational* when they are uncertain what justice entails in the situation. It is entirely possible that on some occasions maximizing *expected* justice would fail actually to achieve justice, just as maximizing *expected* utility sometimes fails to maximize actual utility. Perhaps it is true that inquiring in the proper way about the justiciary merits of the options in a Supreme Court decision requires nonmathematical, qualitative deliberation. However, if the goal is to act *rationally* when we are uncertain about the requirements of justice, then we must adopt methods that are appropriate for rationality. Decision theory is the discipline that investigates and evaluates such methods. Taking uncertainty into account means taking probabilities into account, and reasoning cogently about probabilities cannot always avoid mathematical considerations and methods.

It may be noted that the Supreme Court already uses mathematical methods whenever it renders a decision. That method consists of counting the votes of the justices to determine which opinion is that of the majority. Of course, the mathematical methods described earlier are considerably more complicated than taking a vote among eight or nine Supreme Court justices. But should we rule out complicated methods simply because they are complicated?

The methods I have outlined would normally be used by a single decision-maker to weigh the various pertinent considerations and to take relevant uncertainties into account. For the *Roe v. Wade* case, each Supreme Court justice would have to identify those considerations and make assessments of those probabilities. The decision table for one individual might, and probably would, be substantially different from that for another, at least in the initial stages of deliberation. Perhaps discussions among the members of the Court about the proper form and content of the decision table and the magnitudes of the probabilities and degrees of justice would eventually lead to a consensus. A debate over such details might facilitate resolution of disagreement on at least some occasions on which other methods fail. It would at least encourage disputants to acknowledge their uncertainties about the premises of their arguments and the inferences they contain. This might enable disparate points of view to converge.

A decision-maker may, of course, come to doubt the results of her decision-theoretic analysis and take this as a signal to revise her initial probability and justice assessments and redo the analysis. Adjustments in those assessments might continue until a state of "reflective equilibrium" occurred. Of course, it would be important to guard against self-deception and to minimize the effects of personal bias in estimating or revising estimates of probabilities and degrees of justice. Someone who could not bring her probability and justice measurements into line with her preliminary preference for one option over another might be moved to modify her preference in light of the results of her analysis. And since the Supreme Court normally delivers its decisions in a slow, deliberate fashion, there would ordinarily be enough time for its members to carry out the kind of analysis that I have presented in this chapter.

Of course, there is no guarantee that different individuals would be able to reach agreement on the magnitudes of the probabilities and degrees of justice involved in a particular decision. They might also disagree about what the underlying issues are and thus disagree about the size and shape of the decision table. Consequently, even if they both employed the same method of analysis, the results of their individual analyses might differ. Thus the method of decision-making presented and illustrated in this chapter would contain the same element of subjectivity that we encountered in our discussion of decision-making under moral uncertainty. The reason is that the actions prescribed would depend on decision-makers' individual perceptions of the relative magnitudes of probabilities and degrees of justice. However, it would appear to be considerably less subjective than current methods by which judicial decision-makers arrive at their decisions.

What are the alternatives to the methods I am advocating? One is for decision-makers simply to ignore their uncertainties and reason on the basis of whatever premises they happen to accept. However, ignoring important uncertainties makes no more sense when the goal is to maximize justice than when the goal is to maximize utility. Another approach is for the decision-makers to content themselves with their subjective, intuitive weighings of relevant factors and not even attempt to reconcile their beliefs about probabilities and degrees of justice with their beliefs about which decision alternatives would maximize justice. However, this would mean risking incongruity, if not inconsistency, among one's beliefs and degrees of belief. This could happen insofar as there might sometimes be a course of action that would receive greater support from the "data"—for example, one's probability measurements—than one's chosen course. It is difficult to see how one could rationally defend such a choice.

I conclude therefore that the kind of analysis illustrated here is a reasonable way to examine problematic issues like the *Roe v. Wade* case. It is a more rational approach than others that ignore important uncertainties altogether or inadequately take them into account, and it also offers some hope of resolving disagreements about which judgments should (rationally) be rendered. Of course, some may argue that in *Roe v. Wade* the Court ignored important factors that I should have taken into account in my reconstruction and evaluation. However, even if this is so, I still favor using the maximize-expected-justice approach employed in this chapter, applied to a revised decision table. I recommend it for consideration by decision-makers (and their consultants) for other matters of social, political, and individual decision.

Eight

Long-Run Morality

The decisions that I make today often affect what decisions I shall make tomorrow. For example, if I decide not to go to work today, tomorrow I shall have to decide how to dispatch the tasks that accumulated in my absence. In general, the decisions that we make in the short run often determine to a significant degree the decisions that we shall face in the long run. My present decision whether to become an engineer or a lawyer, assuming that I maintain it, may determine a decade from now whether my decisions then will affect public safety in a significant way or will enable some injured party to obtain just compensation.

These observations are true, in particular, of moral decisions. And I may choose my current or short-term actions with this in mind. For example, I may choose not to become an air traffic controller in order not to have to make the split-second life-or-death decisions that air traffic controllers routinely face. And I do so on moral grounds if my decision stems from my fear that, as an air traffic controller, I would too often fail to meet my moral obligations. I could fail in (at least) two ways: (1) I might fail by doing what I know (or believe) to be morally wrong owing to the weakness of my will; (2) I might fail by having no alternatives the moral rightness of which I was certain. Thus *akrasia* and moral uncertainty are two of the ways in which I may fail to do what is morally right.

Should my expectations about my own future moral behavior affect my current moral decisions? If so, how? Philosophers have by and large ignored these questions.[1] However, it is essential that we give them careful consideration if we hope to make rational decisions. In the following discussion, I shall argue that we should conduct ourselves so that our future actions as a whole achieve maximum expected moral rightness. And I show that if we implement this sort of policy we shall sometimes choose actions that, considered individually, do not maximize expected moral rightness. In other words, in order to maximize the expected degree of moral rightness of our future actions as a whole, it will sometimes be necessary to choose individual actions that we know (or believe) to be morally inferior to other actions we might have chosen. Paradoxically, there can sometimes be moral justification for doing what one knows to be morally wrong.

Courses of Action and Their Morality

Let us use the term *course of action* to mean a sequence of individual actions by an agent.[2] Of course, the concept of an individual action is problematic. For example, is walking across the street an individual action, or is it a sequence of actions that consists of the steps one takes in the order in which they occur? However, I shall ignore these difficulties here. I shall assume only that each individual action involves a decision on the part of its agent and, if questions of moral propriety are raised, the decision is a moral decision.

Imagine that we can foresee and entertain the future lifetime courses of action that we might elect for ourselves. Of course, there may be an infinite number of such courses of action, so for simplicity let us assume that we have somehow eliminated from further consideration all but a relatively small number of candidates. Let us suppose (unrealistically) that we have all relevant information about each course of action, including all of the myriad individual actions that constitute it as well as the degree of moral rightness of each such action. Would it be possible, at least in principle, to make moral comparisons among different courses of action? The answer is "Yes." A course of action 99% of whose individual actions possess maximal moral rightness would appear to be "better," morally speaking, than an equally large course of action 99% of whose components have minimal moral rightness (i.e., maximum moral wrongness).

This illustration suggests one way in which we might conceive degrees of moral rightness of courses of action. The idea is to take the degree of moral rightness of a course of action as the sum of the degrees of moral rightness of all of the individual actions that constitute it. Would this work? Some may claim that we should discount individual actions that would occur in the distant future and weigh their degrees of moral rightness less in our moral appraisals of courses of action. This suggestion would make sense if remotely future actions were less certain to occur than current and short-term actions. However, we are hypothesizing that we know all of the relevant details about the courses of action under consideration and that this includes all of the individual actions that compose them. Later, when we take up the topic of how we should make decisions about courses of action in the "real world," we shall have to contend with uncertainties about the details of their composition. But for the moment, all we are trying to do is get a handle on the *concept* of degrees of moral rightness of courses of action. For that purpose, the agent's temporal proximity to the constituent individual actions is not pertinent.[3]

However, as we saw in our discussion of the VPMR thesis in chapter 4, there is a flaw in the assumption that we may simply add up the degrees of moral rightness of the individual actions to get a total for the composite. This facile procedure is appropriate if we take moral rightness, as it applies to individual actions, to be entirely a matter of conforming to duty and not at all a matter of maximizing some sort of quantity such as intrinsic value.[4] However, if we have a consequentialist theory like act utilitarianism in mind, our main purpose in pursuing a course of action will likely be the same as our main purpose in choosing an individual action—to maximize (expected) utility. It is possible for a course of action to generate more (expected) utility than another even though it includes fewer individual actions that individually maximize (expected) utility. This can happen when more utility is at stake on some occasions than on others. Thus for a consequentialist theory, it is the total utility generated by a course of action that is important and not the number of individual actions that maximize utility.

What if our moral theory includes both duty-fulfilling and utility-maximizing requirements? This occurs in prima facie duties theories, for example. Then we shall need to consider both the degrees of moral rightness of the constituent individual actions and the total (expected) utility generated by the course of action in assessing its overall degree of moral rightness. The weight that each aspect receives will depend on the weight that it has according to the theory. Ascertaining these weights precisely may well present enormous practical difficulties, but there appears to be no serious conceptual problem here.

Let us consider the following simple example: We shall imagine a moral agent who is choosing a course of action. Each available course of action involves choosing an individual action on each of three consecutive occasions, which we shall call t_1, t_2, and t_3. We shall suppose that at t_1 the agent, Nick, will choose between individual actions x_1 and x_2. If Nick chooses x_1 at t_1, then he will choose between individual actions y_1 and y_2 at t_2. But, because what Nick does on a certain occasion affects what decisions he will make on later occasions, if Nick opts for x_2 at t_1, then he will choose between individual actions z_1 and z_2 at t_2. Furthermore, if Nick selects y_1 at t_2, then he will choose between u_1 and u_2 at t_3. And if Nick chooses y_2 at t_2, his alternatives at t_3 are v_1 and v_2. Similarly, if Nick chooses z_1 at t_2, then he will choose either w_1 or w_2 at t_3. And if Nick chooses z_2 at t_2, he will choose either s_1 or s_2 at t_3. Hence, there are eight sequences of individual actions available to Nick—$<x_1\ y_1\ u_1>$, $<x_1\ y_1\ u_2>$, $<x_1\ y_2\ v_1>$, $<x_1\ y_2\ v_2>$, $<x_2\ z_1\ w_1>$, $<x_2\ z_1\ w_2>$, $<x_2\ z_2\ s_1>$, and $<x_2\ z_2\ s_2>$. Nick's choices are represented in Figure 8.1.

Let us suppose that for Nick there are two moral theories in contention—T_1 and T_2. T_1 is a consequentialist theory that always prescribes maximizing utility, while T_2 is a strictly nonconsequentialist theory that says that individual actions must always be either completely right or completely wrong. In other words, according to T_2 there are no intermediate degrees of moral rightness between "right" and "wrong." Kant's theory is the sort of moral theory that T_2 might be. We shall imagine that Nick has complete information about the (expected) utilities of the eight possible courses of action and that they are as follows:

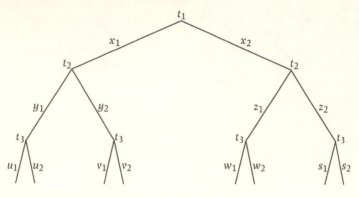

Figure 8.1   Alternative Courses of Action for Nick

$$u{<}x_1\,y_1\,u_1{>} = 20 \qquad u{<}x_2\,z_1\,w_1{>} = 8$$
$$u{<}x_1\,y_1\,u_2{>} = -4 \qquad u{<}x_2\,z_1\,w_2{>} = 5$$
$$u{<}x_1\,y_2\,v_1{>} = -7 \qquad u{<}x_2\,z_2\,s_1{>} = -1$$
$$u{<}x_1\,y_2\,v_2{>} = -10 \qquad u{<}x_2\,z_2\,s_2{>} = 17$$

Furthermore, Nick knows with certainty that, according to T_2, x_1, y_2, u_2, v_2, z_2, w_2, and s_2 would be (completely) right and that y_1, u_1, v_1, x_2, z_1, w_1, and s_1 would be (completely) wrong. He does not know which of the two theories T_1 and T_2 is the true moral theory but judges the probability that T_1 is the true theory to be .6 and the probability that T_2 is the true theory to be .4. Our question is, given this information, which course of action would be the most reasonable for Nick to pursue?

In previous chapters, I argued that in making moral decisions about individual actions we should rationally choose actions that maximize expected moral rightness. The analogous principle for making decisions about courses of action is that the courses of action that are rational for us to choose are those have the greatest expected moral rightness. To apply this principle to our example, we shall calculate EMR$<x\,y\,z> = p(T_1) \cdot m_1{<}x\,y\,z{>} + p(T_2) \cdot m_2{<}x\,y\,z{>}$. In this expressions, $p(T_1)$ and $p(T_2)$ are the probabilities that T_1 and T_2 are, respectively, *the* true moral theory and $m_1{<}x\,y\,z{>}$ and $m_2{<}x\,y\,z{>}$ are the degrees of moral rightness that the course of action $<x\,y\,z>$ would have according to T_1 and T_2, respectively.

Since EMR$<x\,y\,z>$ is a composite measure of moral rightness based on both T_1 and T_2, $m_1{<}x\,y\,z{>}$ and $m_2{<}x\,y\,z{>}$ must be measured on a common scale. We accomplish this by using the normalized values of $m_1{<}x\,y\,z{>}$ and $m_2{<}x\,y\,z{>}$ where each value ranges between 0 (minimum degree of moral rightness) and 1 (maximum degree of moral rightness). The easiest solution is simply to understand $m_1{<}x\,y\,z{>}$ as the normalized utility that would be produced by the course of action $<x\,y\,z>$ and to interpret $m_2{<}x\,y\,z{>}$ as the *average* of the degrees of moral rightness that the individual actions x, y, and z would have according to T_2. We use the *average* values in order to guarantee that $0 \leq m_2 <x\,y\,z> \leq 1$ and thus to avoid what would otherwise be an apples-and-oranges defect in our analysis. We may, of course, want to give one moral theory more weight than another if we regard it as more likely to be the correct theory. In fact, this is the case in our example, where T_1's probability of being true (.6) is judged to be greater than T_2's probability of being true (.4). But this is taken care of already by the terms $p(T_1)$ and $p(T_2)$ in the EMR formula for the alternative courses of action $<x\ y\ z>$. Therefore, we shall let m_1 and m_2 range over the same set of values, which we have arbitrarily chosen to be the interval [0, 1]. Since according to T_2 individual actions must be either completely right or completely wrong, $m_2(x)$, $m_2(y)$, and $m_2(z)$, the respective degrees of moral rightness that x, y, and z would have according to T_2, must each be either 0 or 1. Therefore, for our example each $m_2<x\ y\ z>$ must be either 0, ⅓, ⅔, or 1.

Since the quantities $m_2<x\ y\ z>$ are the normalized values of a utility function, measuring m_2 in a "real-life" situation presents the usual difficulties of utility measurement. Later we shall address some of the practical problems that a decision-maker would encounter in attempting to compare the expected degrees of moral rightness of alternative courses of action. For the moment, however, we are focusing on conceptual matters. We want to know whether it should make a difference to our moral decisions when we consider courses of action rather than just individual actions. Therefore, we shall simply assume that cardinal number measurements of the various quantities that we are considering are available to the decision-maker.

Let us suppose that the values of $m_1<x\ y\ z>$, $m_2(x)$, $m_2(y)$, $m_2(z)$, and $m_2<x\ y\ z>$ for the eight courses of action in our example are as given in Table 8.1. The last column of Table 8.1 contains the values of EMR$<x\ y\ z>$ for the eight courses of action, calculated using the previously stated formula. The table reveals that the course of action that maximizes EMR is $<x_2\ z_2\ s_2>$. This is noteworthy, since $<x_2\ z_2\ s_2>$ does not maximize utility (because $m_1<x_1\ y_1\ u_1>$ exceeds $m_1<x_2\ z_2\ s_2>$) and x_2 does not satisfy T_2. We might expect some course of action that x_1 initiates to maximize EMR because x_1, unlike x_2, satisfies T_2 and the course of action $<x_1\ y_1\ u_2>$ maximizes utility and thus satisfies T_1.

The paradox would be even greater if x_1 individually maximized utility and x_2 did not. This is so because both moral theories T_1 and T_2 would sanction x_1 for the moral decision at t_1 and would disapprove of x_2 at t_1. We have already established that this is true for T_2. But is it true for T_1? To answer this question we must determine which of x_1 and x_2 maximizes utility at t_1. And this raises a

Table 8.1   Values of EMR for Nick's Alternative Courses of Action

x	y	z	$m_1<x\ y\ z>$	$m_2(x)$	$m_2(y)$	$m_2(z)$	$m_2<x\ y\ z>$	EMR$<x\ y\ z>$
x_1	y_1	u_1	1.0	1	0	0	1/3	0.73
x_1	y_1	u_2	0.2	1	0	1	2/3	0.39
x_1	y_2	v_1	0.1	1	1	0	2/3	0.33
x_1	y_2	v_2	0	1	1	1	1	0.4
x_2	z_1	w_1	0.6	0	0	0	0	0.36
x_2	z_1	w_2	0.5	0	0	1	1/3	0.43
x_2	z_2	s_1	0.3	0	1	0	1/3	0.31
x_2	z_2	s_2	0.9	0	1	1	2/3	0.81

puzzling question: What are the utilities that we should associate with x_1 and x_2? The puzzle is that we cannot say how much utility would be generated by acting in a certain way at t_1 unless we know what the agent's actions at t_2 and t_3 will be. Table 8.1 shows that the utility generated depends greatly on Nick's action choices at t_2 and t_3, whatever he does at t_1. Therefore, what assumptions do we make about Nick's actions at t_2 and t_3, if we wish to compare the magnitudes of $u(x_1)$ and $u(x_2)$? And we must answer this question in order to tell whether x_1 and x_2 satisfy T_1.

The alternative that seems more in the "spirit" of utility maximization at t_1 is x_1. This is so because, if Nick were concerned mainly with utility maximization, we would expect him to choose x_1 at t_1, y_1 at t_2, and u_1 at t_3, since the *course of action* $<x_1\ y_1\ u_1>$ alone maximizes utility. Therefore, if we assume that Nick would perform y_1 at t_2 and u_1 at t_3 if he were to choose x_1 at t_1, then it would be appropriate to take $u(x_1)$ (normalized) as 1.0—that is, the utility of the course of action $<x_1\ y_1\ u_1>$. However, it should be noted that different assumptions lead to different results. If we knew somehow both that Nick would choose x_1 at t_1 only if he also chose y_2 at t_2 and that he would choose x_2 at t_1 only if he also chose z_1 at t_2, then we would conclude that $u(x_2) > u(x_1)$. This is so because Table 8.1 implies that the utility generated by any course of action that includes x_2 and z_1 exceeds that generated by any course of action that includes x_1 and y_2. Under these conditions, it would be misleading at best to say that $u(x_1) = 1$.

These questions have considerable *practical* significance for makers of moral decisions. For example, should one who subscribes to an act utilitarian moral theory assume in choosing her actions that all of her future actions will be utility-maximizing, or should she expect herself sometimes to fail to live up to her moral theory and try to take her future failings into account?[5] For most of us, it seems unrealistic to expect oneself *never* to violate one's moral principles, especially if those principles sometimes require us to violate our short-term interests. Even ethical egoism is sometimes difficult to live up to, since it demands that we sacrifice our short-term interests in pursuit of our greater long-term interests (e.g., by giving up cigarettes). These considerations will become important when we attempt to develop useful strategies for real-world moral decision-making. Here let us simply note that the notion of the utility generated by an individual action is not as transparent as is often assumed.[6]

However, let us for the moment bypass these difficulties by making the simplifying supposition that the utility generated by an individual action is to be measured assuming that all the agent's future actions will be utility-maximizing. This means that, for Nick, the utility generated by an individual action is assumed to be the utility of the course of action that includes that individual action and that generates at least as much utility as any other course of action that also includes that action. For example, $u(x_1) = 1.0$, $u(x_2) = .9$, $u(y_2) = .1$, $u(z_1) = .6$, $u(s_2) = .9$, and so forth (where normalized values are assumed). The utilities for all of the possible individual actions in our example are given in Table 8.2.

The expected degrees of moral rightness of the (individual) action alternatives are calculated by using the formula $EMR(x) = p(T_1) \cdot m_1(x) + p(T_2) \cdot m_2(x)$ for each individual action x. As before, $p(T_1) = .6$ and $p(T_2) = .4$. Table 8.2 shows that although x_2 initiates the course of action with the maximum expected degree of

Table 8.2   Values of EMR for Nick's Individual Action Alternatives

x	y	z	$m_1(x)$	$m_1(y)$	$m_1(z)$	EMR(x)	EMR(y)	EMR(z)
x_1	y_1	u_1	1.0	1.0	1.0	1.0	0.6	0.6
x_1	y_1	u_2	1.0	1.0	0.2	1.0	0.6	0.52
x_1	y_2	v_1	1.0	0.1	0.1	1.0	0.46	0.06
x_1	y_2	v_2	1.0	0.1	0	1.0	0.46	0.4
x_2	z_1	w_1	0.9	0.6	0.6	0.54	0.36	0.36
x_2	z_1	w_2	0.9	0.6	0.5	0.54	0.36	0.7
x_2	z_2	s_1	0.9	0.9	0.3	0.54	0.94	0.18
x_2	z_2	s_2	0.9	0.9	0.9	0.54	0.94	0.94

moral rightness, x_1 individually has a greater degree of moral rightness than x_2. Assuming that Nick has all the information contained in Table 8.1 and Table 8.2 and that he can choose any available individual action on each of the three occasions t_1, t_2, and t_3 and also can choose any of the eight available courses of action, what should he do at t_1?

Nick's predicament is this: At t_1 he will choose either x_1 or x_2. *Viewed as an individual action,* x_1 is the option that has the greater expected degree of moral rightness. However, x_2 is the option that initiates the course of action that has the greatest possible expected degree of moral rightness. Since Nick cannot select that course of action without selecting x_2 at t_1, our moral standard for courses of action in effect prescribes that he choose x_2 at t_1. Thus in this example the moral standard for courses of action conflicts with the moral standard for individual actions. The former tells Nick to choose x_2 at t_1 while the latter directs him to choose x_1 at t_1. What should he do?

The *rational* choice of action for Nick, in my judgment, is for him to follow the courses-of-action standard and choose x_2. If we assume that each of the eight courses of action is really available to Nick—that he will definitely perform whichever of the eight courses of action he chooses—then there is no reason for him to regard his decision at t_1 as more important than his decisions at t_2 or t_3. Nick should (rationally) maximize the overall moral rightness of his actions and not just the (expected) moral rightness of his action on a particular occasion. The fact that a decision is being made *now* does not make it more important, morally speaking, than all of one's future decisions. Therefore, Nick should choose x_2 at t_1 in order to initiate the course of action $<x_2\ z_2\ s_2>$.

Let us look more closely at the moral dynamics of Nick's decisions at t_1, t_2, and t_3. Table 8.2 shows that, according to T_1, Nick's moral obligation at t_1 is to choose x_1. And Table 8.1 shows that T_2 also prescribes x_1 for him at t_1. Thus for Nick's decision at t_1 the two moral theories agree in their precriptions. At t_2, if Nick has chosen x_1 at t_1, then T_1 prescribes y_1 while T_2 prescribes y_2. However, if he has chosen x_2 at t_1, then T_1 and T_2 both prescribe z_2 at t_2. Thus if he chooses x_2 at t_1, then one of his alternatives at t_2 will satisfy both moral theories. If Nick chooses x_1 at t_1, then there is no such alternative, although, as just noted, his choosing x_1 at t_1 satisfies both theories. At t_3, if Nick has chosen x_2 at t_1 and z_2 at t_2, then s_2 satisfies both theories. But if he has chosen x_1 at t_1, there is no alternative at

t_3 that satisfies both theories. These observations imply that by choosing x_2 at t_1 Nick enables himself to choose a course of action in which, for two of the three individual decisions, he avoids having to choose between the two moral theories. If Nick chooses x_1 at t_1, then since there would be no alternative at either t_2 or t_3 that satisfies both T_1 and T_2, Nick would risk violating the true moral theory on both occasions. This is so even though at t_1 he can satisfy both T_1 and T_2 only by choosing x_1. In short, by choosing the course of action $<x_2\, z_2\, s_2>$, his actions find the greatest possible common ground between the contending moral theories. This is a strong reason for Nick to choose that course of action.

We should not be surprised at this result. We should expect that, in general, courses of action that capitalize on agreement among competing moral perspectives will also maximize expected moral rightness. This is so because, in general, the more often this agreement occurs the more often the decision-maker assures herself that she is maximally enhancing the expected degree of moral rightness of her course of action. We would live in the best of possible worlds if we always had options that conformed to all competing moral theories, principles, rules, and precepts. Then we would always be able to circumvent any moral uncertainties that we were unable to resolve. It would not matter to us, for purposes of decision-making, which moral theory, principle, rule, or precept were true.

Of course, in the real world, the lifetime courses of action that are available to us never satisfy all the competing moral perspectives. However, we might try to come as close as possible to such a course of action by seeking to *minimize* conflict among rival theories. We might do so by avoiding, as much as possible, situations in which all of our options violate at least one of the moral perspectives that we find plausible. This means that generally we shall try to stay out of *moral dilemmas*, which present us with the most problematic moral decisions.[7]

In the preceding example above, Nick's decision at t_2 between y_1 and y_2 could be a moral dilemma that he bypasses by choosing x_2 at t_1. We shall not always be able to avoid difficult moral decisions, but there may be strategies that we can consider to reduce significantly the number of such decisions that we shall have to make. Thus we may accept as a general guideline the following:

G1
Other things being equal, choose courses of action that minimize conflict among competing moral theories, principles, and rules.

We must remember that the basic principle of rationality enjoins us to maximize the expected moral rightness of our lifetime courses of action. The strategy of minimizing conflict among competing moral perspectives, recommended by G1, will not always accomplish this objective. It would not do so, for example, if minimizing conflicts among competing moral theories would sacrifice too much utility and, as a result, would reduce the expected degree of moral rightness of our course of action below that of some of our other course-of-action alternatives. However, it is a strategy that may be a helpful approximation to the basic maximize-expected-moral-rightness strategy that we may follow when we do not have enough information to carry out the sort of detailed analysis that we performed in the preceding example. We shall come back to this point later when we consider the complexities of real-world decision-making and practical ways of dealing with them.

Let us now consider a possible complication, one that is likely to occur in real-world moral decision-making. In the preceding example, we tacitly assumed that the decision-maker would implement any course of action that he chose at t_1. If, for example, Nick chose the $<x_2\ z_2\ s_2>$ course of action, then there was no doubt that he would perform z_2 at t_2 and s_2 at t_3. However, in reality Nick might not be sure that he would actually perform z_2 when t_2 arrived or that he would in fact perform s_2 when t_3 arrived (provided, of course, that he carried out his intentions to perform z_2 at t_2). There are a number of possible reasons why he might not be sure of his future actions. One reason is that it might not be in Nick's long-term interest to perform z_2 at t_2 and s_2 at t_3. Or, even if it were in his long-term interest, it might conflict with his short-term interest to implement his intended course of action. Anyone who has ever tried to stop smoking cigarettes or to stay on a diet knows the difficulty of carrying out a long-term plan that requires him to postpone rewards until the distant future. One may well have reasonable doubts about how he will make future decisions, even when he has no doubts about his *capacity* to perform the actions that he now envisions as constituting his future course of action. In that event, the agent cannot be sure at the beginning of his chosen course of action that he will actually end up completing it. Therefore, it makes sense for us to take into account our uncertainties about our future action choices in addition to our uncertainties about moral principles, theories, rules, and precepts.[8]

How then should agents take uncertainties about their own future action choices into account in deciding which courses of action to embark upon? Let us modify our previous example that involves Nick and his decisions at t_1, t_2, and t_3. Let us now suppose that Nick assesses the probability that he would actually perform y_1 at t_2 (assuming that he chose x_1 at t_1) to be .9 and, consequently, the probability that he would choose y_2 at t_2 to be .1. Moreover, he rates the probability that he would perform z_1 at t_2 (if he had chosen x_2 at t_1) as .4 and, therefore, the probability that he would choose z_2 at t_2 as .6. To keep things relatively simple, we shall assume that Nick has no uncertainties about his (contingent) choices at t_3.

In this situation, Nick might embark on the $<x_1\ y_1\ u_1>$ course of action, for example, and end up performing the $<x_1\ y_2\ v_2>$ course of action instead. The decision he must make at t_1 is which course of action to initiate. Obviously, this means that he must decide between x_1 and x_2 at t_1. If he wants to base his decision on the expected degree of moral rightness of his course of action, then he wants to know whether the expected degree of moral rightness of the course of action that he would initiate by choosing x_1 at t_1 (whatever it is) would be greater than or less than the expected degree of moral rightness of the course of action that he would initiate by choosing x_2 at t_1 (whatever it is). Since Nick is uncertain which course of action he would actually initiate by selecting x_1 at t_1 or by selecting x_2 at t_1, he cannot choose his course of action by itemizing *in advance* all of its individual action components and comparing its expected degree of moral rightness against other course-of-action alternatives similarly itemized. Somehow he will have to take into account his uncertainty about which course of action he will actually initiate by the action he performs at t_1.

We shall use the expression "EMR$<x$ *>" to represent the expected degree of moral rightness of the course of action that Nick would initiate by choosing individual action x at t_1. If Nick chooses x_1 at t_1, then he will perform one of the two courses of action, $<x_1\ y_1\ u_1>$ or $<x_1\ y_2\ v_2>$. We rule out the other two possibilities by recalling that we are assuming that Nick is certain that he would choose u_1 over u_2 and v_2 over v_1 at t_3. Similarly, if he chooses x_2 at t_1, then he will perform one of the two courses of action, $<x_2\ z_1\ w_2>$ or $<x_2\ z_2\ s_2>$.

One can calculate EMR$<x_1$ *> using the formula EMR$<x_1$ *> $= p<x_1\ y_1\ u_1>\cdot$ EMR$<x_1\ y_1\ u_1> + p<x_1\ y_2\ v_2>\cdot$ EMR$<x_1\ y_2\ v_2>$ where $p<x_1\ y_1\ u_1>$ is the probability that Nick would choose y_1 at t_2 if he were to choose x_1 at t_1, and $p<x_1\ y_2\ v_2>$ is the probability that he would choose y_2 at t_2 if he were to choose x_1 at t_1. We have already assumed that $p<x_1\ y_1\ u_1> = .9$ and $p<x_1\ y_2\ v_2> = .1$. And in our analysis of the original example involving Nick, we calculated that EMR$<x_1\ y_1\ u_1> = .73$ and that EMR$<x_1\ y_2\ v_2> = .4$. Doing the indicated arithmetic reveals that EMR$<x_1$ *> $= .697$. The formula for EMR$<x_2$ *> is EMR$<x_2$ *> $= p<x_2\ z_1\ w_2>\cdot$ EMR$<x_2\ z_1\ w_2> + p<x_2\ z_2\ s_2>\cdot$ EMR$<x_2\ z_2\ s_2>$. We have assumed that the probabilities are .4 and .6, respectively, and Table 8.1 gives us the two EMR values, which are .43 and .81. It turns out that EMR$<x_2$ *> $= .658$. Thus, by a slender margin, the results of our analysis direct Nick to choose a course of action that he will initiate by choosing x_1 at t_1. In short, he should perform x_1 at t_1.

One interesting thing about this result is that if we take into account the agent's uncertainties about his future action choices, the prescribed action at t_1 switches from x_2 to x_1. We reached this result by considering both Nick's moral uncertainty about which moral theory, T_1 or T_2, is correct and his uncertainty about his (contingent) action choices at t_2. We should observe that Nick's uncertainty about his action choice at t_2 is greater if he chooses x_2 at t_1 than if he chooses x_1 at t_1. Although he is 90% certain that he would choose y_1 over y_2 at t_2, he is only 60% certain that he would choose z_2 over z_1 at t_2. Our analysis shows that this greater uncertainty should induce him to favor whichever course of action he would initiate by choosing x_1 at t_1 over whichever course of action he would initiate by choosing x_2 at t_1. This suggests another guideline for moral decisions:

G2
Other things being equal, one should (rationally) choose some course of action that he has the greatest confidence that he would complete if he were to embark upon it.

More succinctly, we should generally avoid embarking on courses of action that we are relatively unlikely to complete. Or, more plainly, we should not start what we probably shall not finish.

We thus have two guidelines that may be useful when we consider more realistic moral choices of courses of action. We should note that G1 and G2 are logically independent of each other and could conceivably conflict in a particular situation. For this reason, decision-makers must be circumspect in applying them, since both have exceptions. However, it is reasonable to expect conflicts to occur relatively infrequently, since there is likely to be a strong correlation between courses of action that frequently present moral agents with moral dilemmas and those that those agents would be discouraged from completing.

In real-world moral decision-making, agents will ordinarily have far less information about alternative lifetime courses of action than we have presumed Nick to have in the preceding examples. Consequently, we shall usually be unable to employ the kind of detailed action-by-action analysis that we performed earlier in this chapter. We shall therefore have to rely on our guidelines to a considerable extent. Let us next consider a more realistic example of moral decision-making and attempt to develop some practical strategies for action choice.

Real-World Moral Decision-making

In the real world, the pertinent uncertainties that surround our moral decisions are often legion. We have already identified some of those uncertainties, including those about moral theories, principles, and rules and their implications for specific moral issues and concrete situations. If we seek to maximize the expected degree of moral rightness of our lifetime courses of action, we compound the uncertainties with which we must deal. In addition, we can usually foresee relatively few of the decisions that we shall make in the future. We know relatively little about the alternatives among which we shall choose and the circumstances under which we shall make our choices. And we know even less what our beliefs and uncertainties will be when we make those future decisions. This means that initially our information about the degrees of moral rightness of the available courses of action will often be meager at best.[9]

Nevertheless, we often make decisions about our future lifetime courses of action. To a great extent, deciding on a job or career is such a choice. This is also true of an individual who adopts a particular "lifestyle" on the basis of the kinds of individual action choices she would expect to face in the future as well as the alternatives that will be available to her when she makes those choices. And though it may be true that we know very few of the details of our future lifetime courses of action, this does not mean that we know nothing about them. In some cases, what we know may be enough for us to conclude that some of them would have greater expected degrees of moral rightness than others. For example, I may know very little about the details of the course of action I would embark upon if I were to decide to become an investment banker. However, I may know enough about it to conclude that I would achieve a greater expected degree of moral rightness if I were to choose some other career.

How then may we take into account the moral rightness of our lifetime courses of action? One approach, which I have already noted, is to employ the two guidelines already discussed. To do so, one would compare how often each course of action under consideration would present her with moral dilemmas and other morally problematic choices. The decision-maker would also gauge the likelihood that she would complete a particular course of action were she to embark upon it. Perhaps these estimates would be enough to eliminate some courses of action from further consideration. Possibly a single course of action would emerge that would both minimize the number of moral dilemmas and maximize the likelihood that the agent would carry it to completion. In some cases, however, there may be enough information about the available courses of action for an agent to estimate their expected degrees of moral rightness directly without appealing directly to G1 and G2. If there is a large difference between the estimate for one course of action and that for another, this may give the agent sufficient confidence to conclude that the course of action associated with the larger estimate is the rational choice.

Let us consider the following somewhat fanciful example: Ophelia, who will soon graduate from college, is deciding whether to apply to medical school to prepare for a career as a primary care physician in an impoverished rural community in which there is a serious scarcity of physicians or apply to graduate school in philosophy to prepare for a career as a philosophy professor. Although Ophelia subscribes to Kant's moral theory, she is not sure that it is the correct theory since she also regards act utilitarianism as a plausible contender. Ophelia knows extremely little about the particular moral decisions that she would make as a physician or as a philosophy professor, although she knows generally what kinds of on-the-job decisions doctors and professors typically face.

One approach that Ophelia might follow is to estimate the degrees of moral rightness of each course of action according to each of the two moral theories and then calculate and compare their expected degrees of moral rightness. This will require her to measure or estimate the probabilities associated with the moral theories. As before, in order to avoid apples-and-oranges problems, Ophelia must have in mind commensurable measures of degrees of moral rightness with respect to the two moral theories. We shall assume normalized degrees of moral rightness with 1 as the maximum and 0 as the minimum. Let us suppose that Ophelia believes that she would maximize utility by choosing a career as a rural physician. We shall assume that this is true not only for these two alternatives but also for any other courses of action she might consider. She might arrive at this judgment on the basis of her belief that since the rural area in which she would practice medicine does not have enough doctors to serve the population, she would often treat illness and injury that would otherwise go untreated and would often prevent suffering and death that would otherwise needlessly occur. She concludes that there is no other lifework she could choose that would lead to the production of more good and the prevention of more evil than the medical career she has in mind.[10] The normalized utility of the "philosophy professor" course of action, in Ophelia's judgment, will be some smaller number between 0 and 1. For the moment, let us call that number u_p.

How about Ophelia's estimates of the degrees of moral rightness of the two courses of action according to Kant's theory? According to Kant's theory, her duty is always to act in accordance with maxims that she can consistently will to be universal laws. In equivalent terms (according to Kant), Ophelia's moral obligation is always to treat persons as ends-in-themselves and never merely as means. Maximizing utility should be no part of her moral deliberations, according to Kant's theory (as she understands it). And Kant's theory, like other standard moral theories, is intended to apply to individual actions and not courses of action. It is possible to interpret Kant as allowing for degrees of moral rightness between maximum rightness and minimum rightness. For example, it seems that we can comply with the Kantian obligation to alleviate the suffering of others to greater or lesser degrees. However, a notion of degrees of moral rightness of *individual* actions seems to violate the spirit of Kant's moral philosophy, given Kant's insistence that moral duty is categorical in nature. Let us, therefore, suppose that Ophelia's concept of Kantian moral obligation recognizes only two degrees of moral rightness—namely, right and wrong.

For courses of action, however, there are obvious discriminations that we can make between those that include a preponderance of individual actions that are morally right according to Kant's theory and those in which there is a dearth of such actions. Let us therefore assume that, with respect to Kant's theory, Ophelia measures the degrees of moral rightness of courses of action according to their proportions of morally right individual actions. The decision table for her decision whether to pursue a career as a rural physician or one as a philosophy professor is Table 8.3.

The quantity u_M is the (normalized) utility that Ophelia would produce by choosing a career as a rural physician, u_P is the (normalized) utility that she would produce by pursuing a career as a philosophy professor, r_M is the relative frequency of her actions that would be morally right according to Kant's theory if she chose a career as a rural physician, and r_P is the relative frequency of her actions that would be morally right according to Kant's theory if she chose to become a philosophy professor. The four quantities—u_M, u_P, r_M, and r_P—are degrees of moral rightness of Ophelia's course-of-action alternatives with respect to the two moral theories under consideration. It can be seen that $EMR(M) = p \cdot u_M + (1 - p) \cdot r_M$ and $EMR(P) = p \cdot u_P + (1 - p) \cdot r_P$, where $EMR(M)$ and $EMR(P)$ are the expected degrees of moral rightness of the "rural physician" and "philosophy professor" options, respectively, and p is the probability that act utilitarianism is the true moral theory. The most straightforward approach to the decision problem would be to measure or estimate the quantities p, u_M, r_M, u_P, and r_P and then calculate $EMR(M)$ and $EMR(P)$ to see which is greater.

As a preliminary step toward cardinal measurements of the five quantities, it may be useful to identify any ordinal comparisons among them that seem reasonable. Since normalized values are assumed, all five quantities will be between 0 and 1. Moreover, since Kant's theory is the moral theory in which Ophelia has the greater confidence, its probability of being the true theory, $1 - p$, is greater

Table 8.3   Decision Table for Ophelia's Career Decision

	act utilitarian theory	Kant's theory
rural physician	u_M	r_M
philosophy professor	u_P	r_P

than the probability p that the act utilitarian theory is the correct theory; therefore, $p < 1 - p$.

How about comparisons among u_M, r_M, u_P, and r_P? Let us hypothesize that Ophelia views the matter in the following way: By becoming a philosophy professor she would not generate nearly as much utility as she would as a rural physician, but she also would not find herself very often in the life-or-death dilemmas that physicians sometimes encounter. In those situations, she would incur substantial risks of violating Kant's moral theory. This is because she would often be torn between respecting her patients' autonomy and relieving their distress and thus would be unsure which action Kant's theory prescribes in such problematic cases. As a philosophy professor, she would encounter such dilemmas much less often. Thus she might reasonably judge that $u_P < u_M$ and $r_M < r_P$.

Since we assume that u_P, u_M, r_M, and r_P are all normalized quantities, Ophelia may venture to make comparisons across the divide between the two moral theories, though such judgments will likely be more tentative than intratheory comparisons. The act utilitarian theory recommends that she choose the "rural physician" option while Kant's theory endorses the "philosophy professor" alternative. It seems reasonable to infer that the degree of moral rightness that a course of action has according to a moral theory that recommends it is greater than the degree of moral rightness that it has according to a theory that does not recommend it. Perhaps this principle has exceptions. However, it is hard to see why it should not apply to the situation in which Ophelia must decide on a course of action. Therefore, let us suppose that $r_M < u_M$ and $u_P < r_P$.

It remains to be seen what comparisons between u_M and r_P and between u_P and r_M can be made, since no such comparisons are implied by the preceding inequalities. Nevertheless, I shall hypothesize that for Ophelia $u_M < r_P$ and $u_P < r_M$. Although there may appear to be an apples-and-oranges character to these assessments, it is possible that she has fairly definite ideas about the degrees of moral rightness of the two courses of action with respect to Kant's theory. She may be relatively sure that, despite the problematic nature of the moral decisions that physicians must make, enough of those decisions are unproblematic to make the degree of moral rightness of the "rural physician" course of action according to the Kantian perspective exceed the degree of moral rightness of the "philosophy professor" course of action according to the utilitarian perspective. Similarly, because of the relatively unproblematic nature of the decisions that she would make as a philosophy professor according to Kant's theory, Ophelia may be fairly confident that the degree of moral rightness of the "philosophy professor" course of action according to Kant's theory would be the largest of the four quantities.

The preceding inequalities may serve to narrow the ranges of specific values to be assigned to p, u_M, u_P, r_M, and r_P. Since for Ophelia $p < 1 - p$, she may infer that $p < .5$. However, let us assume that she is nowhere near being certain that Kant's theory is the true moral theory. She believes that there is a significant possibility that her acceptance of Kant's theory is mistaken and that the act utilitarian theory is the true moral theory. This means that p is closer to .5 than it is to 0. Let us suppose that Ophelia estimates that $p = .4$.

Degrees of moral rightness are somewhat more obscure. However, it is reasonable to hypothesize that by eliminating from further consideration all options except the "rural physician" and "philosophy professor" options, Ophelia has already culled courses of action that would have low degrees of moral rightness according to the two moral theories. For example, she may have excluded the "lawyer" alternative on those grounds. Thus if Ophelia considered all of her options and not just the two that she is *seriously* considering, some would be much worse than the worst that she might do by choosing either of the two. Therefore, she may be quite confident that the least of the four quantities u_M, u_P, r_M, and r_P is more than halfway up the degree-of-moral-rightness scale. Thus she might arrive at the following cardinal measurements of u_M, u_P, r_M, and r_P: $u_P = .6$, $r_M = .7$, $u_M = .8$, and $r_P = .9$. Plugging these values into the expressions for EMR(M) and EMR(P) yields EMR(M) = .74 and EMR(P) = .78. Since EMR(P) > EMR(M), pursuing a career as a philosophy professor would be the rational choice for Ophelia.

It can be argued that Ophelia would reach the same conclusion by consulting the two guidelines G1 and G2. If we assume that she has no reason for thinking that she would not complete either of the two courses of action, then G2 does not apply. However, G1, which directs Ophelia to minimize the frequency of occurrence of moral dilemmas, does apply. We have already determined that she would probably encounter more moral dilemmas by becoming a physician than by becoming a philosophy professor. Thus, according to G1, Ophelia should choose the "philosophy professor" course of action.

These results may not seem very satisfactory, since they are based on estimates of u_M, u_P, r_M, r_P, and p that are, admittedly, very rough. It is not difficult to find values of these quantities that preserve the preceding inequalities but cause EMR(M) to exceed EMR(P). For example, setting $u_P = .6$, $r_M = .75$, $u_M = .85$, $r_P = .9$, and $p = .4$ will cause this to happen. Some may doubt the accuracy or appropriateness of any specific cardinal measurements for such nebulous quantities. The alternative to cardinal measurements is ordinal measurements, represented in the preceding inequalities, and determining which of EMR(P) and EMR(M) has the larger average value over the set of quintuples $<p, u_M, u_P, r_M, r_P>$ that satisfy the preceding inequalities plus, say, $.4 \leq p \leq .5$. If we perform the mathematical analysis (of the kind that we performed in previous chapters), we find that the average value of EMR(P) − EMR(M) is .02.[11] Thus, again, the "philosophy professor" option is more likely to maximize the expected moral rightness of Ophelia's course of action than is the "rural physician" option. Therefore, the "philosophy professor" course of action would still be the prescribed choice.

Until now, we have concerned ourselves with how *individual* moral agents should act in selecting courses of action on the basis of moral considerations. However, sometimes it is possible for *collections* of individuals to act cooperatively to increase the degree of moral rightness of their respective courses of action. For example, cooperative action may be much more effective in preventing moral dilemmas than the independent actions of individuals. Therefore, let us next consider how individuals might act collectively to maximize the expected degree of moral rightness of their lifetime courses of action.

Ultimately I must decide what I shall do. However, what I *should* do may depend in part on what *we* should do. The locution "we should *x*" is ambiguous. It may mean that each of us should *x* as in the sentence "we should all vote in the election." Or it may mean that the end result of our actions collectively should be that *x* is done—as in the sentence "we should eliminate hunger from the face of the earth." Let us call these the *distributive* and the *collective* senses of "we should *x*." The essential difference is that the collective sense of "we should *x*" does not imply that *I* should *x*. In fact, *x* may very well not be within my power to do or bring about.

It is very difficult to say in general what logical connections there are between the collective sense of "we should *x*" and what specifically *I* should do. I shall not propose any solutions to this problem here. However, there is little doubt that what we collectively should do very often has much bearing on what I should do. Is this true if my goal for myself is to maximize the expected degree of moral rightness of my lifetime course of action? The answer is "Yes" if my acting co-operatively with others would enable us to increase the expected degrees of moral rightness of all of our lifetime courses of action. In the following discussion, I shall identify several ways in which cooperative action might secure this mutual advantage.

Consider the following illustration: A number of physicians in a small city work in virtual isolation from one another. Each has her own patients for whose medical care she is responsible. Penelope is one of these physicians. Sometimes Penelope receives phone calls from her patients at night, on weekends, and at other times when she is "off duty." On those occasions she must decide whether her patients' complaints are serious enough to warrant an emergency trip to the hospital or there is no great urgency and the patient may be advised to wait for a day or two and see the doctor during her normal office hours. Penelope is often torn between her concern for her patients and her desire for occasional respite from the rigors of her occupation. On most occasions, Penelope's medical judgment proves correct, but sometimes the complaining patient is more seriously ill than she discerns and her decision to delay treatment leads to a serious worsening of the patient's condition.

These sorts of dilemmas, let us suppose, afflict most of the physicians in this city. In order to forestall them, a number of the physicians agree to install a "doctor-on-call" arrangement so that any patient who seeks emergency medical attention at any time will receive it. In this way the physicians are able to enjoy their leisure time without worrying whether they are depriving any of their patients of urgently needed medical attention. This familiar example of cooperative action illustrates how groups of individuals can sometimes enter into collective arrangements to prevent moral dilemmas that otherwise would arise.

Another medical example: Suppose that a certain disease is moderately contagious and causes all who contract it to die a horrible, painful death. Because of this, people in the final painful stages of the disease often request that their deaths be hastened by the physician's active intervention. Physicians and families of those patients are thus placed in the awful position of having to decide whether to accede to those requests. Researchers have finally produced a vaccine that effectively protects people against infection. Unfortunately, the vaccine brings temporary but severe discomfort to those who receive it. Because of this discomfort and also because many people think (perhaps wishfully) that they will not contract the disease, many individuals do not volunteer to be vaccinated. However, unless a "critical mass" of the population is vaccinated, there will be an ever-worsening epidemic that will cause the painful deaths of many people. These dilemmas would be largely averted if vaccination against the disease were mandatory for everyone. Therefore, even if a mandatory vaccination program would be morally wrong because it would infringe excessively on individual liberty (and this is of course debatable), our moral standard for courses of action might prescribe such a program. It would prescribe the program if the "moral costs" of that infringement were offset by the "moral benefits" derived from preventing moral dilemmas. Thus the morally wrong action of mandating that everyone be vaccinated would be *morally* justified in light of the moral standard for courses of action.

One important way in which individuals can pool their resources to circumvent moral dilemmas is by developing technologies that allow them to avert decisions in which all of the options are morally problematic. However, it is often the opposite claim about technology that is made. Critics of technology point out that new or prospective technologies raise difficult moral questions and insinuate that this is a reason not to develop or introduce those technologies in the first place. Biological or medical technologies like genetic engineering or artificial organs often receive criticism of this sort.[12] At best, the critics' argument is incomplete, for they fail to explain precisely why difficult moral issues should be averted. The best explanation, I have argued, is that problematic moral decisions should generally be avoided in order to maximize the expected degrees of moral rightness of our lifetime courses of action. To accept this explanation, however, brings the following question into relief: If the fact that a technology would create difficult moral decisions is reason to *discourage* the development of that technology, then does it not follow that the fact that a technology would enable us to avert difficult moral decisions is reason to *encourage* its development? Although critics of technology have preoccupied themselves with the antecedent clause in this question, the consequent part appears to be no less interesting and to have no less practical importance.

Let us consider some of the ways in which the development of technologies enables us to avoid moral dilemmas. Some of the best examples of technologies that avert moral dilemmas are biomedical technologies. One is genetic screening, which prevents moral dilemmas associated with aborting fetuses with serious genetic diseases, like Tay-Sachs disease and Lesch-Nyhan syndrome. It does so by warning potential parents who are carriers of those diseases so that they may practice contraception. Another dilemma-averting technology is general anesthesia. Surgery before the advent of anesthesia is vividly depicted in the following nineteenth-century account of the repairing of a dislocated hip:

Big drops of perspiration, started by the excess of agony, bestrew the patient's forehead, sharp screams burst from him in peal after peal—all his struggles to free himself and escape the horrid torture are valueless, for he is in the powerful hands of men then as inexorable as death. . . . At last the agony becomes too great for human endurance, and with a wild, despairing yell, the sufferer relapses in unconsciousness."[13]

As Martin Pernick notes in his essay "The Calculus of Suffering in 19th-Century Surgery," "For many early-19th-century surgical students, learning to inflict pain . . . constituted the single hardest part of their professional training."[14] The development of general anesthesia saved physicians from having to decide whether the torture of surgery outweighed its benefits for their patients.

Other examples of moral-dilemma-averting biomedical technologies abound. Polio vaccination has eliminated the epidemics of polio that terrorized populations only a few decades ago. It has enabled physicians to bypass agonizing decisions about putting polio victims in iron lungs from which they might never escape.[15] And a whole class of technologies that prevent moral dilemmas are those that enable physicians to detect and treat serious illness in its early stages, before people's lives are seriously imperiled. These technologies include biopsies and radiography to detect cancer while it is still operable or otherwise treatable.

However, biomedical technologies are not the only technologies that forestall moral dilemmas. The invention of the safety lamp in the early 1800s dramatically lowered the incidence of mine explosions and thus prevented painful decisions about when to terminate efforts to rescue trapped miners.[16] The invention of the chronometer allowed ships to determine their longitude in the open ocean and thus prevented some of the shipwrecks that lost bearings would have caused in the past. It is likely that this prevented some "sinking lifeboat" dilemmas that would have occurred otherwise.[17] And the development of the air bag for automobiles is today preventing serious injuries in automobile accidents and thus also avoiding the ensuing dilemmas about terminating life support for the victims of those accidents.

Critics of technology will perhaps note that in all of these examples the moral dilemmas that the technologies prevent are themselves the products of technology. For example, the dilemmas averted by genetic screening would not occur in the first place if prenatal diagnosis of genetic disorders had not been developed. These critics may wish to argue that technology at best only fixes problems that it causes.[18] However, even if this were true, it would not mean that technology never produces a net gain, morally speaking. Other considerations may apply. A particular technology may, after all, produce great benefits for those who use it, which may make its development and use *morally* justifiable. Furthermore, even without technology, it may be impossible for us to avoid all moral dilemmas. We must remember that G1 is a guideline that in some situations we may have sufficient reason not to follow. Therefore, we should not jump too quickly to the conclusion that every preventable moral dilemma should be prevented. Even if we could prevent all moral dilemmas by abolishing all technologies, it is extremely doubtful that such a course of action would be morally optimal.

The preceding discussion shows how it is possible for a morally objectionable or dubious technology to be morally justified on the grounds that it enables moral agents to short-circuit recurrent moral dilemmas. This happens whenever averting those moral dilemmas results in courses of action that are "better," morally speaking, than courses of action that do not avert those dilemmas. Can we use this notion of a moral standard for courses of action to resolve current disputes about technology? Are some technologies that are now on the drawing board like the mandatory vaccination program mentioned earlier? In the next section, I shall argue that one such technology is antiaging technology, which biomedical research may deliver to us in the foreseeable future.

Antiaging Technologies

Among the most heartrending moral decisions that we ever have to make are decisions about medical or custodial care of an aging spouse or parent. Too often old age brings serious debilities, such as Alzheimer's disease or crippling arthritis. It also makes us increasingly vulnerable to such assaults as heart attacks, strokes, and cancer. Decisions about continuing heroic and costly medical intervention when the patient has little or no chance of returning to reasonably good health often present moral dilemmas of the most distressing sort.

Deciding whether to commit one's aging spouse or parent to a nursing home is another tragic choice that many of us have to face. Often the only alternatives to the nursing home option are (1) caring for the spouse or parent oneself and (2) hiring professional nurses or custodians to provide at-home care. However, even if the demands of one's job do not make the first alternative impossible, taking on such a task may quickly lead to physical or emotional exhaustion. And the second alternative is often prohibitively expensive. But living in a nursing home is rarely as desirable as living in one's own home or in that of a close relative. Spouses and parents who are placed in nursing homes often feel abandoned by and resentful of their families, whom they may perceive as selfish and ungrateful. And nursing homes are often dismal environments with high concentrations of people with serious physical or mental impairments.

These are the sad facts of life for many of us today. In the industrialized world, where hunger and poverty have been subdued to a considerable degree, the tribulations associated with growing old are a major source of people's unhappiness and anxiety. And as populations age the problems will only get worse. Demographers predict that early in the twenty-first century, when the vanguard of the first–World War II generation reaches retirement age, the demand for medical and economic resources will greatly increase at a time when the ratio of the labor force size to the over-65 population will be small by historical comparison.[19] These changes threaten to cause considerable social, political, and economic upheaval.

The "moral costs" of allowing these trends to continue will be enormous. The number of decisions that we shall have to make about who will receive expensive long-term medical or custodial care will increase dramatically. Many of these will be agonizing decisions that will test our emotional capacities. One solution that has been suggested is limiting access to highly costly biomedical technologies, such as dialysis and organ transplantation, on the basis of age. Some countries have already enacted such policies.[20] However, even if imposing age restrictions on certain kinds of medical procedures becomes the accepted norm, this will not resolve the *moral* dilemmas associated with such practices. We shall continue to have serious moral misgivings, for example, about denying a heart transplant to a 66-year-old retiree who has just begun to enjoy the retirement that she has long worked for and looked forward to.

We can reasonably expect therefore that, without some radical departure from the path we are on, moral dilemmas associated with medical care for the aged will occur with increasing frequency in the coming decades. Is there a way in which technology might allow us to avert some of these awful decisions? Quite possibly there is. Although scientists are not yet sure what causes us to age, evidence indicates that the maximum life span of some species, including some mammals, can be significantly lengthened by relatively simple methods.[21] With the acceleration of progress that has occurred in the biological sciences in recent years, there is a reasonable chance that within the next two or three decades or, with a concerted, adequately financed research effort, perhaps even sooner, scientists will understand the aging process well enough to design an effective life-span-extending technology for human beings.[22]

A number of objections have been raised to any attempt to interfere with the human aging process. Some critics have noted the effects on overpopulation and the economic and social disruptions that an effective antiaging technology would cause. Others have claimed that intellectual and cultural stagnation would result from the strict limits that would have to be placed on reproduction if an antiaging technology were widely used.[23] Another objection alleges that a research program to develop an effective antiaging technology would unjustly divert resources from more important and urgent biomedical needs.[24] Yet another criticism is based on the notion of a "natural death."[25] And no doubt many people would oppose antiaging technology on the grounds that its development would be an act of hubris and an illicit violation of our nature as mortal beings.

Although I do not find any of these arguments convincing, I grant that the issue of the moral rightness of developing antiaging technologies is problematic and that its correct resolution is uncertain. However, if what I have said about courses of action is correct, the critical issue is whether the moral standard for courses of action supports developing such a technology. To decide, we must determine whether courses of action that include developing life-span-extending technologies would be "better," morally speaking, than courses of action that do not include developing those technologies.

We must bear in mind that an effective life-span-extending technology would spare us many agonizing life-and-death decisions about medical and nursing care for the aged. It would do so by significantly increasing the human life span, thus greatly increasing people's opportunities for reaching their life goals.[26] Once an individual has reached her main goals, it may be easier for her and for others to accept her death. We shall still have to make life-and-death decisions, but, generally speaking, they will less often be the tragic choices that our brief life span forces on us in the current era.[27]

Of course, we can foresee only very few of the details of the lifetime courses of action that we shall set into motion by our collective decision to develop or not develop an antiaging technology. Consequently, we shall have to apply the moral standard for courses of action on the basis of our imprecise and indefinite perceptions of the available alternatives and our summary judgments about which ones are "best," morally speaking. However, we must consider the magnitude of the problems that our aging populations present now and will increasingly present in the future, as well as the risks that we shall make bad decisions when we decide matters of life and death for the aged. I believe that if we do so, we shall conclude that seeking to avert or minimize those dilemmas is likely to be the "better" course of action. The long-term "moral benefits" of reducing the number of those life-and-death decisions that we shall have to make will outweigh any short-term moral improprieties.

Utopian Implications

We have seen how collective action directed toward the prevention of moral dilemmas can be the best strategy for morally optimizing *individuals'* lifetime courses of action. We have also seen how the individual action components of those courses of action need not always possess the maximum degree of expected moral rightness *as individual actions*. This means that from the customary perspective that considers moral rightness to come in only two sizes (viz., right and wrong), it is possible for an individual action component of a morally optimal course of action to be morally wrong. In this way, moral agents can sometimes be morally justified in acting in ways that are morally wrong. In those instances, not only are these agents morally justified in acting wrongly, but their actions are also justified *all things considered*. This is true because the moral standard for courses of action is, in the final analysis, the standard that we should (rationally) follow.

What would happen if individuals cooperated to implement a policy of minimizing the frequency with which moral dilemmas and morally problematic situations occur? Conceivably a world would evolve in which those dilemmas and situations would no longer arise at all. What would such a world be like? Problematic moral issues concern, among other things, various kinds of conflicts. They include conflicts among the interests of different individuals and, in particular, conflicts between the interests of the moral agent herself and those of others; conflicts among specific moral duties such as respecting the autonomy of others and preventing harm; conflicts among various moral rights such as the right to free expression and the right not to be slandered; as well as conflicts among those interests, duties, and rights. Hence, a world in which those issues no longer arise would be a world in which people's interests are always in harmony and in which they are never forced to choose which moral duties or rights to violate. It would also be a world in which pursuing their interests never required them to violate their moral duties or anyone's moral rights.

It seems apt to characterize such a world as utopian. And to the extent to which our actions, when they accord with our moral standard for courses of action, should be aimed at realizing that world, we are enjoined by what we might call a utopian imperative. This depiction of utopia resolves what may appear to be a kind of dissonance between morality and utopian ideals. The dissonance is that utopia, conceived as a world whose inhabitants live in complete harmony, seems incompatible with what we know about human beings and human nature. From that perspective, realizing a utopian world would require nothing less than transforming human nature—a project that both inherently and because of the measures that would be necessary in order to achieve it would be morally unjustifiable. Since morally unjustifiable measures are always unjustified *all things considered*, the argument goes, utopia must remain forever an unattainable ideal—one that is *essentially* unreal and that therefore must not be taken too seriously as a model for political or social reform.

One problem with this argument is that it implies the implausible proposition that even if the world of human beings could be transformed into a utopian world by someone's committing just one morally wrong act, it would still be wrong, *all things considered*, to commit that act. If we accept the ordinary standard of moral rightness as the ultimate authority for moral decisions, then the only way to avoid the conclusion that a utopia generated by a single morally wrong act would be morally illegitimate is to deny that such an act could conceivably bring utopia into existence. Most act utilitarians would perhaps not find it difficult to deny this, since they would argue that any act that would realize utopia would necessarily maximize utility. And some proponents of other moral theories, Robert Nozick for example, argue that utopia can be brought about entirely by morally acceptable means.[28]

However, even if we grant that a particular moral theory sanctions the means that would be necessary to realize a utopian world, to bridge the gap between the real world and utopia in this way would require us to subscribe to that theory *without any reservation*. If we had doubts about it, it would behoove us to consider rival theories and to ask whether the *individual* action(s) that would get us to utopia would have maximal expected moral rightness. I suspect that for many moral agents the answer would be "No." But if we recognize a distinction between the ordinary moral standard of right and wrong for individual actions and a moral standard for courses of action that directs us, both individually and collectively, to maximize the expected degree of moral rightness of our lifetime courses of action, then it is very easy to overcome the sort of moral barrier to utopia just described. We need only recall that the moral standard for courses of action always sanctions certain *individual* actions, as initial actions in morally optimal courses of action, which need not themselves be morally optimal (i.e., maximize expected moral rightness). Thus a course of action that leads to the realization of a utopian world could be the "best" available course of action, morally speaking, even though it includes individual actions that, with respect to the ordinary moral standard for individual actions, are morally deficient to some degree. If I am correct in claiming that, in the final analysis, we should (rationally) make our action choices on the basis of the moral standard for courses of action, then we are morally justified, in the most important sense of "morally justified," in directing our actions toward the creation of a utopian world.

This argument works, however, only if we accept the preceding characterization of utopia as a world in which morally problematic situations have been eliminated. This does not mean, of course, that in utopia all moral questions have been conclusively answered or that no one has any doubt about which moral theory is *the* true theory. It means only that for every moral decision that any moral agent has to make there is at least one alternative such that the agent is certain that its degree of moral rightness is maximal and that the intended lifetime course of action of which it is a part is also morally optimal.

The suggestion that utopia be conceived as containing no unavoidable moral conflict is, to the best of my knowledge, novel.[29] It is not included in, or at least is not emphasized in, other utopian philosophies. One consequence of this conception is that unavoidable conflicts among the interests of the inhabitants of utopia are eliminated. This is the way in which social harmony would be secured. Social harmony is, of course, a common theme in utopian writings. Thus the utopian vision that I propose is continuous in at least one significant respect with other utopias. The important difference is that the utopia that I envision comes with its own built-in moral justification in the following respect: If the eventual outcome of individuals' implementing morally optimal courses of action would be the creation of a world in which unavoidable moral conflict has been eliminated, then the creation of that world is morally justified. This is, of course, a very big "if." And while I shall not attempt here to present a conclusive argument for its truth, we already have evidence for it in the form of G1, which says that, in general, we morally optimize our courses of action by minimizing the number of moral dilemmas and other morally problematic situations that we have to confront. It is at least plausible that by creating a world in which moral dilemmas and morally problematic situations do not arise at all, we would minimize their occurrence in the long run.

It is important to note, however, that the end of eliminating moral dilemmas and morally problematic situations would not justify all effective means to that end. For example, a proposal to create a world without moral dilemmas by eliminating enough of the world's people so that the interests of the survivors would all be compatible would obviously not satisfy the terms of our moral standard for courses of action. In this instance, the liabilities of G1 as a strategy for morally optimizing our courses of action are evident. However, the previous discussion does open the door, morally speaking, to some measures for eliminating or minimizing moral dilemmas that, considered as individual actions, are morally dubious. For example, one proposal with utopian intentions would impose state control on human reproduction in order both to combat overpopulation and to improve the intellectual, physical, and perhaps psychological capacities of human offspring. A minimally coercive eugenics program, relying mainly on economic incentives to encourage individuals to reproduce only via in vitro fertilization so that the quality of the resulting embryos could be assured, might mitigate somewhat the moral objections that are usually raised against eugenics. We must, of course, distinguish the goals of eugenics from the means by which some might try to attain them, such as those that the Nazis employed in the Third Reich. However, even with the most benevolent eugenics program, the moral objections to eugenics would not disappear entirely, and probably very few people would regard the *individual* actions of those who carried out such a program as morally justified.

Nevertheless, if we became convinced that a minimally coercive eugenics program would accomplish its intended mission, then it might be possible to defend its implementation as part of a morally optimal course of action. This means that it is not enough for critics to dismiss eugenics proposals by raising the usual moral criticisms that eugenics violates human dignity or individual liberty. Even if those criticisms are successful in demonstrating the *inherent* moral deficiencies of eugenics, the crucial question that, in the final analysis, should (rationally) determine our action choices is whether the course of action that they, in part, would constitute would be morally optimal. If I am right about courses of action and the cardinal importance of the moral standard that should govern their selection, then ending our moral discussion and deliberation at the stage at which one makes the usual moral judgments about individual actions is premature and very possibly reaches the wrong decision.

The line of argument that I have just sketched might be applied to other "brave new world" projects like genetic engineering and behavior control/modification. My purpose here is not to argue that those projects would in fact be (rationally) justified. Rather, it is to contend that because the pertinent moral issues have not been explored in light of an appropriate moral standard for courses of action, previous discussion of those issues is incomplete and inadequate. Serious proposals for radical changes in human nature and in the human condition, such as a greatly extended human life span and greatly improved intellectual and physical capacities, are usually dismissed out of hand both by "common sense" and by "mainstream" moral philosophy. By paying attention to the utopian implications of our moral standard for courses of action, we can give those proposals their due consideration and overcome some of the superficiality of the current discussion of the moral issues that they raise.

Finally, it should be noted that our utopian vision lends itself to a political philosophy that is unique in several significant respects. Instead of prescribing how the conflicting interests of individuals are to be resolved in a just manner, our theory, which is based on cooperative action toward the minimization or, ideally, the elimination of morally problematic situations, directs us collectively to pursue the eradication of situations in which those interests are not aligned. Instead of prescribing a "minimal state" that could have arisen from an original position by measures that violate none of the moral rights of those who form it, our theory accepts temporarily the violation of rights in order to create a world in which no one has any reason or incentive to violate anyone's rights. In the utopian world that we envision, government would be needed at most to coordinate individuals' actions so that individuals can determine how to serve the interests of others while at the same time serving their own interests. There would be no incentive for anyone to refuse such coordination, since it would not be in anyone's interest to do so and there would be no moral purpose served by doing so. Ideally, coordination would simply be a matter of suggesting to individuals how they can cooperatively morally optimize their courses of action. In such a world, force and coercion would be unnecessary.

Consider the decision problem represented in the three-dimensional Table 8.4. The table is for an imaginary world (society, game) whose inhabitants are Rikki, Sylvia, and Tess. Each agent has three course-of-action alternatives labeled x, y, and z. The labels with the subscript 1 indicate Rikki's alternatives, those with subscript 2 refer to Sylvia's alternatives, and those with subscript 3 indicate Tess's alternatives. The rows in each part of the table correspond to Rikki's alternatives, the columns in each part correspond to Sylvia's alternatives, and the three separate parts of the table represent Tess's three alternatives.

The three numbers in each box of the table are the "payoffs" for Rikki, Sylvia, and Tess, respectively. Each "payoff" is a measure of the degree of moral rightness

Table 8.4   Collective Moral Decision-making

$Tess(x_3)$:

		Sylvia		
		x_2	y_2	z_2
Rikki	x_1	$-7,12,3$	$1,0,-8$	$3,-5,-6$
	y_1	$-9,12,4$	$0,10,-5$	$8,12,10^*$
	z_1	$8,12,6$	$8,-1,-1$	$8,-6,-3$

$Tess(y_3)$:

		Sylvia		
		x_2	y_2	z_2
Rikki	x_1	$7,12,7$	$8,12,10^*$	$-3,0,6$
	y_1	$5,12,3$	$-5,4,5$	$0,-1,9$
	z_1	$8,12,-4$	$8,-6,-5$	$8,11,7$

$Tess(z_3)$:

		Sylvia		
		x_2	y_2	z_2
Rikki	x_1	$3,12,-2$	$-7,10,-1$	$7,12,10$
	y_1	$0,12,0$	$8,12,10^*$	$6,-1,-7$
	z_1	$8,12,-9$	$8,-11,-3$	$8,-10,1$

of the agent's course of action according to some criterion that the agents regard as one of the competing moral criteria. For example, the numbers in each box of the table might represent respectively the utilities of the agents' corresponding course-of-action choices, where it is assumed that the maximization of personal utility is one of the moral criteria that the agents regard as plausible. Let us assume that this is the case. Since the utility that each agent receives depends not only on which course of action the agent chooses but also on the other agents' courses of action, the agents must be circumspect in making their choices.

It is easy to see that the $(8,12,10)$ outcome is the optimal outcome for all three agents, but there are a variety of ways in which it might be obtained. It can be obtained by Rikki, Sylvia, and Tess choosing x_1, y_2, and y_3, respectively. But it can also be obtained by their choosing y_1, y_2, and z_3 or y_1, z_2, and x_3. Furthermore, Rikki can maximize her utility by choosing z_1, whatever the other two agents choose to do. The same is true of Sylvia if she chooses x_2. However, by doing so they would deprive Tess of the opportunity to maximize her utility. Since Rikki and Sylvia would also maximize their utilities by coordinating their action choices with Tess in order to achieve the optimal outcome, they have no incentive (with respect to utility maximization) not to do so. In simple cases, like the one we are examining here, this coordination might be accomplished by direct communication and cooperation among the agents. In more complicated cases, however, that involve many agents who have no effective ways of communicating and interacting with one another, coordination by designated coordinators may be needed.

In our example, we have considered only one criterion of moral rightness—utility maximization. In the sort of utopia that I have in mind, in which several such criteria operate, it would always be possible for every individual to conform to all criteria in choosing her actions. Coordination of actions among the inhabitants of that world would be required not only to identify action choices for each moral agent that would allow everyone to maximize utility but also to determine which individual actions would enable everyone to attain maximal moral rightness with respect to all competing moral criteria. That such alternatives would always be available to moral agents is the condition that would make the world utopian.

An interesting question arises here. I have already mentioned that before embarking on the construction of a world in which moral problems can always be circumvented, we must first convince ourselves that in that way we would most likely morally optimize our lifetime courses of action. But here we run into an ambiguity. In asking whether we would morally optimize our courses of action by acting in a certain way, we may be asking either of two quite different things. We may be asking whether *each of us individually* would morally optimize her courses of action by her acting in that way. Or we may be asking whether the composite of our courses of action would be morally optimal if *we collectively or cooperatively* acted to produce a certain result, even though some of us individually might fail to optimize our courses of action. It is conceivable that the "best" way, morally speaking, for *us* to bring about a utopian world would require me to settle for a lifetime course of action that was less than morally optimal. It might require me, for example, to do some of the "dirty work" connected with altering human nature and human behavior that must be done if a utopian world is to eventuate. May I (rationally) sacrifice some of the moral rightness of my own course of action for the greater moral rightness of the composite of everyone's courses of action? Or must I morally optimize my own lifetime course of action regardless of the moral effects on other lifetime courses of action?

I have no answers to offer to these questions. I lean toward the view that each of us individually should (rationally) morally optimize her lifetime course of action. However, I know of no convincing argument for this conclusion. Therefore, I shall simply leave these issues for the reader to ponder. I also have no argument either for or against the view that we would morally optimize our lifetime courses of action by directing our actions toward the realization of the sort of utopian world that I have described in this chapter. My intuition is that the view is correct—that is, by attempting to bring such a utopia into existence we would morally optimize our courses of action. However, I suspect that a successful argument for either side of the issue would be complicated, and I shall not embark upon the construction of such an argument here. It is possible that we shall not be able to adduce enough information to settle the issue in some conclusive or convincing way and that therefore we have no choice but to follow our hunches about how to proceed in morally optimizing our lifetime courses of action.

Nine

Retrospective

I hope that at this point it is clear to the reader how the main themes of this book relate to one another. I began in chapter 1 by posing the problem of decision-making under moral uncertainty and claiming that the problem is a prevalent, if not ubiquitous, one for moral agents. I then argued in chapter 2 that insofar as moral considerations preempt nonmoral considerations in our action choices, we should (rationally) follow PR2 and choose actions that have maximum probability of being morally right. In situations in which individuals lack the information needed to apply PR2 directly, the proper strategy is to maximize the probability that one's actions conform to PR2. This latter injunction is PR3.

In chapter 3, we saw in considerable detail how both PR2 and PR3 can be applied to women's decisions whether to have abortions. I then argued in chapter 4 that, from some theoretical perspectives, it is reasonable to think of moral rightness as a many-valued rather than a two-valued (right or wrong) quantity. This meant that my initial principle for decision-making under moral uncertainty, PR2, is really a special case of the more general principle, PR4, which advises us to maximize the expected degrees of moral rightness of our actions. We saw how using PR4 instead of PR2 would in some instances make a difference in which actions we should (rationally) choose, and we reconsidered women's abortion decisions in light of that result. We also found it necessary to formulate another principle, PR5, for use in situations in which decision-makers do not have the information needed in order to apply PR4 directly. In those situations, PR5 advises us to maximize the probabilities that our actions accord with PR4.

Chapter 5 anticipated and forestalled a criticism of PR2–PR5 and, particularly, of their common injunction to optimize with respect to moral rightness. That criticism is closely related to supererogationism, which distinguishes actions that are morally "sufficient" from those that are morally supreme. I argued that supererogationism itself is fundamentally flawed and therefore lends no support to a satisficing conception of rationality. I also showed how for perhaps typical moral uncertainties, abandoning supererogationism does not commit us to an extreme altruism.

Although PR2–PR5 do not provide the means of resolving agents' moral uncertainties, we found that they may in some instances enable the parties in moral disputes to reach agreement on a particular action as *rational* to choose. As we saw for the medical ethics case we examined in chapter 6, by identifying pertinent uncertainties and adopting a concept of degrees of moral rightness it may sometimes be possible to reach agreement about what should be done even though the moral issues pertinent to the decision remain unresolved. And we found in chapter 7 that the same thing may be possible for some nonmoral normative disputes, such as those among the Supreme Court justices that were evident in the *Roe v. Wade* case.

In chapter 8, I argued that we can sometimes be justified, all things considered, in choosing individual actions that, although they conform to the courses-of-action principle, are not morally optimal as individual actions. I offered two guidelines for implementing the courses-of-action standard and speculated that one way in which we might cooperate to minimize the frequency with which moral dilemmas and problematic moral decisions arise would be to create a utopian world in which those situations never occur. I suggested also that, from this perspective, projects to which there are strong moral objections, like eugenics and genetic engineering, may nonetheless be morally justified as means to utopian ends.

If my arguments are sound, they expose major deficiencies in prevailing philosophical accounts of moral deliberation and decision-making. In particular, they invalidate what I have called the my-favorite-theory approach, which many ethicists assume in offering and defending their solutions to various problems of moral decision-making. I have tried to show how correcting those deficiencies will lead to substantial changes in our views about how, in the final analysis, we individually should conduct our lives and what goals we collectively should set for ourselves. Perhaps this book will dispose some to embark on courses of action that will advance us toward those goals.

Appendix: Decisions with Uncertain Probabilities

The decision theory for decisions with uncertain probabilities (sometimes referred to as decisions with *unreliable* probabilities) used in this book is, to the best of my knowledge, novel. Therefore, an explanation why this particular theory was chosen over other theories is in order.

Among theories that take uncertain probabilities into account are those that require as part of the deliberation process the identification of an a priori Bayesian probability distribution. These include the theories of J. L. Hodges Jr. and E. L. Lehman and of Daniel Ellsberg.[1] This requirement appears not to be reasonable for decisions with unknown *objective* probabilities (such as that of Table 3.3) for which the available information does not select a particular probability distribution. And if the probabilities are *subjective*, it is unclear how the problem of uncertain probabilities comes up at all if a single Bayesian distribution is discernible. For it would appear that, on the subjectivity hypothesis, such a distribution would *necessarily* be the "true" distribution. Of course, subjective probability assessments are notoriously unstable, and one might argue that a range of values is needed because decision-makers would be unsure which of the hypothetical gambles they used in order to measure their subjective probabilities they would actually accept and which they would decline. But then it is unclear why one should accord a particular Bayesian distribution any special significance. Should the decision-maker regard it as the most likely value of the uncertain probability? If so, it is doubtful that decision-makers would always or even usually be able to settle on a single most likely value.

Another kind of theory for decisions with uncertain probabilities makes use of parameters that represent decision-makers' degrees of optimism and pessimism about the outcomes of their decisions. One such theory is that of Leonid Hurwicz,[2] who advocates calculating an "a-index," $a \cdot m_x + (1-p) \cdot M_x$, for each alternative x where m_x and M_x are the minimum and maximum expected utilities of x over the range of admissible probability distributions. The alternative(s) with the maximum a-index are identified, and the decision-maker is permitted to choose any of them. The parameter a may change from one decision to another. Its value represents the decision-maker's *feelings* of optimism/pessimism about the outcome. One criticism of this sort of approach is that judgments about rational choice should not depend on decision-makers' *moods*. There is also the problem of measuring the parameter a for each decision. The methods that have been proposed assume that decision-makers can discern precise points of indifference for certain hypothetical choices among actions. This seems no more plausible than the claim that decision-makers can make the precise discriminations involved in measuring Bayesian subjective probabilities. And there are some counterintuitive implications of the Hurwicz criterion for decisions where the decision-maker is completely ignorant of the magnitudes of the probabilities.[3] These would apply to the "partial ignorance" case as well.[4]

Two theories have more recently been proposed by Isaac Levi[5] and by Peter Gärdenfors and Nils-Eric Sahlin.[6] Levi's theory sanctions actions that have a property he calls "S-admissibility." In order to be S-admissible, an alternative must first maximize expected utility for some set of "permissible" probability distributions. Alternatives that meet this requirement are then compared with respect to their "security levels" (which may be thought of as "worst cases" in some respect), and the decision-maker is advised to choose some alternative that has a maximum such level. Levi distinguishes "chance" probabilities ("objective statistical" probabilities) from "credal" probabilities (subjective probabilities). Beliefs about the former have truth value, but beliefs about the latter do not, according to Levi. For this reason he views it as a mistake to think of the latter as having possible (i.e., possibly true) values and entertain second-order probabilities with respect to those values. Ranges of "permissible" values of credal probabilities, however, are acceptable as long as those values represent a decision-maker's "state of suspense between two or more credal probability distributions."[7] Rather than being uncertain which probability distribution is the *true* distribution, the agent is simply *uncommitted* among the members of a set of distributions for purposes of calculating expected utilities. The MEU standard is sufficiently heeded, Levi believes, as long as the action chosen maximizes expected utility for at least one permissible probability distribution.

For Levi, there is no single way of determining "security levels" for the decision alternatives, which "is a matter of the agent's goals, values, moral commitments, professional obligations and the like."[8] Gärdenfors and Sahlin charge that this relativism in Levi's theory deprives it of any predictive power or normative content.[9] And if we bar all restrictions on ways of determining the security levels of one's alternatives, their criticism seems cogent. A natural way of conceiving security levels is to take the security level of each alternative as its minimum possible payoff over the possible states. If we do so, then for the kinds of decisions with which we are concerned Levi's theory advises us to choose some alternative that (1) maximizes the expected payoff for some "permissible" probability distribution and (2) maximizes the minimum payoff among the alternatives that satisfy (1).

Gärdenfors and Sahlin show that Levi's theory fails to satisfy an "independence of irrelevant alternatives" condition, which is analogous to the social choice theory condition of the same name.[10] Moreover, for some of the decisions under moral uncertainty discussed in this book, Levi's theory is much too ecumenical. For those decisions, each alternative would maximize the expected (moral) payoff for some set of "permissible" probabilities, so requirement (1) would eliminate none of the alternatives. Unfortunately, neither would requirement (2), since the minimum (moral) payoff for almost every alternative is the same—0. Therefore, if we believe that some alternatives are (rationally) better than others, Levi's theory will not help us discern them. Perhaps a different way of figuring security levels would overcome this criticism.[11]

The theory of Gärdenfors and Sahlin advises us first to identify a set of probability measures with "a 'satisfactory' degree of epistemic reliability" and then to choose some alternative with the largest minimal expected utility over that set. They characterize their theory as a "maximize-the-minimum-expected-utility" (MMEU) theory. The set of probability measures to be used is determined on the basis of a "measure . . . of epistemic reliability." Each decision-maker selects a "*desired level . . . of epistemic reliability*" and includes all candidate probability distributions that reach or surpass that level. Since there are no rules that the decision-maker must follow in choosing this minimum level, there is an element of subjectivity in the deliberation process. However, since we must somehow distinguish the probability values that we take seriously from those that we do not, it is difficult to see how we can avoid subjective judgment altogether.

Gärdenfors and Sahlin do not require the set of probability distributions on which the decision is based to be convex. For this reason, their theory sometimes produces counterintuitive results: Consider Table A.1. Let the range of values of the probability p_1 that s_1 is the true "state of nature" be the set $\{.1\} \cup [.5, 1]$, and let p_2, the probability that s_2 is the true state, be $1 - p_1$ for each value of p_1. It turns out that the minimum expected utility of a_1 is 0, which occurs when $p_1 = 1.0$, and the minimum expected utility of a_2 is -0.1, which occurs when $p_1 = .1$. Therefore, Gärdenfors and Sahlin's theory prescribes a_1. However, for values of p_1 in the interval $[.5, 1]$, $EU(a_1)$ ranges from 0 to 5 while $EU(a_2)$ ranges from 7.5 to 17. Throughout the interval, $EU(a_2)$ exceeds $EU(a_1)$ by a margin of at least 2.5. Only when $p_1 = .1$ is $EU(a_1)$ larger than $EU(a_2)$, and then only by a margin of 0.1. This appears not to be the right result.

One might object to this argument on the grounds that it assumes that the interval of p_1 values $[.5, 1]$ should be accorded greater weight than the single point $p_1 = .1$. And we may not assume this unless we have reason to accept a principle of indifference (principle of insufficient reason) that regards each real number in the range of p_1 values as equally likely to be the "true" value of p_1. Moreover, in the case of subjective probabilities, this would involve the dubious hypothesis (which Gärdenfors and Sahlin, as well as Levi, reject) that statements

Table A.1   Decision with Nonconvex Set of Probability Distributions

	s_1	s_2
a_1	0	10
a_2	17	−2

about the magnitudes of subjective probabilities can be true or false. However, it is not at all clear that the MMEU criterion avoids such a hypothesis, since the motivation for its use seems to be the idea that we should (rationally) avoid the "worst case" consequences that would occur if pertinent subjective probabilities were to have certain *true* values. For the MMEU criterion, the "worst case" result is that one's action will have an avoidably small expected utility. Perhaps there is some other motivation behind the MMEU criterion, but it is not obvious what it might be. Proponents of that criterion would seem to bear the burden of proof.

The point just made about a principle of indifference is an important one for the topic of decisions with uncertain probabilities. It is important because PR3 and its later refinement PR5 advise us to choose some alternative with the maximum average expected (moral) payoff over the set of probability values. This suggests that we should regard all of those values as equally likely to be the *true* values of the probabilities—a conclusion that a principle of indifference would support. More precisely, each one of an infinite number of equally likely probability values would have 0 probability of being *the true* value. Therefore, if carefully formulated, a principle of indifference for an (uncountably) infinite set of possible values would assign probabilities to intervals of real-number values in proportion to the lengths of the intervals. For example, if the range of possible values included the intervals [0, .4] and [.5, .7], the probability that the *true* value is contained in the former would be twice the probability that it is contained in the latter. This means that the second-order probability distribution is a uniform distribution over the interval(s) of possible values.[12] Let us interpret our principle of indifference in this way.

For a variety of reasons, principles of indifference have been rejected by many decision theorists and philosophers of science (such as Levi). One of the difficulties they present is that in cases in which evidence accumulates over time it is extremely difficult to use a principle of indifference to assign a priori probabilities without violating Bayesian conditionalization of posterior probabilities.[13] Another difficulty is that for many decisions there are often several apparently reasonable ways of partitioning the pertinent "states of the world," and the assignments of probability values via the principle of indifference depend on one's choice of partition. Neither of these problems arises for PR3, however. No posterior probabilities are being calculated, and the only natural partition of the "states of nature" is that dictated by the moral considerations that the individual decision-maker recognizes as relevant.[14]

There is, however, a generic objection to principles of indifference that does apply to the uses that I make of them in this book. Suppose that we know about a certain quantity x only that it is contained in the interval [0, 1]. The principle of indifference says that we should assume a uniform probability distribution for x over that interval. But then we also know that the range of x^2 is the same interval. And if we have no information about x^2 except its interval of possible values, we may apply the principle of indifference and infer a uniform probability distribution for it as well. However, a uniform distribution for x^2 is inconsistent with a uniform distribution for x. Therefore, the principle of indifference leads to an inconsistency.

Some regard this argument as a conclusive refutation of all principles of indifference that are intended to apply to quantities whose possible values vary continuously over intervals of real numbers. If it is sound, then it certainly casts doubt on PR3 and PR5. However, the argument is unsound. The mistake is to suppose that we can have no better reason to assume a uniform distribution for x over the interval $[0, 1]$ than to assume such a distribution over that interval for x^2, x^3, or any other function of x whose possible values we also know to range over that interval. Of course, if we had no information about x^2 other than its range of possible values, the principle of indifference would prescribe a uniform distribution for it. In this respect, what is true about x^2 is also true about x. However, our judgments about the probability distribution for x^2 in $[0,1]$ would normally be derived from our initial judgment about the probability distribution for x, which, without more information than we are given, we reasonably assume to be uniform.

Of course, we may consider the questions in the reverse order. That is, we may first consider a number y about which we know only that it is contained in a certain interval and then consider what sort of probability distribution to assign to the square root of y. In that case, we would assume a uniform distribution for y and then derive a nonuniform distribution for its square root. It seems that because of symmetry considerations we should assign the same distribution to the square root of y that we assigned to x in the previous instance. But this reasoning ignores the differences between the epistemic conditions under which the assignments occur. In the case of x and x^2, we assign the nonuniform distribution to x^2 *after having already assigned a uniform distribution to x*. In the case of y and the square root of y, we assign the nonuniform distribution to the square root of y *after having already assigned a uniform distribution to* y. For this reason, the cases are not analogous.

I contend that the order of assignment is important for the (second-order) probability distributions we assign to the various "component probabilities" that we encounter in moral decision-making. We naturally entertain possible values of those probabilities rather than of their squares, square roots, and so forth. If for some strange reason we were first to consider the latter in a particular instance, it is highly likely that we would insist on first assigning a (second-order) distribution to the unknown probabilities and then deriving the distribution for the quantity in question. It is puzzling why this is true. Perhaps the explanation has something to do with natural kinds. However, for practical purposes, we need not explain why it is true in order to recognize that it is true.

We may note that to accept the generic argument against principles of indifference would disqualify its application to the decision represented by Table 3.5, repeated here as Table A.2. According to that argument, we have no better reason

Table A.2   Reproduction of Table 3.5

	white ball from urn A (p_1)		black ball from urn A ($1 - p_1$)
	red ball from urn B (p_2)	blue ball from urn B ($1 - p_2$)	
gamble X	0	$1,000	$1,000
gamble Y	$1,000	0	0

to assign a uniform probability distribution to the possible percentages of white balls in urn A than to assign a uniform distribution to the squares or cubes of those percentages. This would mean that our analysis of that decision in chapter 3 and our recommendation that the decision-maker choose gamble X are faulty. The alternative, maximin approaches advocated by Levi and by Gärdenfors and Sahlin would counsel indifference between the two gambles. But such advice seems unreasonably cautious and appears not to make the best use of the available information. Assuming a uniform probability distribution over the possible percentages of white balls in urn A seems a more reasonable reaction to that information.

Perhaps the decision criterion to which mine is most similar is M. K. Starr's "Domain Criterion."[15] It prescribes an alternative A if the size of the region in the probability vector space $<p_1, \ldots, p_n>$ in which A's expected utility exceeds (or is not exceeded by) the expected utility of any other alternative is greater than the sizes of the corresponding regions of the other alternatives. This amounts to choosing alternatives that, based on available information, are most likely to maximize expected utility. In applying Starr's criterion, one generally assumes a uniform second-order distribution of the possible values of the first-order probabilities in the region determined by the constraints. The mathematical problem is to calculate, for each alternative, the size of the region in which its expected utility is maximal. One then compares the results to determine which alternative's region is largest. The main difference between Starr's criterion and PR5 is that in order to apply PR5 one calculates, for each alternative, its *average expected utility* over the region determined by the partial information about (first-order) probabilities and utilities. PR5 prescribes an alternative if its average expected utility is maximal. It can be shown that, in general, alternatives that are most likely to maximize expected utility do not necessarily have maximum average expected utility.

I believe that the decision theory represented by PR3 and its variants is the most satisfactory theory for decision-making under moral uncertainty. It avoids the shortcomings of rival theories, and the arguments against it, particularly those based on criticisms of the principle of indifference, are not successful. There are metaphysical puzzles about the notion of the *true* value of a subjective probability that may arise for the theory. However, I believe that similar puzzles arise for other theories as well. Perhaps decision-makers should be agnostics on this issue.

Notes

Chapter 1

1. I assume that I cannot do both y and z in the situation and, moreover, that it is not the case that I should, all things considered, perform each of two mutually exclusive alternatives. One who denies the latter claim must hold that there can be dilemmas in which one should, all things considered, do each of two or more mutually exclusive things. Since such a notion of what we should do, all things considered, would sometimes tell us to do the impossible, it is not particularly helpful to decision-makers. Therefore, I shall conceive "all things considered" so that there cannot be such situations. However, this says nothing about moral dilemmas of other types, which I shall discuss later on.

2. However, I should warn the reader that in later discussion I shall identify multiple moral standards for action choice/appraisal. Thus there will be a sense in which an action can be morally permissible, i.e., morally right, according to the ordinary moral standard of right and wrong, without being morally permissible according to a different moral standard, and conversely.

3. Peter Singer in his writings has advocated radically altruistic reforms in our (i.e., Americans' and members of other modern industrialized countries') views about our moral obligations *as individuals* to help relieve poverty and suffering in underdeveloped countries. A sizable philosophical literature on the subject has developed in recent years. See, for example, Peter Singer, "Famine, Affluence, and Morality," *Philosophy and Public Affairs* 1 (1971–1972), pp. 229–243, and *Practical Ethics* (Cambridge: Cambridge University Press, 1979), chap. 8. More recently, Shelly Kagan has defended

what he terms "extremist morality," which enjoins us to make "optimal use" of our time and resources and which, therefore, prescribes considerably greater altruism than ordinary, commonsense morality requires. See *The Limits of Morality* (Oxford: Clarendon Press, 1989). Those who employ a commonsense, nontheoretical approach to ethics, like Stephen Toulmin ("The Tyranny of Principles," *Hastings Center Report* 11 [December 1981], pp. 31–39), sometime seem oblivious to the controversial nature of their views about our obligations to the world-at-large. For example, Toulmin appears to see little need to defend his judgment that "in these transient encounters [with strangers], our moral obligations are limited and chiefly negative—for example, to avoid acting offensively or violently" (p. 35).

4. Alasdair MacIntyre, "Why Is the Search for the Foundations of Ethics So Frustrating?" *Hastings Center Report* 9 (August 1979), p. 18.

Several philosophers have commented on uncertainty in ethical theory and its significance for applied ethics: Michael Bayles in "Moral Theory and Application," *Social Theory and Practice* 10 (1984), pp. 97–120, has observed that "applied ethics cannot provide a clear-cut decision procedure that easily grinds out answers for all situations, no matter how hard or borderline they may be. . . . The exercise of moral judgment will always be necessary" (p. 115). Hugh La Follette in "Applied Philosophy Misapplied," in *The Applied Turn in Contemporary Philosophy*, ed. Michael Bradie, Thomas W. Attig, and Nicholas Rescher (Bowling Green, OH: Applied Philosophy Program, Bowling Green State University, 1983), pp. 88–96, echoes these sentiments concerning the importance of moral judgment, although neither he nor Bayles explains precisely how one determines whether one's faculty of moral judgment is working properly except by checking it against some accepted ethical theory or principle. Mike W. Martin in "Applied and General Ethics: Family Resemblances and Tensions," in *The Applied Turn in Contemporary Philosophy*, pp. 41–42, observes that applied ethicists "may find it permissible to work with several of the traditional ethical theories if they provide concrete insights or complementary frameworks for approaching concrete issues" (p. 42). However, he provides no details of the sort of reasoning that would be employed.

5. See Toulmin, "Tyranny," and Albert R. Jonsen and Stephen Toulmin, *The Abuse of Casuistry* (Berkeley: University of California Press, 1988). Toulmin concluded that in moral discourse, such as that which has engaged the members of the U.S. National Commission for the Protection of Human Subjects of Biomedical and Behavioral Research, moral principles "serve less as foundations, adding intellectual strength or force to particular moral opinions, than they do as corridors or curtain walls linking the moral perceptions of all reflective human beings with other, more general positions—theological, philosophical, ideological, or *Weltanschaulich*" ("Tyranny," p. 32).

6. Prominent philosophers who have expressed antitheory sentiments include Annette Baier, John McDowell, Stuart Hampshire, and Martha Nussbaum. Bernard Williams has strong reservations not only about the search for a universally true moral theory but also about moral theory itself as a philosophical enterprise. (See Bernard Williams, *Ethics and the Limits of Philosophy* [Cambridge, MA: Harvard University Press, 1985].) A useful anthology on this topic is Stanley G. Clarke and Evan Simpson, eds., *Anti-Theory in Ethics and Moral Conservatism* (Albany: State University of New York Press, 1989). For a defense of the protheory view, see Robert B. Louden, *Morality and Moral Theory* (New York: Oxford University Press, 1992).

7. This view is defended by Tom L. Beauchamp and James F. Childress, who in *Principles of Biomedical Ethics*, 3d ed. (New York: Oxford University Press, 1989), claim that some forms of rule utilitarianism and rule deontology "lead to virtually identical principles and rules and recommended actions" (p. 44). Thus it is unnecessary, for practical purposes, to determine which theory is the correct theory.

8. This was the principal conclusion in my doctoral dissertation "Moral Quandaries and Disagreements" (University of Rochester, 1977).

9. In chapter 8 of *Ethics and the Limits of Philosophy*, Bernard Williams contrasts

scientific inquiry with ethical inquiry in terms of the "coherent hope" that inquiry will lead to "convergence on an answer, where the best explanation of convergence involves the idea that the answer represents how things are" (p. 136). He argues that in the case of scientific inquiry such a "coherent hope" exists, while for ethical inquiry it does not. He infers that we cannot plausibly expect "reflective ethical thought" to converge on any "ethical reality" and that this fact discredits "the objectivist view of ethical life as . . . a pursuit of ethical truth" via "a process that substitutes knowledge for beliefs attained in unreflective practice" (p. 152). He sees a similar disanalogy between ethics and mathematics in that while "every non-contradictory piece of mathematics . . . not every noncontradictory structure of ethical reflection can be part of one such subject" (p. 152). However, if Williams is claiming that every noncontradictory mathematical statement is mathematically true, then he is simply mistaken, since it is well-known that some noncontradictory mathematical statements are neither provable nor disprovable (e.g., the generalized continuum hypothesis) and there seems to be no other way of determining their truth/falsity. If Williams had noticed this similarity between ethical inquiry and mathematical inquiry, then it might have occurred to him that the absence of any "coherent hope" that ethical inquiry will converge on "a determinate set of ethical conclusions" indicates not the nonexistence of ethical reality, but rather the impossibility of knowing everything we would like to know about it. Thus even if Williams's claims about the nonconvergence of ethical inquiry are true, ethical skepticism seems to be as plausible an explanation as the one he accepts.

10. The reader may note that according to my use of "rational," someone may conceivably act rationally in doing x without having specific reasons for doing x.

11. Derek Parfit, *Reasons and Persons* (Oxford: Oxford University Press, 1984), p. 129. Parfit seeks to discredit the "self-interest theory" as a correct account of what reason requires.

12. W. K. Frankena takes this position in *Ethics*, 2d ed. (Englewood Cliffs, NJ: Prentice-Hall, 1973). Susan Wolf, in "Moral Saints," *Journal of Philosophy* 79 (August 1982), pp. 419–439, reprinted in *The Virtues: Contemporary Essays on Moral Character*, ed. Robert B. Kruschwitz and Robert C. Roberts (Belmont, CA: Wadsworth, 1987), describes the moral point of view as "the point of view one takes up insofar as one takes the recognition of the fact that one is just one person among others equally real and deserving of the good things in life as a fact with practical consequences, a fact the recognition of which demands expression in one's actions and in the form of one's practical deliberations" (pp. 436–437).

13. In his book, *Human Morality* (New York: Oxford University Press, 1992), Samuel Scheffler defends the "moderate" view of morality according to which "although morality sometimes requires significant sacrifices of us, nevertheless the most demanding moral theories are mistaken" (p. 6). According to the moderate view, it is "inappropriate . . . to infer . . . that morality is always or usually hostile to conduct that promotes the agent's well-being" (p. 113). Moreover, it is clear from Scheffler's discussion that morality is egoistic to the extent that it permits us on occasion to pursue our interests even when *other* moral considerations oppose our doing so.

14. One form that the debate about the overridingness of moral considerations has taken recently is the "admirable immorality" debate. Williams, Michael Slote, Wolf, and others who defend the admirable immorality thesis generally do so by offering what they regard as clear instances of immoral action that nonetheless deserve our admiration and are therefore justified in an important respect. Critics of the thesis typically argue, for each such example, either that the action described is not immoral or that it is not admirable. They generally dispute the assertions of immorality by arguing for the moral rightness of the action on the basis of some moral perspective to which they subscribe. Their approach is different from that of Lawrence Becker and others who regard the finality thesis as *necessarily* true and who therefore deny the

intelligibility of any notion of admirable immorality having any sort of practical (i.e., decision-making) significance. (Writings of proponents of the admirable immorality thesis include Williams, "Moral Luck," *Proceedings of the Aristotelian Society* supplementary vol. 50 [1976], pp. 115–135, and *Moral Luck: Philosophical Papers 1973–1980* [New York: Cambridge University Press, 1981]; Thomas Nagel, "Moral Luck," in *Mortal Questions* [Cambridge: Cambridge University Press, 1979], chap. 3, pp. 24–34; Michael Slote, *Goods and Virtues* [Oxford: Clarendon Press, 1983], especially chap. 4 ["Admirable Immorality"], pp. 77–107; and Wolf, "Moral Saints." Critics of the admirable immorality thesis are represented by Robert B. Louden, "Can We Be Too Moral?" *Ethics* 98 [January 1988], pp. 361–378; Marcia Baron, "On Admirable Immorality," *Ethics* 96 [1986], pp. 557–566; and, somewhat ambivalently, Owen Flanagan, "Admirable Immorality and Admirable Imperfection," *Journal of Philosophy* 83 [1986], pp. 41–60.)

Although Flanagan rejects Slote's argument for the admirable immorality thesis, he believes that Slote's examples do, in a way, discredit the overridingness thesis: "Even when there is agreement that moral considerations reign supreme there may not be agreement about what the moral considerations are or how they are to be weighted, and this suggests that the overridingness thesis is not particularly contentful, action-guiding, or dispute-resolving" (p. 49). However, I doubt that, with the possible exception of Kant, proponents of the overridingness thesis would claim that it has these characteristics. The purpose of the thesis is not to resolve any particular moral dispute or to prescribe any particular action but rather to assess the importance that moral considerations should, in the final analysis, have in our choices and evaluations of actions.

Interestingly, advocates of the admirable immorality thesis have missed what seems to me the most plausible example of admirable immorality—viz., the morally conscientious agent who regards moral considerations as supreme but who commits immorality because of her mistaken moral beliefs.

15. One possible example of a philosopher who accepts this version is Philippa Foot, who in "Morality as a System of Hypothetical Imperatives," *Philosophical Review* 81 (July 1972), pp. 305–316, defends the view that whether one should act morally in a particular situation depends on whether she has "moral ends," such as liberty, justice, and the happiness of others. Since a person may have such ends at some times and not at others, whether moral rightness is the determinative decision criterion will vary from case to case.

16. Flanagan ("Admirable Immorality and Admirable Imperfection") suggests that moral considerations might not override nonmoral considerations even if the former are not overridden by the latter. He conjectures that the moral and the nonmoral may represent "incommensurable points of view," neither of which overrides the other. Furthermore, "once both points of view have been put on the same level . . . there is no longer any a priori answer . . . to the question of which set of requirements, which set of claims, is overriding" (p. 55). However, since the lexicographical model permits ties among decision criteria at the top of the ranking, Flanagan's notion of incommensurable criteria on the same level can be accommodated within that model.

17. In chapter 4, we shall consider relaxing this condition and contemplate "degrees of moral rightness" between 0 and 1.

18. Without this assumption, R_1 and R_2 would not be commensurable criteria.

19. George Sher, in "Subsidized Abortion: Moral Rights and Moral Compromise," *Philosophy and Public Affairs* 10:4 (Fall 1981), pp. 361–372, proposes moral compromise as a possible response to moral conflict, such as that arising over the question of whether the state should subsidize abortions for poor women. Such compromise may be appropriate, Sher believes, because of "the complexity and uncertainty of the subject" (p. 369). He explains: "If one's convictions involve principles whose grounding is itself problematical, if the opposing view is also supported by plausible-sounding ar-

guments, and if thoughtful and intelligent persons are unable to agree about the issues, then only a dogmatist will deny that he may well be mistaken, and his adversary correct." Of course, not all instances of moral uncertainty involve adversaries, and in such cases there will be no one with whom to compromise. However, moral uncertainty will often involve adversarial positions on the issue in question, and therefore one might argue that it is possible to identify action alternatives that represent a sort of compromise among those positions. I believe that such a notion of compromise, if worked out carefully, would coincide with my notion of rational decision-making under moral uncertainty.

20. This is slightly misleading. For Kant, because human beings are imperfectly rational beings, morality takes the form of imperatives to act out of respect for and in conformity with the moral law. A perfectly rational being would act in the same way but would do so purely because of its nature as a rational being and not because of its being subject to the moral law. Thus, for Kant, morality and rationality operate in different spheres. However, the important fact is that for Kant, a person who does the morally right thing necessarily does what she might naturally do if she were a perfectly rational being. In this respect, morality and rationality in action coincide.

21. One prominent philosopher who views morality as a proper subset of rationality is Kurt Baier, who in *The Moral Point of View* (Ithaca, NY: Cornell University Press, 1958) argues that moral questions arise only in interpersonal contexts. An agent in a situation in which her decision will have no effect on others may still have better reason (e.g., because of self-interest) for choosing one action than for choosing another. Thus, for Baier, rationality extends further than morality.

22. Lawrence Becker, "The Finality of Moral Judgments: A Reply to Mrs. Foot," *Philosophical Review* 82 (1973), p. 367. Becker is criticizing Foot's position in "Morality as a System of Hypothetical Imperatives."

23. Another ethicist who appears to subscribe to the finality thesis is Louden ("Can We Be Too Moral?"), who writes, "What gives ethics and politics supreme importance, once their architechtonic or comprehensive role is granted, is that they tend to have the 'last word' in all practical decisions concerning the overall bearing of individual and/or public life . . . All serious questions about what to do and how to live are (by definition, on this view) ethical and/or political questions" (p. 375). Curiously, Louden agrees "to an extent . . . that one ought not to beg the question here by superimposing a metaethical theory which dictates an automatic answer concerning what morality is when one asks 'can we be too moral?'" It is unclear why conceiving ethics as playing an "architechtonic role" by virtue of which it tends "to have the 'last word' in all practical decisions concerning the overall bearing of individual and/or public life" should not be regarded as a metaethical position.

24. The same basic point applies to noncognitivistic metaethical positions (e.g., emotivism, prescriptivism). In general, decision-makers will have varying degrees of approval/disapproval toward their action alternatives or will judge their rightness/wrongness more or less emphatically. The effects of these variations on agents' decisions should be analogous to the effects of moral uncertainty according to PR2.

25. Alasdair MacIntyre, *After Virtue: A Study in Moral Theory*, 2d ed. (Notre Dame, IN: University of Notre Dame Press, 1984), p. 214.

26. Ibid., p. 216.

27. One puzzle for proponents of virtue ethics who believe it to provide guidance for action choice is whether we should (1) act virtuously (i.e., as a perfectly virtuous agent would act) even if we ourselves are imperfectly virtuous or (2) act to improve ourselves with respect to virtue, postponing virtuous action until the point at which we become disposed to perform it. It seems clear that these two alternatives are capable of conflicting. For example, consider the question of what one should do personally about Third World poverty and suffering. If we assume that a truly virtuous person would make substantial, self-sacrificing efforts at relieving poverty and suffering, an

imperfectly virtuous person would have to decide whether to undertake such efforts, even though disinclined to do so, or attempt to effect the character transformation that would eventually dispose her to take such actions.

28. A closely related view is that moral obligation is best understood in terms of virtue and that moral appraisals of acts can best be explained in terms of more basic appraisals of persons or their character traits. For a recent discussion and criticism of this view, see Phillip Montague, "Virtue Ethics: A Qualified Success Story," *American Philosophical Quarterly* 29:1 (January 1992), pp. 53–61.

Chapter 2

1. This assumption is almost always tacit, rather than explicit, in the applied ethics literature. It is taken for granted that the solution that is being proposed to the moral problem being addressed is to be implemented by moral agents in their decisions and that a satisfactory solution requires a conclusion that a certain type of action would be right or ought to be done under the circumstances in question. An ethicist who comes relatively close to stating the assumption explicitly is R. M. Hare, who in his essay "Abortion and the Golden Rule" (*Philosophy and Public Affairs* 4 [Spring 1975], pp. 201–222) declared his intention to be that of applying ethical theory to "practical issues" and later observed, "We shall get the issues in better focus if we discuss them directly in terms of what we ought or ought not to do, or what it would be right or wrong to do, to the fetus or the mother in specified circumstances" (p. 204). Obviously, Hare is supposing that if something is right to do or ought to be done, then it is rational to do it.

2. The expected morality expressions presuppose that $c_1, c_2, \ldots, c_n$ are mutually exclusive and collectively exhaustive.

3. Although I refer to moral statements as being true or false, I do not wish to rule out noncognitivist or nondescriptivist metaethical perspectives according to which ascribing truth or falsity to moral judgments, principles, theories, and so on, is, strictly speaking, incorrect. My analysis applies to any conception of moral statements for which the issue of which moral theory, principle or procedure is to be accepted, consulted, or used arises. For my purposes, "true" and "false" when applied to moral locutions should be understood in an extremely broad sense.

4. To the best of my knowledge, the only philosopher who has developed a decision-theoretic approach to decision-making under moral uncertainty is Graham Oddie in his essay "Moral Uncertainty and Human Embryo Experimentation" (in *Medicine and Moral Reasoning*, ed. K. W. M. Fulford, Grant Gillett, and Janet Martin Soskice, [Cambridge: Cambridge University Press, 1994], pp. 144–161). He recommends maximizing the expected "overall goodness or value" of one's actions based on one's "best estimate" of pertinent "objective chances" and "real values." By "overall goodness or value," he means whatever it is that determines moral rightness/wrongness, and he regards both deontological and consequentialist considerations as eligible. An action that maximizes expected value (in this sense), he says, is "morally justified" whether or not it is "objectively right." As we shall soon see, an action that maximizes expected value (in Oddie's sense) might or might not also have maximum probability of being morally right. Therefore, Oddie's "expected value" principle is not equivalent to PR2. However, if we were to replace the binary hypothesis with a many-valued conception of moral rightness (as we shall consider doing in chapter 4), then Oddie's principle would express a plausible interpretation of "maximizing expected moral rightness."

5. We might compare this criticism of PR2 with the criticism that Williams and others have raised against morality itself that is based on "moral luck." Their view, which we shall examine later in this chapter, is that by strictly adhering to moral

requirements one may deprive herself of the opportunity to live the kind of life that she will retrospectively judge to have been significant.

6. A somewhat technical argument that some important senses of "obligatory" imply doing the best that one can is given in Fred Feldman, *Doing the Best We Can* (Dordrecht: Reidel, 1986).

Holly M. Smith has suggested, for reasons that are somewhat different from mine, that it may be appropriate for an agent to follow a moral principle other than his/her preferred principle if he/she has limited confidence in the correctness of the latter and believes that there is some chance that the former is correct. Such a strategy might appeal to the agent if the prescriptions of the preferred principle are unclear while those of the alternative principle are clear. (See Holly M. Smith, "Making Moral Decisions," *Noûs* 22 [1988], pp. 89–108.) Interestingly, she regards the rule of maximizing expected utility as just one of a number of possible "auxiliary rules" that utilitarians might employ in the absence of sufficient information about the consequences of their action alternatives. She argues that, in general, such auxiliary rules do not solve the practical problems faced by agents who are uncertain of the concrete implications of their preferred moral principles. She would perhaps criticize, on similar grounds, my assumption that maximizing expected moral rightness is the most reasonable approach to decision-making under moral uncertainty. However, R. Eugene Bales in "Act-Utilitarianism: Account of Right-making Characteristics or Decision-making Procedure," *American Philosophical Quarterly* 8 (1971), pp. 257–265, expresses a view that appears to have some affinity with PR2: "[Rules of thumb and moral codes] are successful the adoption of which tends to maximize the performance of acts pronounced right by the account [of right-making characteristics]" (p. 264).

7. David G. Thomasma in "The Role of the Clinical Medical Ethicist: The Problem of Applied Ethics and Medicine," in *The Applied Turn in Contemporary Philosophy*, ed. Michael Bradie, Thomas W. Attig, and Nicholas Rescher (Bowling Green, OH: Applied Philosophy Program, Bowling Green State University, 1983), pp. 136–157, urges applied ethicists to disavow the role of "moral expert" in favor of that of "moral consultant"—i.e., someone "who makes recommendations based on the literature and discipline of ethics and medical ethics" (p. 149). Such recommendations, Thomasma says, "are not the same as judging the moral right and wrong of a course of action" (p. 151). Rather, "the recommendation is . . . based on a community of values, some shared and some not, in the practice, that is, in the relationship of healing. . . . The moral right or wrong according to theory is not at issue" (p. 152). Arthur Caplan, in "Ethical Engineers Need Not Apply: The State of Applied Ethics Today," *Science, Technology, and Human Values* 6 (1980), pp. 24–32, identifies what he calls the "engineering model of applied ethics," in which "practitioners of applied ethics depict themselves as moral 'engineers' who take theoretical insights from the basic researchers and apply them to the resolution of concrete moral dilemmas" (p. 26). He argues that this model has serious shortcomings and urges that applied ethicists consider other roles that they may perform, including "theoretician, diagnostician, educator, coach, conceptual policeman, and skeptic" (p. 30). A useful anthology of articles on the relationship between ethical theory and applied ethics is David M. Rosenthal and Fadlou Shehadi, eds., *Applied Ethics and Ethical Theory* (Salt Lake City: University of Utah Press, 1988).

While I do not deny that there are many dimensions to applied ethics, it seems obvious that decision-makers who wish to enlist moral considerations in their choices of action will find an applied ethics that refuses to offer any recommendation or suggestion about what is to be done in morally problematic situations to be unsatisfactory.

8. By "moral luck," I mean simply luck in choosing an action that turns out to be morally right. My meaning is obviously very different from Williams's in his influential essay "Moral Luck." Williams has in mind a kind of luck that he believes a certain conception of morality (which he goes on to criticize) precludes. See Williams, "Moral

Luck," *Proceedings of the Aristotelian Society* supplementary volume 50 (1976), pp. 115–135, reprinted in *Moral Luck: Philosophical Papers 1973–1980*, (New York: Cambridge University Press, 1981), pp. 20–39.

9. This example is taken from Donald Hubin's commentary on my colloquium paper "Abortion, Moral Uncertainty, and Rational Decision-making" at the Spring 1987 Central Division meeting of the American Philosophical Association.

10. This statement assumes that endangering possible others does not by itself diminish the utility of the action. Utility is diminished only when someone is directly harmed. If this assumption is denied, then the example does not work. However, it would not be difficult to construct other examples that would prove the point.

11. Decision theorists have discussed at great length whether expected utility theory is an adequate normative account of decision-making under risk. Much of that discussion has revolved around certain paradoxes—the Allais and the Ellsberg paradoxes, in particular—that some theorists view as exposing the inadequacy of standard expected utility theory. For our current discussion of rational decision-making under moral uncertainty, the Allais paradox does not apply, since it does not arise when the binary hypothesis is in force. (However, we shall suspend that hypothesis in later discussion.) The Ellsberg paradox involves unknown probabilities, which we shall not consider until chapter 3. In my adaptations of decision-theoretic techniques for application to moral decision-making, I shall largely ignore the technical adjustments that may be needed in order to avoid the problems for expected utility theory raised by these and similar paradoxes. See Paul J. H. Schoemaker, "Subjective Expected Utility Theory Revisited: A Reductio Ad Absurdum Paradox," *Theory and Decision* 33 (1992), pp. 1–21, for a new paradox and an addition to the literature on this subject.

12. An extensive survey of subjective expected utility theories to 1980 may be found in Peter C. Fishburn, "Subjective Expected Utility: A Review of Normative Theories," *Theory and Decision* 13 (1981), pp. 139–199.

13. This analysis requires us to reject the inference from the obligatoriness of an action to its rightness, since otherwise each of two alternative obligatory acts x and y would be both right and wrong. For discussions of various aspects of the contemporary debate about the existence of moral dilemmas, see Christopher W. Gowans, ed., *Moral Dilemmas* (New York: Oxford University Press, 1987), and Walter Sinnott-Armstrong, *Moral Dilemmas* (Oxford: Basil Blackwell, 1988).

14. Sinnott-Armstrong, *Moral Dilemmas*.

15. This statement assumes that supererogatory actions must be morally right. Frances Myrna Kamm in her essay "Supererogation and Obligation" (*Journal of Philosophy* 82 [March 1985], pp. 118–138) has argued that superogatory acts can fail to be morally permissible. Kamm contends that three criteria—moral duty, supererogation, and personal preference—have moral status in the following respect: There are decision situations in which supererogation "may take precedence over" moral duty. There are also decisions for which personal preference "may take precedence over" supererogation. However, the "may take precedence over" relation is intransitive in that personal preference "may not take precedence over" moral duty. (Surprisingly, Kamm argues that superogatory acts may violate moral duty. I shall discuss her argument for this in chapter 5.)

The practical problem for Kamm is that decisions for which all three criteria apply seem to be quite common. Often we must decide among alternatives among which are some that satisfy our moral obligation, others that go beyond duty and are thus supererogatory, and still others that serve our personal interests but fail to satisfy moral duty or to be supererogatory. In such cases, how are we to decide what to do? If we understand Kamm's "may take precedence over" relation as bearing on our choices of action, then there is no criterion among the three that "may take precedence over" the other two. Whichever criterion I choose, there is another criterion that "may take precedence over" it. Therefore, it is problematic which criterion or criteria I may, all things considered, choose as the basis of my action.

Perhaps Kamm would say that when all three criteria apply to our decision, personal preference should be eliminated from consideration, since personal preference "may not take precedence over" moral duty. This would leave duty and supererogation as possible criteria for my choice of action. However, this unveils another puzzle: how should I choose between duty and supererogation? According to Kamm, supererogation "may take precedence over" duty. But because the "may take precedence over" relation is intransitive, we may not conclude that duty "may take precedence over" supererogation. This would leave supererogation as the only rational basis for my decision. In other words, I should *always* act supererogatorily whenever I must choose among supererogation, moral duty, and personal preference. It is unlikely that Kamm or any other ethicist who subscribes to the view that supererogatory actions are possible would accept this result. However, for her conceptual scheme it is difficult to see how one would rationally choose among the three criteria. (I shall argue in chapter 5 that we should jettison the whole notion of supererogation.)

16. If we assume that A is justified in believing a proposition if and only if A justifiably assigns to it a probability greater than .5 and that the probabilities that A assigns to the various propositions in Example 2.3 are (epistemically) justified, then A *justifiably* believes that doing x would accord with T1 and also *justifiably* believes that T1 is the true moral theory but *justifiably* denies that x would be morally right. This would mean that A is not necessarily justified in believing propositions entailed by those that A justifiably believes. More generally, the attribute (of propositions) of being justifiably believed by a rational agent is not closed under entailment. For a defense of the nonclosure thesis, see Richard Foley, "The Epistemology of Belief and the Epistemology of Degrees of Belief," *American Philosophical Quarterly* 29 (1992), pp. 111–124.

17. If we broaden the concept of a subjective theory to include theories that allow agents to have uncertainties about some aspects of their application, then it is not difficult to imagine situations in which the alternative action most likely to conform to the subjective moral theory that is most likely to be "true" is *proscribed* by PR2.

18. "Moral certainty" can be interpreted in two ways: (1) as *objective* moral certainty, which implies the correctness of the agent's moral belief, or (2) as *subjective* moral certainty, which leaves open the question of whether the agent's moral belief is correct. One can be *subjectively* certain that act x is morally right even if in fact x is morally wrong. Generally speaking, it is subjective moral uncertainty that I have in mind. However, in general, my arguments should work even if moral certainty/uncertainty is understood as objective moral certainty/uncertainty.

19. See Williams, *Moral Luck*, p. 39.

20. Ibid., p. 22.

21. "For many decisions which are part of the agent's ongoing activity . . . we can see why it is that the presence or absence of regrets is more basically conditioned by the retrospective view of the deliberative processes than by the particular outcomes. Oneself and one's viewpoint are more basically identified with the dispositions of rational deliberation, applicable to an ongoing series of decisions, than they are with the particular projects which succeed or fail on those occasions" (ibid., p. 35).

22. "But there are certain other decisions . . . which are not like this. . . . In these cases, the project in the interests of which the decision is made is one with which the agent is identified in such a way that if it succeeds, his stand-point [*sic*] of assessment will be from a life which then derives an important part of its significance for him from that very fact; if he fails, it can, necessarily, have no such significance in his life. If he succeeds, it cannot be that while welcoming the outcome he more basically regrets the decision. If he fails, his standpoint will be of one for whom the ground project of the decision has proved worthless, and this . . . must leave him with the most basic

regrets. So if he fails, his most basic regrets will attach to his decision, and if he succeeds, they cannot. That is the sense in which his decision can be justified, for him, by success" (Ibid., pp. 35–36).

23. Williams admits that "deliberative rationality" applies to agents' decisions whether to embark on long-term projects. But he believes that, in general, the more important standard of evaluation will be the retrospective one: "There is indeed some room for the presence and subsequent assessment of deliberative rationality. The agents in our cases might well not be taken as seriously as they would otherwise if they did not, to the limited extent that the situation permits, take such rational thought as they can about the realities of their situation. But this is not the aspect under which they will primarily look back on it, nor is it as a contribution to a series of deliberative situations that it will have its importance for them. Though they will learn from it, it will not be in that way." (Ibid., p. 35). It is unclear what Williams means by "taken as seriously as they would otherwise" in the second sentence in the preceding passage. If he has in mind the evaluation of the agent's decision by others, then he apparently overlooks the main reason that deliberative rationality, which takes into account the likelihood that the envisioned project will be successfully completed, should be important to the decision-maker—i.e., that the agent must decide one way or another and that it (usually) matters, all things considered, what the agent does.

24. If Williams would accept my suggestion that the all-things-considered propriety of an agent's choice of project is affected by the worthiness of that project and the likelihood that the agent would successfully complete it, then this would suggest that a utilitarian standard is being appealed to. However, Williams considers and rejects a utilitarian framework for his ideas. He does so partly on the grounds that a utilitarian perspective has no means of distinguishing cases of project failure in which the agent has no knowledge of or control over the cause of failure from cases in which the failure is properly ascribed to the agent herself. Perhaps this distinction is important for the agent's retrospective evaluation of herself in having failed to complete the project. It is unclear, however, whether or why this distinction is relevant to the agent's decision whether to take on the project in the first place. If it is not relevant to the agent's *prospective* evaluation of the project, then it is no obstacle to regarding the decision criterion being employed as utilitarian. However, if it is relevant to the agent's initial decision, then it should be possible to incorporate the distinction into the decision criterion, perhaps by giving greater weight to the likelihood that if the project fails, the principal cause of failure will be the agent herself than to the likelihood that the cause of failure will be of an "external and incident kind" (ibid., p. 25). In either event, there is no reason to suppose that no standard of *prospective* evaluation of projects exists.

Chapter 3

1. One proabortion argument based on certain kinds of moral uncertainty is proposed by James R. Greenwell in "A Probabilistic Justification for Abortion,"*Philosophy Research Archives* 2 (1976), pp. 182–195. His analysis unfortunately is marred by his failure to notice an ambiguity in the crucial phrase "is called for," which in the context may be taken as meaning either "is morally right" or "is morally required." Some of his statements are plausible only if the phrase is interpreted one way, while some of his inferences are valid only if it is understood the other way.

Raymond S. Pfeiffer, in "Abortion Policy and the Argument from Uncertainty," *Social Theory and Practice* 11 (1985), pp. 371–386, criticizes several antiabortion arguments that he characterizes as arguments from uncertainty. They are different from the arguments developed in this chapter in at least one important respect: His arguments' conclusions appear to say that abortion should be *legally* prohibited or restricted, while the arguments in this chapter say nothing about legal considerations. Also, it is not clear from Pfeiffer's article whether the "oughts" and "shoulds" in the conclusions of the arguments he attempts to refute are moral terms or fall into some other normative category. He refers to the arguments as "pragmatic" but does not say enough to enable this reader to tell whether the conclusions are intended to express moral judgments. If he intends his conclusions to refer to moral obligations, then this would be another important difference between the arguments he considers and the arguments I present here.

2. Judith Jarvis Thomson's landmark essay "A Defense of Abortion" (*Philosophy and Public Affairs* 1 [1971], pp. 47–66) has spawned the debate, which still rages, over the significance of the personhood issue for the abortion issue itself. Among those who generally accept her argument and conclusion are Mark Strasser ("Dependence, Reliance, and Abortion," *Philosophical Quarterly* 35 [1985], pp. 73–82) and Holly M. Smith ("Intercourse and Moral Responsibility for the Fetus," in *Abortion and the Status of the Fetus*, ed. William B. Bondeson, H. Tristram Englehardt Jr., Stuart F. Spicker, and Daniel H. Winship ([Dordrecht: Reidel, 1985], pp. 229–245). Among those who find fault in Thomson's arguments, but not necessarily in her main conclusions, are Nancy Davis ("Abortion and Self-Defense,"*Philosophy and Public Affairs* 13 [1984], pp. 175–207), Michael Davis ("Fetuses, Famous Violinists, and the Right to Continued Aid,"*Philosophical Quarterly* 33 [1983], pp. 259–278), Steven L. Ross ("Abortion and the Death of the Fetus," *Philosophy and Public Affairs* 11 [1982], pp. 232–245), James P. Sterba ("Abortion, Distant Peoples, and Future Generations,"*Journal of Philosophy* 77 [1980], pp. 424–439), Jean Beer Blumenfeld ("Abortion and the Human Brain,"*Philosophical Studies* 32 [1977], pp. 251–268), Hugh V. McLachlin ("Must We Accept Either the Conservative or the Liberal View on Abortion?" *Analysis* 37 [1977], pp. 197–204), I. S. Carrier ("Abortion and the Right to Life," *Social Theory and Practice* 3 [1975], pp. 381–401), Richard Werner ("Abortion: The Moral Status of the Unborn," *Social Theory and Practice* 3 [1974], pp. 201–222), and B. A. Brody ("Thomson on Abortion," *Philosophy and Public Affairs* 1 [1972], pp. 335–340).

It is not my purpose to defend a particular approach to the morality of abortion question or to claim that certain forms of moral uncertainty are more reasonable than others. My goal are only to consider several typical kinds of moral uncertainty that concern abortion and to outline and illustrate a general approach to decision-making about abortion that can be applied to various kinds of moral decisions.

3. See Mary Anne Warren, "On the Moral and Legal Status of Abortion," *Monist* 57 (1973), pp. 43–61, and Michael Tooley, *Abortion and Infanticide* (Oxford: Oxford University Press, 1983) and "Abortion and Infanticide," *Philosophy and Public Affairs* 2 (1972), pp. 37–65. Tooley's bold (or reckless) acceptance of the moral rightness of infanticide as an implication of his views on abortion has particularly engendered philosophical controversy and discussion. Some of Tooley's critics, like Carrier ("Abortion and the Right to Life") and Loren E. Lomasky ("Being a Person—Does it Matter?" *Philosophical Topics* 12 [1982], pp. 139–152), regard the fact that Tooley's proabortion argument would support infanticide as sufficient to discredit that argument, while others apparently would be willing to accept the infanticide implication if the argument could not be refuted independently. For an exchange between Warren and Tooley, see Warren, "Reconsidering the Ethics of Abortion," *Philosophical Books* 26 (1985), pp. 1–9, and Michael Tooley, "Response to Mary Anne Warren's 'Reconsidering the Ethics of Infanticide,' " *Philosophical Books* 26 (1985), pp. 9–14.

4. Several writers have expressed doubts about the very possibility of rationally resolving the personhood issue. See Jane English, "Abortion and the Concept of a Person," *Canadian Journal of Philosophy* 5 (1975), pp. 233–243; Meredith W. Michaels, "Abortion and the Claims of Samaritarianism," in *Abortion*, ed. Jay Garfield and Patricia Hennessey (Amherst: University of Massachusetts Press, 1984), pp. 213–226; Robert C. Solomon, "Reflections on the Meaning of Fetal Life," in Bondeson, et al.,

Abortion and the Status of the Fetus, pp. 209–226; and Grant Crosby, "Abortion: An Unresolved Moral Problem,"*Dialogue* 17 (1978), pp. 106–121.

One direction that the debate about the personhood of fetuses has taken is to try to define more clearly the relevant meaning of "person" for the abortion question and, particularly, to determine whether the appropriate concept of personhood is itself a moral concept in the sense that to ascribe personhood to something is to make a moral or normative judgment. I shall not here attempt to detail the large body of literature that exists on this topic. In the examples that I use in this essay, I shall not specify all the uncertainties that may underlie decision-makers' uncertainties about fetal personhood. A full representation of a decision-maker's beliefs and uncertainties that relate to the morality of abortion may be considerably more complicated than as presented in these examples.

5. Many references on dominance and other concepts and methods of decision theory exist. One of the most useful is the standard text by R. D. Luce and H. Raiffa, *Games and Decisions* (New York: John Wiley and Sons, 1957). Another is Michael D. Resnik, *Choices: An Introduction to Decision Theory* (Minneapolis: University of Minnesota Press, 1987).

6. One philosopher who apparently is willing to countenance the possibility that having an abortion in normal circumstances may be morally obligatory is Donald Hubin, who made such a suggestion in his commentary on my colloquium paper "Abortion, Moral Uncertainty, and Rational Decision-making" at the Spring 1987 Central Division meeting of the American Philosophical Association.

7. Judith Thomson appears to take this position herself in the following: "The woman who allows the pregnancy to continue, at great cost to herself, is entitled to praise in the same amount, and, more important, of the same kind, as is the man [the Good Samaritan] who sets forth, at great cost to himself, to give aid" ("Rights and Deaths," in *Rights and Wrongs of Abortion*, ed. Marshall Cohen, Thomas Nagel, and Thomas Scanlon, [Princeton, NJ: Princeton University Press, 1974], p. 124).

8. Some philosophers conceive supererogatory actions as possibly violating their agents' moral duties. For example, Frances Myrna Kamm in her essay "Supererogation and Obligation" (*Journal of Philosophy* 82 [March 1985], pp. 118–138) claims, "In doing a supererogatory act we may have permissibly failed to do our duty" (p. 121). Not only does such a point of view complicate the relationships among the concepts of permissibility and duty, but it also may sometimes force decision-makers to resolve conflicts between supererogation and moral obligation in choosing their actions. I shall argue in chapter 5 that the disadvantages of adopting such a conceptual scheme outweigh any advantages.

9. R. M. Hare ("Abortion and the Golden Rule," *Philosophy and Public Affairs* 4 [Spring 1975], pp. 201–222) believes that there is a general obligation to procreate but argues that, under certain circumstances, abortion is permissible if the would-be parents intend to bring to birth at a later time a child who will not be born if the present fetus is not aborted. Hare bases his argument on a "logical extension" of the Golden Rule that directs us to "do to others what *we are glad was* done to us" (p. 208). Since most of us are glad that our parents did not abort us but brought us into the world, we have an obligation to do the same for others. However, if there is evidence that the present fetus is defective and would lead a miserable life, would die before birth, or would in some other way be much less likely to have a life worth living than the next fetus that could otherwise be brought into existence, then, according to Hare, the Golden Rule allows the would-be mother to abort the present fetus. He believes that such a moral perspective bypasses the personhood issue entirely. However, this is not the case. If the present fetus is a person and the possible future fetus is not, then the Golden Rule applies to the former but not to the latter. Hare's argument thus makes the unwarranted assumption that the present fetus and the possible future fetus have the same personhood status. See George Sher, "Hare, Abortion, and the Golden

Rule,"*Philosophy and Public Affairs* 6 (Winter 1977), pp. 185–190, and Richard Werner, "Hare on Abortion,"*Analysis* 36 (June 1976), pp. 177–181, for critical discussions of Hare's views on abortion.

10. James L. Hudson, in "Subjectivization in Ethics," *American Philosophical Quarterly* 26 (1989), pp. 221–229, points out that for subjective moral theories it is frequently unnecessary to actually calculate the value of consequences or of any other morally significant quantity in order to apply the theories to concrete situations, since it may be enough just to have estimates of the magnitudes of the quantities involved. A similar observation may be made about the rationality principles that I propose.

11. The method is described in Luce and Raiffa, *Games and Decisions*, pp. 301–302. There is considerable opposition among philosophers of probability to the whole notion of subjective probability. (See, for example, Henry E. Kyburg, Jr., "Subjective Probability: Criticisms, Reflections, and Problems,"*Journal of Philosophical Logic* 7 [1978], pp. 157–180.) Clearly, practical and philosophical difficulties connected with subjective probabilities may cause us to opt for objective probabilities. However, for such uncertain "events" or "states of the world" as those associated with the truth of a particular moral statement or the moral status of a particular entity, it may be difficult to find plausible objective interpretations of the pertinent probabilities. One option is to conceive such probabilities as epistemic probabilities, representing the likelihoods of the truth of various moral claims with respect to available information. The key point here is that we need not settle on a particular philosophy of probability in order to appreciate that the general notion of probability is deeply implicated in moral uncertainty and to employ that notion in practical strategies for moral decision-making. (See also H. E. Kyburg, Jr., and Howard E. Smokler, eds., *Studies in Subjective Probability* [Huntington, NY: Krieger, 1980].)

12. See Donald Davidson and Patrick Suppes, *Decision Making* (Palo Alto, CA: Stanford University Press, 1957), for further discussion of the practical and theoretical problems of subjective probability measurement.

13. For a recent discussion of the objective/subjective value issue and an argument in favor of objective value and objective probability in moral decision-making, see Graham Oddie and Peter Menzies, "An Objectivist's Guide to Subjective Value," *Ethics* 102 (April 1992), pp. 512–533.

14. We may obtain this result by using geometrical considerations and evaluating $25\int_R [1/(2p_1)-.7]dp_1$. Alternatively, we may calculate $25\int_R dp_1 \, dp_2$, where R is the region in $<p_1 \, p_2 \, p_3>$ space determined by the constraints on p_1, p_2, and p_3— $.6$, $< p_1 < .8$, $.7 < p_2 < .9$, and $p_1 p_2 < .5$.

15. Since for this example exactly one alternative can be prescribed by PR2, the probability that the "no abortion" alternative is prescribed by PR2 is approximately $1 - .18 = .82$.

16. The idea of a second-order subjective probability, measuring one's subjective uncertainty about the magnitude of a first-order subjective probability, raises conceptual difficulties. For if a probability is truly subjective, then, it would seem, there is no objective probability about which one could be mistaken and thus uncertainty about its magnitude is misplaced. One way we might try to avoid this puzzle is by following the practice of defining subjective probabilities in terms of betting behavior under appropriate conditions. Then individuals can be mistaken about betting behavior, even their own, if those conditions do not yet exist and they are predicting or hypothesizing precisely what forms of betting behavior will, or would, actually occur. The difficulties reappear, however, if the conditions cannot actually be created—for example, if the proposition whose truth is being gambled on cannot be verified or falsified. This is, in fact, the sort of situation that arises in decision-making about abortion, since there is no way to conclusively verify or falsify a claim of fetal (non-)personhood, for instance. See Jacob Marshak, "Personal Probabilities of Probabilities," *Theory and Decision* 6 (1975), pp. 121–153, and Karl Borch, "Probabilities of Probabilities: A Comment on

Jacob Marshak," *Theory and Decision* 6 (1975), pp. 155–159, for a discussion of these and related matters.

17. Decision theorists have proposed several theories for decision-making with uncertain probabilities, and a number of interesting and perplexing problems arise for theories of this sort. Readers who wish to know what alternatives to the approach embodied in PR3 exist and why I have chosen that approach over those alternatives may consult this book's appendix.

18. The mathematical problem is to calculate the average value of $E(X)-E(Y)$ over the region R determined by the inequality $0 < p_1 < p_2 < 1$. That is,

$$\text{AVE } [E(X)-E(Y)] = \frac{\int_R (1-2p_1p_2) \, dp_1 dp_2}{\int_R dp_1 dp_2} \times \$1,000.$$

It should be noted that, in general, the average value of a function $f(x_1, x_2, \ldots, x_n)$ over some set of values of $x_1, x_2, \ldots, x_n$ is not the value of f at the average values of $x_1, x_2, \ldots, x_n$ over that set. Therefore, we could not have calculated AVE $[E(X) - E(Y)]$ by first calculating the average values of p_1 and p_2 and then evaluating $1 - 2p_1p_2$ at those values.

19. The mathematical problem is to calculate the average value of $p(A) - p(\text{not-}A)$ over the region R determined by the constraints on p_1 and p_2. That is,

$$\text{AVE } [p(A)-p(\text{not-}A)] = \frac{\int_R (1-2p_1p_2) \, dp_1 dp_2}{\int_R dp_1 dp_2}$$

20. The mathematical problem is to calculate the average value of $p(A) - p(\text{not-}A)$ over the region R determined by the constraints on p_1, p_2, p_3, and p_4—viz., $0 \le p_1 \le p_4 \le p_3 \le p_2 \le 1$—where $p(A) - p(\text{not-}A) = 2p_1p_2p_4 - p_1p_3p_4 - 2p_1p_2 - p_4 + 1$. That is,

$$\text{AVE } [p(A)-p(\text{not-}A)] = \frac{\int_R (2p_1p_2p_4 - p_1p_2p_3p_4 - 2p_1p_2 - p_4 + 1) \, dp_1 dp_2 dp_3 dp_4}{\int_R dp_1 dp_2 dp_3 dp_4}$$

21. This is determined by calculating

$$\text{AVE } (p_1) = \frac{\int_R p_1 \, dp_1 dp_2 dp_3 dp_4}{\int_R dp_1 dp_2 dp_3 dp_4},$$

where R is the region determined by the constraints on p_1, p_2, p_3, and p_4, including $p \ge .5$.

22. The mathematical calculation is the same as in note 20 except that $p \geq .5$ is added as a condition that determines the region R.

23. Among the many ethicists who emphasize the indispensability of keen moral judgment for moral decision-making are ethical intuitionists like G. E. Moore, Ross, and Frankena and, more recently, ethical casuists like Jonsen and Toulmin. Bayles has argued that moral judgment is necessary because there is no available "decision procedure" for the complex tasks of applying moral theories, principles, and rules to concrete decisions. (For references, see notes 3, 4, 5, and 12 in chapter 1.)

24. It is, of course, possible to consider the calculating quality of consequentialist ethical theories as reasons not to accept them.

25. The mathematical computation is $25 \int_R dp_2 dp_3$, where R is the region in $<p_2, p_3>$ space determined by the constraints $.4 \leq p_2 \leq .6$, $.2 \leq p_3 \leq .4$, and $p_3 - p_1 p_2 - p_1 p_3 \geq 0$ with $p_1 = .4$. Otto Ruehr has discovered an ingenious method for evaluating this and other integrals in this book where the regions R are determined by somewhat complicated constraints on the variables of integration.

26. My approach of regarding the personhood of a fetus at a certain stage of development as an object of uncertainty may be contrasted with the views of those who regard personhood as a "fuzzy" property that fetuses, and presumably other things as well, may possess to varying degrees. The latter approach is taken by L. W. Sumner in *Abortion and Moral Theory* (Princeton, NJ: Princeton University Press, 1981). The reader must bear in mind that I am mainly concerned with rational decision-making under moral uncertainty and not directly with resolving the ethical and metaphysical issues themselves, which is what Sumner is concerned with. The sorts of decisions that I am considering in this book are assumed to be made by persons who have certain kinds of beliefs and uncertainties pertinent to those decisions. I am not recommending those beliefs to decision-makers, and there will, no doubt, be many such persons who have very different views from those that I hypothesize. I would still recommend the same rationality principles for those decisions, although obviously the results of applying those principles may turn out quite different.

27. The mathematical calculation is $\int_R dp_1 dp_2 dp_3$, where R is the region in $<p_1, p_2, p_3>$ space determined by the constraints $.4 \leq p_1 \leq .6$, $.4 \leq p_2 \leq .6$, $.2 \leq p_3 \leq .4$, and $p_3 - p_1 p_2 - p_1 p_3 > 0$.

28. Since in this example exactly one of the two alternatives must be prescribed by PR2, the probability that the "no abortion" alternative is prescribed by PR2 is approximately $1 - .055 = .945$.

29. The mathematical computation is

$$\text{AVE } [p(A) - p(\text{not-}A)] = \frac{\displaystyle\int_R (p_3 - p_1 p_2 - p_1 p_3) \, dp_1 dp_2 dp_3}{\displaystyle\int_R dp_1 dp_2 dp_3},$$

where R is the region determined by the constraints $0 \leq p_1 \leq p_2 \leq p_3 \leq 1$.

30. The mathematical computation is the same as in note 27 except that the region R is determined by the constraints $0 \leq p_3 \leq p_1 \leq p_2 \leq 1$.

31. The mathematical computation is the same as in note 27 except that the region R is determined by the constraints $0 \leq p_1 \leq p_3 \leq p_2 \leq 1$.

32. The mathematical computation is the same as in note 27 except that the constraint $p_3 - p_1 < 1 - p_3$ is added to those that determine the region R.

Chapter 4

1. See note 10 of chapter 3.

2. James L. Hudson, "Subjectivization in Ethics," *American Philosophical Quarterly* 26 (1989), p. 221.

3. In the first part of his essay, Hudson conceives "expected utility" to be "the amount of utility actually expected by the agent" (ibid., p. 223). This means that, for Hudson, the "maximize expected utility" rule directs agents to select actions such that the utility that the agent actually expects them to produce is at least as great as the utility that the agent expects from any alternative act. It should be noted that this is very different from the usual formulation, which defines the expected utility, EU, of an act x as $EU(x) = p(c_1, x) \cdot u(c_1) + \ldots + p(c_n, x) \cdot u(c_n)$. For the latter version, all sorts of uncertainties may abound—for example, about the $p(c_i, x)$s, the $u(c_1)$s, and so forth. Hence, the standard "maximize expected utility" rule would not qualify as a subjective theory according to Hudson's definition, since in order to be a subjective theory, the ability of agents to use the theory to guide their actions must be guaranteed.

Later on, Hudson apparently changes his concept of a subjective theory to one that "requires merely that the agent have an estimate of the relative utility of the action she performs" (p. 225). Subjective utilitarianism appears now to say to the agent, "Choose an act that you estimate to produce at least as much utility as any alternative act." But what if one currently has no such estimate? Does one simply assume that all actions under serious consideration would produce equal amounts of utility, or is this a situation where Hudson's subjective utilitarian principle fails to prescribe at all (and thus fails to be a subjective theory)? One example of such a decision would be someone's deciding on investments in the stock market without believing of any potential investment that the utility produced would be at least as great as that produced by any other investment.

4. Ibid., p. 224.

5. Ibid.

6. Ibid.

7. Mill (*Utilitarianism*, ed. George Sher [Indianapolis: Hackett, 1979 (1861)]) is usually interpreted as having misstated his real views and not having meant what he wrote. See, for example, Fred Feldman, *Introductory Ethics* (Englewood Cliffs, NJ: Prentice-Hall, 1977), p. 21.

8. Alan Donagan, in *The Theory of Morality* (Chicago: Chicago University Press, 1977), writes, "Although wrongness, or moral impermissibility, does not have degrees, impermissible wrongs are more or less grave. . . . And, given that wrongs can differ in gravity, it quite obviously follows from the fundamental principle of morality that, when through some misdeed a man is confronted with a choice between wrongs, if one of them is less grave than the others, he is to choose it" (p. 152). Thus Donagan's notion of the gravity of a moral wrong may perform roughly the same function as my notion of degrees of moral rightness. I prefer to observe the principle that for every possible moral decision, at least one alternative action must be morally optimal.

9. W. D. Ross, *The Right and the Good* (Oxford: Clarendon Press, 1946).

10. I would analyze "x is more reasonable than y" in a way analogous to my explanation of "x has greater moral rightness than y"—i.e., x is more reasonable than y for agent A in situation S if and only if, if A's options in S were confined to just x and y, then x would be reasonable and y would be unreasonable for A to choose in S.

11. Hudson, "Subjectivization in Ethics," p. 224.

12. Two well-known examples of interval scales are the Fahrenheit and Centigrade scales for temperature. Among the characteristics of interval scales are that the 0 point is arbitrary and that equivalent scales are related by positive linear transformations.

13. Another, perhaps more controversial, argument for assuming equal maximum and minimum possible degrees of moral rightness for different moral theories is based on the principle of insufficient reason.

14. In conversation, Derek Parfit expressed doubts about the PEMT, which led me to identify the preceding objections and to offer the preceding analysis. I do not know, however, whether he will be satisfied with my discussion. I am grateful to him for pointing out the need to say more about the PEMT than I had previously thought necessary.

15. For subjective ethical theories, it is the gap between the maximum and minimum expected quantities of intrinsic value that would be relevant.

16. For a discussion of the rank-order method and the independence condition, see Michael D. Resnik, *Choices: An Introduction to Decision Theory* (Minneapolis: University of Minnesota Press, 1987), pp. 183–185.

17. It should be noted that this does not mean that one must believe of some identifiable action that it would actually lead to the worst possible consequences. One may be able to say of an action x that there is no other identifiable action y in the situation the consequences of which she would expect to be worse than x's consequences without being able to say that there is no possible action in the situation that would actually lead to consequences worse than x's consequences. (Compare this to my believing that at least one of my current beliefs is false, although there is no identifiable belief x of mine that I believe to be false.)

18. This result is produced by evaluating

$$\text{AVE } [\text{EM}(A)-\text{EM}(\text{not-}A)] = \frac{\int_R [\text{EM}(A)-\text{EM}(\text{not-}A)] \; dp \; dm}{\int_R dp \; dm}$$

where $dp = dp_1 dp_2 dp_3 dp_4$, $dm = dm_1 dm_2 dm_3$, and R is the region determined by the constraints on p_1, p_2, p_3, p_4, m_1, m_2, and m_3.

Chapter 5

1. See, for example, Michael Slote, *Beyond Optimizing* (Cambridge, MA: Harvard University Press, 1989).

2. Ibid.

3. David Heyd, in his book *Supererogation* (Cambridge: Cambridge University Press, 1982), originated the term "supererogationism." Marcia Baron adopted it also in her essay "Kantian Ethics and Supererogation" (*Journal of Philosophy* 84 [1987], pp. 237–262).

4. In A. I. Melden, ed., *Essays in Moral Philosophy* (Seattle: University of Washington Press, 1958).

5. "Supererogation is justified by showing that some supererogatory acts must exist because society cannot require of the individual every act that would promote the general good, and because the individual has the right to satisfy his wants and to achieve his ends and ideals regardless of their social utility" (Heyd, *Supererogation*, p. 166).

6. For example, Heyd writes, "The way a theory treats the problem of supererogation and whether it can be adjusted to contain it serve as criteria for its adequacy" (ibid., p. 10).

7. Heyd argues that some utilitarian ethical theories are more accommodating of a concept of supererogatory actions than others. However, he concludes that ultimately the problem of demarcating between supererogatory and nonsupererogatory actions cannot be satisfactorily solved within the context of utilitarianism. For his discussion of supererogation in relation to utilitarianism, see ibid., chap. 4.

8. For example, Marcia Baron, in "Kantian Ethics and Supererogation," argues that Kant's concept of imperfect duties suffices to serve the main purposes for which the concept of supererogation is intended. Susan Hale argues for essentially the same conclusion in "Against Supererogation," *American Philosophical Quarterly* 28:4 (October 1991), pp. 273–285.

9. For examples, see Peter Singer, "Famine, Affluence, and Morality," *Philosophy and Public Affairs* 1 (1971–1972), pp. 229–243, and *Practical Ethics* (New York: Cambridge University Press, 1979), and also Elizabeth M. Pybus, " 'Saints and Heroes,' " *Philosophy* 57 (1982), pp. 193–199.

I have chosen to conceive of supererogatory actions as "going beyond" moral rightness rather than as "going beyond" moral duty. Much confusion has occurred, in my view, because philosophers have adopted the latter conception. It is far more natural, I believe, to think of supererogatory actions as being morally right actions that both fulfill our moral obligations and possess greater amounts of moral value than other morally right actions one might have chosen.

10. See Patricia M. McGoldrick, "Saints and Heroes: A Plea for the Supererogatory," *Philosophy* 59 (1984), pp. 523–528; Elizabeth M. Pybus, "A Plea for the Supererogatory: A Reply," *Philosophy* 61 (1986), pp. 526–531; and Russell A. Jacobs, "Obligation, Supererogation and Self-sacrifice," *Philosophy* 62 (1987), pp. 96–101.

11. Joseph Raz, "Permissions and Supererogation," *American Philosophical Quarterly* 12 (1975), pp. 161–168.

12. See Heyd, *Supererogation*, p. 168, and Robin Attfield, "Supererogation and Double Standards," *Mind* 88 (1979), pp. 481–499.

13. See Heyd, *Supererogation*, p. 171.

14. I invite the reader to invent her own explanations for why only these options are available.

15. Heyd, *Supererogation*, p. 5.

16. This restatement is needed because if more than one supererogatory action is available to the moral agent, it may be optional which of them she chooses. The interesting question is whether it would be optional whether she chooses any supererogatory action at all.

17. Heyd emphasizes the "logical relation" between supererogation and moral rightness, which he claims to have two "features" that he calls "correlativity" and "continuity." "Correlativity means that acts of supererogation derive their special value from their being 'more than duty requires'; i.e., they have meaning only relatively to obligatory action." (*Supererogation*, p. 5). Continuity has to do with supererogatory actions' having an excess of the same kind of value that makes morally right actions valuable.

18. See Gregory Mellema, *Beyond the Call of Duty: Supererogation, Obligation, and Offence* (Albany: State University of New York Press, 1991), chap. 5.

19. Ibid., p. 124.

20. Ibid.

21. It should be noted that my argument does *not* imply that moral agents would have better reasons to perform *each* supererogatory action than to perform any other action. For it is possible for there to be more than one supererogatory alternative in a decision situation. However, my argument does assert that moral agents would have better reasons to perform a supererogatory action than to perform any nonsupererogatory action. Thus it would follow that one could not have sufficient reason to perform any nonsupererogatory action if supererogatory action alternatives were available.

22. In her essay "Supererogation and Obligation" (*Journal of Philosophy* 82 [March 1985], pp. 118–138), Frances Myrna Kamm argues that supererogatory actions can violate agents' moral obligations. She gives the example of an agent who must decide between donating a kidney to save the life of an accident victim that the agent has just encountered and keeping a lunch appointment. Kamm contends that it would be supererogatory of the agent to donate the kidney and, since the agent's only moral duty is to keep the lunch appointment, doing what is supererogatory would mean failing to discharge her moral duty. However, I see no reason to accept Kamm's claim that the agent's duty is *entirely* to keep her lunch appointment. It seems much more plausible to regard the agent's duty as being discharged if she either donates her kidney or keeps her lunch appointment. It may be difficult to articulate accurately and comprehensively what the agent's moral duty would be in such a situation. However, I see no reason not to stipulate that whatever our moral duties are, they cannot be violated by our acting supererogatorily.

23. See Singer, *Practical Ethics*, chap. 8.

24. Readers who find ethical egoism to be a totally discredited theory may substitute a moral theory that has an egoistic component, such as the sort of theory that Samuel Scheffler has advocated in *Human Morality* (New York: Oxford University Press, 1992). Susan Hale ("Against Supererogation") has argued that actions are often mistakenly regarded as supererogatory because they are the most onerous among the alternatives that satisfy conflicting imperfect moral duties in the situation. She claims that in such cases the overriding duties are often those of self-interest. She believes that she can account for the moral status of purportedly supererogatory actions and for their optionality without recognizing a separate category of supererogatory actions. While I am sympathetic to her antisupererogationist point of view, I think that her argument relies too heavily on her controversial claims about moral duties of self-interest. One advantage of the argument I propose here is that it assumes only that such claims have at least a small measure of plausibility, which decision-makers should take into consideration in their deliberations.

Chapter 6

1. The published codes of ethics of many professional organizations recognize an obligation of confidentiality that is qualified in a variety of respects. For example, the American Bar Association's "Model Rules of Professional Conduct" allows attorneys to reveal confidential information in order to prevent clients from committing crimes that are "likely to result in imminent death or substantial bodily harm." The American Medical Association's "Principles of Medical Ethics" states that a "physician . . . shall safeguard patient confidences within the constraints of the law." The American Nurses' Association "Code for Nurses" states, "The nurse safeguards the client's right to privacy by *judiciously* protecting information of a confidential nature." (emphasis added). The American Psychological Association's "Ethical Principles of Psychologists" directs psychologists to "respect the confidentiality of information obtained from persons in the course of their work." However, they may "reveal such information . . . in those unusual circumstances in which not to do so would result in clear danger to the person or to others."

Medical ethicists typically contend that physicians' confidentiality obligations are on occasion outweighed by other considerations. For example, see Leo J. Cass and William J. Curran, "Rights of Privacy in Medical Practice," *Lancet* 2 (October 16, 1965), pp. 783–785; LeRoy Walters, "Ethical Aspects of Medical Confidentiality," in *Contemporary Issues in Bioethics*, ed. Tom L. Beauchamp and LeRoy Walters (Belmont, CA: Wadsworth, 1978), pp. 169–175; and Raanan Gillon, "AIDS and Medical Confidentiality," *British dentiality,*" *British Medical Journal* 294 (June 27, 1987), reprinted in *Contemporary Issues in Bioethics,* ed. Tom L. Beauchamp and LeRoy Walters, 3d ed. (Belmont, CA: Wadsworth, 1989), pp. 408–411.

2. See California Supreme Court, 1 July 1976, 131 *California Reporter,* pp. 14–42, for the majority and dissenting opinions, reprinted in *Ethical Issues in Professional Life,* ed. Joan C. Callahan (Oxford: Oxford University Press, 1988), pp. 239–248. The facts in *Tarasoff* are in some ways similar to those of the medical ethics case examined in this chapter. In both cases, a physician's patient threatens the physical well-being of a third party and the physician must decide whether to warn the threatened person and, in so doing, divulge confidential information about the patient. Among the differences between the two cases, possibly ethically significant, are that in one case the patient threatens homicide while in the other the patient threatens infection with the HIV virus. In the former the patient confides his violent intentions as part of psychotherapy, while in the latter psychotherapy is not involved.

3. "AIDS and a Duty to Protect," *Hastings Center Report* 17 (February 1987), pp. 22–23, commentaries by Morton Winston and Sheldon H. Landesman.

4. In an essay titled "AIDS, Confidentiality, and the Right to Know" (*Public Affairs Quarterly* 17 [April 1988], pp. 91–104, reprinted in *Biomedical Ethics,* ed. Thomas A. Mappes and Jane S. Zembaty, 3d ed. [New York: McGraw-Hill, 1991], pp. 173–180), Morton Winston presents a somewhat more elaborate argument for his views about physicians' informing the sex partners of AIDS patients. The "duty to protect" is now based on the "Harm Principle," which "requires moral agents to refrain from acts and omissions which would foreseeably result in preventable wrongful harm to innocent others," and the "Vulnerability Principle," according to which "the duty to protect against harm tends to arise most strongly in contexts in which someone is specially dependent on others or in some way specially vulnerable to their choices and actions." In my discussion, I shall consider only Winston's arguments as presented in the *Hastings Center Report.*

5. This appears to be very close to the position of the AMA in its "Principles of Medical Ethics," which acknowledges only the "constraints of law" as limiting the physician's obligation to "safeguard patient confidences."

6. One view about medical confidentiality is that while the physician's obligation of confidentiality to the patient is not absolute, the burden of proof is on one who claims that some other obligation outweighs it. For example, see Walters, "Ethical Aspects of Medical Confidentiality."

7. In "AIDS, Confidentiality, and the Right to Know," Winston considers the view that "programs of partner notification and limited contract tracing are unwise on the grounds that they will tend to deter individuals from being tested in the first place." He replies that "such programs will not deter individuals who are socially responsible and are willing to take steps to protect themselves and others from HIV infection, and it will tend to increase compliance with voluntary disease control measures among identified HIV-infected members of risk groups who are reluctant to accept their social responsibilities." However, this reply appears to ignore the fact that it is the *unidentified* HIV-infected individuals who present the greatest threat to those with whom they have intimate contact.

8. The decision-maker may, of course, be more inclined to doubt his initial assessments of $p_1, p_2 \ldots, p_5$ than to doubt his preconceptions about which alternative has the greater probability of being morally right. In this event, revising his measurements of $p_1, p_2, \ldots, p_5$ may be in order. Such a back-and-forth process might continue until "reflective equilibrium" is reached. However, if he is unable to bring his measurements of $p_1, p_2, \ldots, p_5$ into line with his initial judgment about which course of action is likelier to be morally right, then he should seriously consider abandoning that judgment.

9. This may be shown as follows: $p(not\text{-}I) - p(I) = 2p_1p_2p_3(p_4 - 1) + 2p_1(1 -$

p_5) $+ 2p_5 - 1$. The factors in the addend that contain p_2 besides p_2 itself are 2, p_1, p_3, and $p_4 - 1$. All are positive quantities except the last. Thus p_2 is multiplied by a non-negative number in its addend, which means that if p_2 is decreased from its maximum value of .8 the effect on p(not-I) $- p(I)$ cannot be to decrease its magnitude since the addend that contains p_2 will either become larger (i.e., become a smaller negative number) or be unchanged (if $p_4 = 1$). A similar analysis produces the same conclusion for p_3. If the preceding expression for p(not-I) $- p(I)$ is rewritten slightly, p_4 occurs only in an addend whose other factors are 2, p_1, p_2, and p_3. All are greater than or equal to 0, so if p_4 is increased from its minimum of .2 the effect on p(not-I) $- p(I)$ cannot be to decrease its magnitude since either the addend remains at 0 or a larger positive quantity contributes to the sum. Another rewriting of the expression for p(not-I) $- p(I)$, installing p_5 as a term in a single addend, shows that the other factor in that addend is $2 - 2p_1$. Since $p_1 \leq .8$, $2 - 2p_1 \geq .4 > 0$. Thus increasing the value of p_5 from its minimum value of .6 can only have the effect of increasing the magnitude of p(not-I) $- p(I)$. Therefore, given the constraints on $p_1 - p_5$, for any given value of p_1, p(not-I) $- p(I)$ will be a minimum when $p_2 = p_3 = .8$, $p_4 = .2$, and $p_5 = .6$. To determine the effect of p_1 on p(not-I) $- p(I)$, we need only express the preceding statement mathematically—i.e., p(not-I) $- p(I) \geq 2p_1(.8)(.8)(.2 - 1) + 2p_1(1 - .6) + 2(.6) - 1$. Doing some algebra shows that p(not-I) $- p(I) \geq .2 - .224p_1$. Obviously, decreasing p_1 from its maximum value of .8 will increase the magnitude of p(not-I) $- p(I)$. Thus the minimum value of p(not-I) $- p(I)$ occurs when $p_1 = .8$ and $= .2 - (.224)(.8) = .0208$. Therefore, with our limits (maxima and minima) on $p_1 - p_5$, p(not-I) $- p(I)$ must be a positive number, which implies that p(not-I) $> p(I)$.

10. The mathematical problem is to find the average value of $p(I) - p$(not-I) over the region R determined by the inequalities involving the ps. That is,

$$\text{AVE } [p(I) - p\text{(not-I)}] = \frac{\int_R [p(I) - p\text{(not-I)}] \, dp}{\int_R dp},$$

where $dp = dp_1 dp_2 dp_3 dp_4 dp_5$.

11. The mathematical problem is to find the average value of EMR(I)−EMR(not-I) over the region R determined by the inequalities involving the ps and ms. That is,

$$\text{AVE } [\text{EMR}(I) - \text{EMR(not-I)}] = \frac{\int_R [\text{EMR}(I) - \text{EMR(not-I)}] \, dp \, dm}{\int_R dp \, dm},$$

where $dp = dp_1 dp_2 dp_3 dp_4 dp_5$ and $dm = dm_1 dm_2 dm_3 dm_4 dm_5 dm_6$.

12. Obviously, theoretical perspectives other than those employed by Winston and Landesman are possible. One such view is that HIV patients who refuse to inform their sex partners of their medical status and who will not agree to other persons' doing so thereby forfeit their right of confidentiality, and thus their physicians do nothing impermissible in informing the endangered individuals. This position is taken by Gillett Grant ("AIDS and Confidentiality," *Journal of Applied Philosophy* 4 [1987], reprinted in *Ethical Issues in Modern Medicine*, ed. John Arras and Nancy Rhoden, 3d ed., [Mountain View, CA: Mayfield, 1989], pp. 123–127) and by Sissela Bok (*Secrets: The Ethics of Concealment and Revelation* [New York: Random House, 1983], pp. 116–135, reprinted in Callahan, *Ethical Issues in Professional Life*, pp. 230–239). Bok suggests that a phy-

sician's promise to maintain confidentiality under such extreme circumstances is a promise wrongly made and is therefore not binding. Alan Donagan makes a similar argument regarding attorneys' confidentiality obligations to their clients in "Confidentiality in the Adversary System," in *The Good Lawyer: Lawyers' Roles and Lawyers' Ethics,* ed. David Luban (Totowa, NJ: Rowman and Allanheld, 1984), pp. 123–149 (reprinted in *Ethical Issues in Professional Life,* pp. 250–255). There are clearly difficulties with the general thesis that wrongly made promises should never be kept.

Chapter 7

1. This is not to say that the Supreme Court continues to subscribe to the reasoning in *Roe v. Wade.* One commentator has claimed that in the more recent abortion rulings "the reasoning on which the original *Roe* decision rested has largely been abandoned by the Court" (Ian Shapiro, ed., *Abortion: The Supreme Court Decisions* [Indianapolis: Hackett, 1995], p. 2).

2. From Justice Blackmun's opinion in *Roe v. Wade,* 410 U.S. 159 (1973).

3. Ibid.

4. See Baruch Brody, *Abortion and Sanctity of Human Life* (Cambridge: MIT Press, 1975), p. 127.

5. There is an interesting question of semantics about the meaning of "person" as it appears in the U.S. Constitution: Is its meaning such that beings of a certain kind could conceivably be *discovered* to be persons even though they were previously believed not to be persons? Or is "person" a technical term the meaning of which is fully stipulated or implied by the Constitution?

6. See Mary B. Mahowald, "Is There Life after *Roe versus Wade?*" *Hastings Center Report* 19 (July–August 1989), pp. 22–29.

7. See Mary Anne Warren, "On the Moral and Legal Status of Abortion," *Monist* 57 (1973), pp. 43–61. David Algeo in "Abortion, Personhood, and Moral Rights," *Monist* 64 (1981), pp. 543–549, disputes Warren's principle.

8. Dissenting opinion, *Doe v. Bolton,* 410 U.S. 222 (1973).

9. There is an interesting, related conceptual issue here. Does the hunter in our example endanger a person's life if his target turns out not to be human? More generally, does one endanger an object of kind A only by endangering some x where x is an A? Or does one endanger an A by endangering some x where x *may* be an A? What if x is incapable of being harmed—e.g., because it is an inanimate object? Should we say then that one endangers an A if one acts toward some x in such a way that x would be harmed if it were an A? But this ignores the possibility that the agent may know with sufficient certainty that x is not an A.

Perhaps we should say that one endangers an A if one is not sufficiently certain that x is not an A and she acts toward x in such a way that x would be harmed if x were an A? But what would be meant by "sufficiently certain"? Perhaps one endangers an A by subjecting some x to some probability p of serious harm where x *is* an A and p is sufficiently large? Or maybe one endangers an A by subjecting some x to some probability p_1 of serious harm where x has a probability p_2 of being an A and $p_1 \cdot p_2$ is sufficiently large? Another possibility is that one endangers an A by subjecting some x to some probability p_1 of harm of degree h where x has a probability p_2 of being an A and $p_1 \cdot h \cdot p_2$ is sufficiently large.

If either of the last two options is selected, then conceivably even if p_2 is relatively small p_1 could be large enough to compensate sufficiently so that the product $p_1 \cdot p_2$ is larger than the level required for reckless endangerment. (In the case of abortion, p_1 would be relatively large, since the probability of abortion's leading to serious harm [death] of the fetus is exceedingly high.) For example, if one drives through a red light at high speed without checking to see whether other motorists or pedestrians are present, does she avoid endangering people's lives if it turns out that no one was nearby at the time?

10. A being may fail to have a certain right either (1) because it is not the sort of being that may have that right or (2) because the alleged right does not exist. A right to smoke cigarettes in enclosed public places is an example of an alleged right that, in my view, does not exist.

11. See Nancy Rhoden, "A Compromise on Abortion?" *Hastings Center Report* 19 (July–August 1989), pp. 32–37.

12. Ibid., p. 35.

13. The Court did not rule that pregnant women's right to abortions, which it based on their right to privacy, was absolute but rather that the right to abortions must be weighed against states' interest in protecting the health of pregnant women and in protecting "the potentiality of human life." It was that interest on which the Court based its conclusion that states may regulate abortion after the fetal viability stage.

14. See Lisa Newton, "Abortion in the Law: An Essay on Absurdity," *Ethics* 87 (1977), pp. 244–250.

15. See note 13.

16. From Justice Blackmun's opinion in *Roe v. Wade*, 410 U.S. 153.

17. Concurring opinion, *Doe v. Bolton*, 410 U.S. 210.

18. Majority opinion, *Roe v. Wade*, 410 U.S. 153.

19. In his dissenting opinion in *Roe v. Wade*, Justice Rehnquist expressed doubt that the right to privacy was even involved in the case. There is considerable difference of opinion among philosophers about what privacy is and what a right to privacy would entail. See W. A. Parent, "Recent Work on the Concept of Privacy," *American Philosophical Quarterly* 20 (1983), pp. 341–356, and "Privacy, Morality, and the Law," *Philosophy and Public Affairs* 12 (1983), pp. 269–288; Ferdinand Schoeman, "Privacy: Philosophical Dimensions," *American Philosophical Quarterly* 21 (1984), pp. 199–214; H. J. McCloskey, "Privacy and the Right to Privacy," *Philosophy* 55 (1980), pp. 17–38; and J. H. Reiman, "Privacy, Intimacy, and Personhood," *Philosophy and Public Affairs* 6 (1976), pp. 26–44, for discussions of the conceptual issue. One of the issues that arises in connection with the right to privacy is whether the right is fundamental or "derivative" from more basic rights. That debate occurs in Judith J. Thomson, "The Right to Privacy," *Philosophy and Public Affairs* 4 (1975), pp. 295–314; Thomas Scanlon, "Thomson on Privacy," *Philosophy and Public Affairs* 4 (1975), pp. 315–322; and James Rachels, "Why Privacy Is Important," *Philosophy and Public Affairs* 4 (1975), pp. 323–333.

20. Raymond M. Herbenick in "Remarks on Abortion, Abandonment, and Adoption Opportunities," *Philosophy and Public Affairs* 5 (1975), pp. 98–104, explores the idea of regarding abortion as a form of abandonment and considers what public policy responses would be appropriate.

21. From Justice Blackmun's opinion in *Roe v. Wade*, 410 U.S. 159.

22. Another issue, not addressed in this discussion, is whether aborting a fetus violates the fetus's right to life, assuming that it possesses such a right. It has been argued by Judith Jarvis Thomson that no such violation need occur because the fetus's right to life is, if anything, the right not to be killed *unjustly* and aborting a fetus need not involve killing unjustly ("A Defense of Abortion," *Philosophy and Public Affairs* [1971], pp. 47–66). See also Holly M. Smith, "Intercourse and Moral Responsibility for the Fetus," in *Abortion and the Status of the Fetus*, ed. William B. Bondeson, H. Tristram Englehardt Jr., Stuart F. Spicker, and Daniel H. Winship (Dordrecht: Reidel, 1985), pp. 229–245.

23. I ignore, for simplicity, the various ways in which the Court could have ruled the statute unconstitutional. A more detailed analysis would consider different kinds of restrictions that the Court might place on states' regulation of abortion.

24. In general, different agents (e.g., different justices of the Supreme Court) would

have different subjective probabilities or different estimates of the objective probabilities. Thus the method outlined here would not necessarily resolve disagreements about what is to be done (although it might do so) but would be useful in enabling individual agents to reach conclusions about each's contribution to the collective decision.

25. The "if-then" statement is to be understood as a subjunctive conditional. Its probability as a material conditional of being true would actually increase as the probability that its antecedent is true decreased.

26. The mathematical problem is to find the expected value of EJ(uphold) − EJ(disallow) over the region R determined by the inequalities involving the ps. Specifically,

$$\text{AVE [EJ(uphold)} - \text{EJ(disallow)]} = \frac{\int_R f(p) \ dp}{\int_R dp},$$

where $f(p) = p_1 p_2 p_3 + p_1 p_2 + p_1 - \frac{1}{2}$ and $dp = dp_1 dp_2 dp_3$.

27. I am grateful to an anonymous referee for Oxford University Press for pointing out that in an earlier version of this chapter I needed to give a better explanation of my claim that j_1 is closer to 1 ("perfect justice") than to any of the other j quantities.

28. The method is to find the expected value of EJ(uphold)−EJ(disallow) over the region R determined by the inequalities involving the ps and the js. Specifically,

$$\text{AVE [EJ(uphold)} - \text{EJ(disallow)]} = \frac{\int_R f(p,j) \ dp \ dj}{\int_R dp \ dj},$$

where $f(p,j) = p_1 p_2 p_3 (2 - j_1 - j_3) + p_1 p_2 (j_1 + j_4 - 2) + p_1 (2 - j_2 - j_4) + j_2 - 1$, $dp = dp_1 dp_2 dp_3$, and $dj = dj_1 dj_2 dj_3 dj_4$.

29. The mathematical operations are the same here as for note 28 except that R is now the region determined by the new constraints on the ps and js.

Chapter 8

1. Philosophers who have not done so include Lars Bergström ("On the Formulation and Application of Utilitarianism," *Noûs* 10 [1976], pp. 121–144 and "Utilitarianism and Future Mistakes," *Theoria* 43 [1977], pp. 85–102), Holly S. Goldman ("Dated Rightness and Moral Imperfection," *Philosophical Review* 85 [1976], pp. 449–487, "Doing the Best One Can," in *Values and Morals*, ed. A. I. Goldman and J. Kim [Dordrecht: Reidel, 1978], pp. 185–214, and "Moral Realism, Moral Conflict, and Compound Acts," *Journal of Philosophy* 88 [1986], pp. 341–345), Eric B. Dayton ("Course of Action Utilitarianism," *Canadian Journal of Philosophy* 9 [1979], pp. 671–684), Jordan H. Sobel ("Utilitarianism and Past and Future Mistakes," *Noûs* 10 [1976], pp. 195–219), and Torbjörn Tännsjö ("Moral Conflict and Moral Realism," *Journal of Philosophy* 82 [1986], pp. 113–117). However, none of their discussions address the question of how agents' moral and nonmoral uncertainties should enter into their practical deliberations, as I shall do in this chapter.

2. In adopting this terminology, I follow Dayton ("Course of Action Utilitarianism"). Dayton also distinguishes between "complex acts" and the "particular acts" that are their constituents, and he regards courses of action as a certain kind of complex act.

While the distinction between particular acts and complex acts may ultimately be arbitrary, to me it seems unnatural and awkward to think of courses of action that extend over months or years as individual actions. I shall therefore assume that, for the most part, the distinction is unproblematic.

3. The courses of action we are interested in here are those of individual moral agents. According to some views of personal identity that emphasize psychological continuity, some of our commonsense beliefs about ourselves are mistaken. For example, we are not the same persons as 70-year-olds that we were as infants or young children, since there is insufficient continuity of our thoughts, feelings, dispositions, etc., over such a span of time. If we adopt a theory of personal identity of this sort, then it follows that courses of action cannot extend beyond the periods of time over which persons exist. In general, this will be a shorter period of time than the lifetime of a particular human body, and this must be taken into consideration in the following discussion. A contemporary philosopher who defends a psychological continuity conception of personal identity is Derek Parfit (*Reasons and Persons* [Oxford: Oxford University Press, 1984], part 3).

4. Although intrinsic value is what moral agents are most often called on to maximize, there are other morally significant quantities, such as freedom, justice, and virtue, that we might also maximize. Of course, we might regard intrinsic value as multifaceted, so that it encompasses freedom, justice, and so on. However, some moral pluralists conceive intrinsic value more narrowly—hedonistically, for instance. In their view, our moral obligations with respect to freedom, justice, virtue, and so on, are not subsumed under our obligation to promote intrinsic value. We should note that such obligations need not be obligations to maximize. For example, the obligation to act justly is not the same as the obligation to maximize justice.

5. In his essay "Moral Conflict and Moral Realism," Tännsjö claims that we should "adapt actions to our future moral mistakes" but denies that this means that we should deliberate in any particular way. His purpose is to reconcile the existence of moral conflicts with moral realism rather than to propose a theory of moral deliberation.

6. Act utilitarianism and other act consequentialist moral theories are usually formulated so that they prescribe *individual* actions without taking into account course-of-action considerations. Actions are sanctioned if and only if they maximize (expected) utility given whatever information agents have about the world, *including their own future action choices*. However, this leads to the following counterintuitive result:

Suppose that agent A is to choose between actions x_1 and x_2 at t_1 and between y_1 and y_2 at t_2 (where A's alternatives at t_2 are not affected by what A does at t_1). Suppose that the utilities of the total consequences of the two actions are as given here:

x	y	$u<x\ y>$
x_1	y_1	1.0
x_1	y_2	.1
x_2	y_1	.5
x_2	y_2	.7

According to consequentialism, A should choose x at t_1 so that $u(x)$ is maximized. But what is $u(x)$? The table gives explicit information only about $u<x\ y>$. It would appear that $u(x)$ can be determined only by anticipating what A will choose at t_2. What will A choose at t_2 if she wishes to maximize $u(y)$? This depends on what A will have chosen at t_1. Suppose that A predicts that she will choose y_2 at t_2. Based on this prediction, A should choose x_2 at t_1 since $u<x_2\ y_2> > u<x_1\ y_2>$. Furthermore, assuming that A has chosen x_2 at t_1, she should (according to consequentialism) choose y_2 at t_2 since $u<x_2\ y_2> > u<x_2\ y_1>$. A's prediction that she will choose y_2 at t_2 is a self-fulfilling prophecy because, by making that prediction at t_1 and acting on it, A becomes obligated at t_2 to do as predicted.

Thus, on the usual formulation of consequentialism, it appears that the course of action $<x_2\ y_2>$ would be sanctioned in the previous situation. However, if A's overriding objective is to maximize utility, then surely she should choose the course of action $<x_1\ y_1>$, since $u<x_1\ y_1>$ is greater than $u<x_2\ y_2>$. (It may readily be verified that A's choosing x_1 at t_1 and y_1 at t_2 also satisfies the consequentialist criterion as usually formulated.) The problem is that the usual formulation apparently does not *disallow* the $<x_2\ y_2>$ course of action, since it does not require that we choose individual actions according to which courses of action are optimal. The moral here is that moral theories that include utility maximization or other types of optimization as criteria for action choice should be formulated so that they take course of action considerations into account. The literature on this topic includes the previously referenced articles by Bergström, Dayton, and Sobel.

7. In this discussion of courses of action, I am (for the most part) using the term "moral dilemma" broadly to describe situations that are morally problematic because of agents' difficulties in bringing themselves to do what they believe to have maximum expected moral rightness or in knowing which of their alternatives have maximum moral rightness. Most often I am not using the term in its more recent sense—i.e., to refer to decisions in which agents morally ought to perform each of two mutually exclusive actions.

Ruth Barcan Marcus argues in "Moral Dilemmas and Consistency," *Journal of Philosophy* 77 (1980), pp. 121–136, reprinted in *Moral Dilemmas*, ed. Christopher Gowan (New York: Oxford University Press, 1987), pp. 188–204, that "the recognition of . . . [the] . . . reality [of moral dilemmas] . . . motivates us to arrange our lives and institutions with a view to avoiding such conflicts. It is the underpinning for a second-order regulative principle: that as rational agents . . . we ought to conduct our lives and arrange our institutions so as to minimize predicaments of moral conflict" (pp. 188–189). It should be noted that Marcus is using the term "moral dilemma" in its more recent meaning.

8. Holly S. Goldman ("Doing the Best One Can") argues that agents' choices among sequences of actions should be limited to those that they have the ability to perform. She defines an agent's present ability to perform a sequence of actions as the condition that occurs exactly when "a present desire on his part to perform it would lead to its performance" (p. 209). She allows the fading of the agent's present desire to perform a certain later action x to disqualify the sequence of actions that includes x as one that the agent has the ability to perform. However, Goldman's scheme appears not to allow the agent's uncertainty about whether he would actually perform the later action to enter into his deliberations. Since we shall rarely be certain that we would actually perform all the actions we envision as parts of any extended course of action, it seems essential that this uncertainty be recognized and considered in our deliberations.

9. Obviously there are many other forms of uncertainty that may affect the expected degree of moral rightness of one's lifetime course of action, including uncertainty about one's future abilities to perform certain actions in future situations, uncertainty about the number and kinds of moral decisions one will have to make in the future, and uncertainty about the physical, psychological, and social conditions under which future action choices will have to be made.

10. In an early draft of this chapter, Ophelia's alternative was simply that of becoming a physician; I did not stipulate that she was specifically considering serving a population that was medically disadvantaged because of a physician shortage. As an anonymous referee for Oxford University Press correctly pointed out, Ophelia's choosing a medical career *sans stipulation* would not necessarily maximize utility if some other equally able and motivated person would otherwise take her place in medical school.

11. The mathematical problem is to evaluate

$$\text{AVE } [\text{EMR}(P) - \text{EMR}(M)] = \frac{\int_R [p \cdot (u_p - u_M) + (1-p) \cdot (r_P - r_M)] \, du_M du_P dr_M dr_P dp}{\int_R du_M du_P dr_M dr_P dp},$$

where R is the region in $<u_P, u_M, r_P, r_M, p>$ space determined by the constraints on u_P, u_M, r_P, r_M, and p.

12. For example, Jeremy Rifkin in several of his writings has raised ethical questions about genetic engineering, where it is clear from his rhetorical style that, at the very least, he is proposing that research be suspended until those questions are resolved. Given the likelihood that any publicly debated ethical question can ever be answered to the satisfaction of the vast majority of the population, his proposal amounts to suspending genetic engineering research indefinitely. See *Declaration of a Heretic* (Boston: Routledge and Kegan Paul, 1985) and *Algeny* (New York: Viking, 1983). David Suzuki and Peter Knudtson also express moral trepidation about biotechnology in *Genethics*, rev. ed. (Cambridge, MA: Harvard University Press, 1990), in which they write, "The clash between genetics technologies and human values has already resulted in a deluge of difficult ethical problems. And it will continue to do so in the future, in ways that are simply impossible to anticipate" (p. 333). Their rhetorical purpose appears to be the same as Rifkin's.

13. Quote attributed to a nineteenth-century anesthesia promoter by Betty MacQuitty in *The Battle for Oblivion: The Discovery of Anaesthesia* (London: George G. Harrap, 1969), p. 68, and quoted in Martin S. Pernick, "The Calculus of Suffering in 19th-Century Surgery," *Hastings Center Report* 13 (April 1983), pp. 26–36. Pernick's essay is reprinted in *Sickness and Health in America*, ed. Judith Walzer Leavitt and Ronald L. Numbers (Madison: University of Wisconsin Press, 1985), pp. 98–112. The quote appears on p. 99 of *Sickness and Health in America*.

14. Pernick, "The Calculus of Sufferings," in Leavitt and Numbers, *Sickness and Health in America*, p. 99.

15. The notion that permanent incarceration in the iron lung was the usual fate of polio victims before the advent of polio vaccine is convincingly discredited by James H. Maxwell in "The Iron Lung: Halfway Technology or Necessary Step?" *Milbank Quarterly* 64 (1986), pp. 3–29. For an interesting discussion of the merits of the iron lung as a medical technology, see Maxwell's essay and Lewis Thomas, "Response to James H. Maxwell's Essay, 'The Iron Lung,' " *Milbank Quarterly* 64 (1986), pp. 30–33.

16. See Arthur Birembant, "The Mining Industry," chap. 2 of part 6 of *A History of Technology and Invention*, vol. 3: *The Expansion of Mechanization*, ed. Maurice Daumas, trans. Eileen B. Hennessy (New York: Crown, 1979), pp. 505–526 (especially pp. 518–519).

17. See Harold L. Burstyn, "What Can the History of Technology Contribute to Our Understanding?" in *The History and Philosophy of Technology*, ed. George Bugliarello and Dean B. Doner (Urbana: University of Illinois Press, 1979), pp. 57–80, especially pp. 62–64.

18. Jacques Ellul has recently argued, in *The Technological Bluff* (Grand Rapids, MI: William B. Eerdmans, 1990), that technology *always* creates greater "problems" than it solves. (See pp. 51–54.) For Ellul, "problem" sometimes seems to mean harm or disadvantage. However, it is clear that he sometimes has *dilemmas* in mind. For example, he writes, "We have here a typical case of the *insoluble dilemmas* that technique thrusts upon us when it is applied to some problems" (p. 54, emphasis added). If Ellul's conclusion were true of *moral* dilemmas, then introducing new technologies would always produce a deficit, morally speaking. However, Ellul gives no convincing reasons to believe that his conclusion is true of *all* technologies.

19. See Jacob S. Siegel and Cynthia M. Taeuber, "Demographic Dimensions of an Aging Population," in *Our Aging Society*, ed. Alan Pifer and Lydia Bronte (New York: W. W. Norton, 1986), pp. 79–110.

20. Arguments for age-based restrictions on access to medical technologies are made by Daniel Callahan in *Setting Limits* (New York: Simon and Schuster, 1987).

21. See Albert Rosenfeld, *Prolongevity II* (New York: Alfred A. Knopf, 1985), for a discussion of future prospects in gerontological science and antiaging technology.

22. Ibid., chap. 18.

23. See, for example, Robert L. Sinsheimer, "The Presumptions of Science," in *Limits of Scientific Inquiry*, ed. Gerald Holton and Robert S. Morison (New York: W. W. Norton, 1979), p. 30, and Robert S. Morison, "Misgivings about Life-extending Technologies," in *Limits of Scientific Inquiry*, pp. 285–286.

24. See Robert Veatch, "Justice and Valuing Lives," in *Life Span*, ed. Robert Veatch (New York: Harper and Row, 1979), pp. 197–224.

25. See Daniel Callahan, "Natural Death and Public Policy," in Veatch, *Life Span*, pp. 162–175.

26. *Life span* should be distinguished from *life expectancy*. Life span is the maximum lifetime that the members of a species are biologically capable of living—for humans, about 110 years. Life expectancy is the average lifetime of a group of individuals. For example, Americans born in 1992 can expect on average to live about 75 years. While life expectancy has increased dramatically in recent times—it was about 49 years for Americans born in 1900—the human life span has not changed at all. Antiaging technologies are directed at increasing human *life span*.

27. Since accidents and disease will always occur, some life-and-death decisions would be tragic even if an effective antiaging technology were universally employed. However, the frequency with which such decisions would arise would be greatly reduced.

28. In the seldom-discussed part 3 of *Anarchy, State, and Utopia* (New York: Basic Books, 1974), Robert Nozick argues that the minimal state, which is the only kind of state that can come into existence without violating Lockean rights, is "the one that best realizes the utopian aspirations of untold dreamers and visionaries" (p. 333).

29. By "unavoidable moral conflict," I mean a moral decision in which every alternative under consideration by the decision-maker fails to be morally optimal according to at least one criterion of moral rightness that the decision-maker regards as having a greater than 0 probability of being correct. This notion would allow there to be conflict among the criteria for some of the alternatives as long as at least one alternative avoided such conflict.

Appendix

1. See J. L. Hodges, Jr., and E. L. Lehmann, "The Uses of Previous Experience in Reaching Statistical Decisions," *Annals of Mathematical Statistics* 23 (1952), pp. 396–407, and Daniel Ellsberg, "Risk, Ambiguity, and the Savage Axioms," *Quarterly Journal of Economics* 75 (1961), pp. 643–669, reprinted in *Decision, Probability, and Utility*, ed. Peter Gärdenfors and Nils-Eric Sahlin (Cambridge: Cambridge University Press, 1988), pp. 245–269. A useful but somewhat dated discussion of decision-making under "partial ignorance" is given in R. Duncan Luce and Howard Raiffa, *Games and Decisions* (Mineola, NY: Dover, 1989), pp. 299–306.

2. See Leonid Hurwicz, "Some Specification Problems and Applications to Econometric Models," *Econometrica* 19 (1951), pp. 343–344 (abstract).

3. See Luce and Raiffa, *Games and Decisions*, pp. 282–284.

4. I disregard theories that attempt to accommodate "risk aversion" and "ambiguity aversion" characteristics in actual decision-makers. I am not convinced that

those features should be parts of *normative* decision theories of any sort, and I am convinced that they should not be parts of normative theories of decision-making under moral uncertainty. I also ignore theories that distinguish between the notion of *accepting* a statement and that of believing (or disbelieving) a statement more or less strongly. Decision theories of these types have been proposed by Ronald P. Loui ("Decisions with Indeterminate Probabilities," *Theory and Decision* 21 [1986], pp. 283–309), Edward Kofler and Peter Zweifel ("One-shot Decisions under Linear Partial Information," *Theory and Decision* 34 [1993], pp. 1–20), and Donald P. Davis and M.-Elizabeth Paté-Cornell ("A Challenge to the Compound Lottery Axiom: A Two-stage Normative Structure and Comparison to Other Theories," *Theory and Decision* 37 [1994], pp. 267–309).

5. See Isaac Levi, "On Indeterminate Probabilities," *Journal of Philosophy* 71 (1974), pp. 391–418, reprinted in Gärdenfors and Sahlin, *Decision, Probability, and Utility*, pp. 287–312; *Hard Choices* (Cambridge: Cambridge University Press, 1986), chap. 7; and "Ignorance, Probability and Rational Choice," *Synthese* 53 (1982), pp. 387–417.

6. See Peter Gärdenfors and Nils-Eric Sahlin, "Unreliable Probabilities, Risk Taking, and Decision Making," *Synthese* 53 (1982), pp. 361–386, reprinted in Gärdenfors and Sahlin, *Decision, Probability, and Utility*, pp. 313–334, and "Reply to Levi," *Synthese* 53 (1982), pp. 433–438. Also see I. J. Good, *Probability and the Weighing of Evidence* (London: Charles Griffin, and New York: Hafner, 1950).

7. Levi, "Ignorance, Probability and Rational Choice," p. 389.

8. Ibid., p. 404.

9. See Gärdenfors and Sahlin, "Reply to Levi," p. 436.

10. See Gärdenfors and Sahlin, *Decision, Probability, and Utility*, p. 332.

11. The same difficulty arises in Henry Kyburg's decision theory ("Tyche and Athena," *Synthese* 40 [1979], pp. 415–438). Kyburg adopts interval-valued probabilities, resulting in interval-valued expected utilities. Alternative A is to be preferred over alternative B only if the *entirety* of A's EU interval exceeds the *entirety* of B's EU interval. For problematic moral decisions, this condition will rarely, if ever, occur among the alternatives among which agents wish to decide.

If we construe the "security level" for each alternative as its minimum expected utility over the range of probability values, then the main difference between Levi's theory and that of Gärdenfors and Sahlin is that Levi requires that decision-makers choose alternatives that maximize expected utility for some "permissible" probability distribution, while Gärdenfors and Sahlin impose no such requirement.

12. To be precise, for the decisions under moral uncertainty that we are primarily interested in, the uniform probability distributions that we have in mind are (second-order) probabilities over the n-tuples $<p_1, p_2, \ldots, p_n>$ of "component probabilities" that satisfy whatever constraints are imposed on $p_1, p_2, \ldots, p_n$.

13. For an informative but quite technical discussion of the problems of initializing probabilities prior to the collection of evidence on the basis of a priori principles akin to the principle of indifference, see Teddy Seidenfeld, "Why I Am Not an Objective Bayesian: Some Reflections Prompted by Rosenkrantz," *Theory and Decision* 11 (1979), pp. 413–440, and a reply by R. D. Rosenkrantz, "Bayesian Theory Appraisal: A Reply to Seidenfeld," *Theory and Decision* 11 (1979), pp. 441–451.

14. For a fairly elementary discussion of several paradoxes associated with the principle of indifference, see Colin Howson and Peter Urbach, *Scientific Reasoning: The Bayesian Approach* (La Salle, IL: Open Court, 1989), pp. 45–48.

15. See M. K. Starr, *Product Design and Decision Theory* (Englewood Cliffs, NJ: Prentice-Hall, 1962), and G. O. Schneller IV and G. P. Sphicas, "Decision Making under Uncertainty: Starr's Domain Criterion," *Theory and Decision* 15 (1983), pp. 321–336.

Index

abortion, 3, 49, 50–73, 92–96, 124–142, 169–170
  and consequentialism, 55–56, 65–66
  as morally obligatory, 53–55, 67–68, 73
  and nonconsequentialism, 55, 65–66
  rationality of, 52, 69–73
abortion, forgoing
  general agreement about the moral rightness of, 51
  as having greater probability of being morally right, 52
  rape victim's as supererogatory, 54–55
  as rational, 52
abortion, moral rightness of
  argument from uncertainty, 52, 186–187 n
  certainty about as a sign of ignorance or fanaticism, 51
  conflicting and misleading advice from ethicists concerning 52

contentiousness of debate about, 51
  and moral safety argument, 52, 186–187 n
actor perspective, 101, 104
admirable immorality debate, 179 n
admirable immorality thesis, 179–180 n
aging process, human, objections to attempts to alter, 162
AIDS, 113–122
air bag for automobiles, 160
akrasia, 143
altruism, radical, 108
anesthesia, 159–160
antiaging technologies
  as means of avoiding life–and–death decisions, 162–163
  prospects for, 162
applied ethics
  flaw in customary approach to, 6
  methodology of, 34
artificial organs, 159
Attfield, Robin, 100

Becker, Lawrence, 16
behavior control and modification, 166
binary hypothesis, 27, 29–30, 75, 78–79, 82, 90–95, 115
  pragmatic argument for, 79–81
  semantic argument for, 79–81
biomedical technologies, 159–163
  age-based rationing of, 161–162
biopsy, 160
Blackmun, Harry, 125–128, 131
Borda count method, 89
Brody, Baruch, 126

career, choice of, 153
categorical imperatives, 104
chess strategy, compared to moral decision strategy, 4
chronometer, 160
commonsense view about supererogatory actions, 100, 102–103, 107–108, 110
confidentiality, obligations of, 111–123
  and professions, 112
conflict among competing moral theories, principles, and rules, 150
consequentialism, 201–202 n
continuity, as characteristic of the relationship between obligation and supererogation, 104
cooperative action, 158, 166–167
coordination of actions of individuals, 166–168
courses of action
  collective decision-making about, 158–161
  contrasted with individual actions, 144
  lifetime, 150, 153, 158, 162–164, 168
  morality of, 144–153

decision-making under moral uncertainty as a problem, 4–9, 16–21, 46–49
  arguments against the recognition of, 5–8, 46–49
  why ethicists have ignored, 16–21
decision-making under moral uncertainty as unavoidable, 8, 50–51
decision principle, second-order, 51

decision theory and abortion policy, 133
"degree of rationality," 14
dialysis, 161
dilemmas, moral. *See* moral dilemmas
disagreements, moral, practical resolutions of, 111–142
disagreements among ethicists, advice to moral agents in, 111–112
disagreements among Supreme Court justices, possibility of resolving, 141–142
Doe v. Bolton, 128, 130
dominant strategy, "no abortion" alternative as, 53–54
Douglas, William O., 130–131

egoism
  as a moral theory, 10, 108–109
  as a nonmoral standard, 9–10
ethical egoism. *See* egoism, as a moral theory
ethical nihilism, 19
ethical skepticism, 8
eugenics, 165–166, 170
"exclusionary permission," 100
expected utility formula, 27, 57

"finality thesis," and flaw in, 16
foundationalism, ethical, 7
future action choices, uncertainty about, 151–152

G1, 150, 154, 160, 165
  stated, 150
G2, 152, 154
  stated, 152
genetic engineering, 159, 166, 170
genetic screening, 159

Hare, R. M., 13
Hastings Center Report, 112, 113
hedging, moral. *See* moral hedging
Heyd, David, 100, 102
HIV, 113–122
Hubin, Donald, 35
Hudson, James L., 74–75, 89–90, 96
human reproduction, state control of, 165

identity, personal. *See* personal identity
ignorance, decision-making under, 37

independence condition in decision theory, 89
insufficient reason, principle of, 37
international relief, 101–110
intrinsic value, incommensurability of different conceptions of, 77

justice
    as excellence in judicial decision-making, 133–134
    expected degree of, 134–135, 141–142
    many-valued conception of, 137–138
    ordinal measurement of degrees of, 137–140

Kant, Immanuel, 15

Landesman, Sheldon H., 113–114, 116–117, 122–123
life, right to. *See* right to life
life span, distinguished from life expectancy, 204 n
lifestyle, choice of, 153
long-run morality, 143–168

MacIntyre, Alasdair, 7, 19, 20
Mahowald, Mary B., 127
mathematics
    appropriateness of use in moral decision-making, 66–67
    and judicial decision-making, 140–141
maximin principle, 37, 45
maximize-expected-justice approach, 140, 142
maximize-expected-moral-rightness strategy, 150
maximize-expected-utility (MEU) principle
    as a decision principle, 57
    as a moral principle, 58, 78
    uncertainty about correct application of, 58
maximize-utility principle
    as a moral principle, 58–64
    uncertainty about correct application of, 59–64
medical ethics, case study in, 113–123
Mellema, Gregory, 105–107
Mill, John Stuart, 79

mine explosions, 160
"minimal state," 166
minimax-regret principle, 37
moral controversies and quandaries, 3, 7
    reasons for the frequent occurrence of, 7
moral dilemmas, 39–40, 150, 156, 158–163, 170, 202 n
    avoiding, 150, 156, 158–163
moral failure, risk of, 4
moral hedging
    for axiological uncertainty, 74–76
    for ethical uncertainty, 74–75, 83
    possibility of, 76–80
    as unnecessary, 75–76
moral judgments, methods of justifying, 7
moral luck, 34, 46–49
moral point of view, 9
moral relativism, 17–19
moral rightness, expected
    contrasted with expected utility, 58
    defined, 27
    maximizing, 78–79, 82–83, 90, 95–96, 109–110, 122, 144, 146–152, 155, 157, 163–164
moral rightness, many-valued
    conception of, 74–97, 101, 155–156, 166–167, 169–170
    and abortion, 92–96
moral subjectivism, 17–18
moral theories, objective. *See* objective moral theories
moral theories, subjective. *See* subjective moral theories
"morality," indefinability of as reasonableness in action, 5
morality-can-be-overridden thesis
    lexicographical version of, 11–12, 15, 22, 32
    weighted sum version of, 11–12, 14–15, 22–23
"morality is paramount" doctrine, 4, 9
"morally right," as used in this book, 5
my-favorite-theory approach, 42–43, 91, 108–109, 170
    shortcomings of, 42–43, 91

"natural death," 162
Newton, Lisa, 130
nihilism, ethical. *See* ethical nihilism

noncognitivism, ethical, 13
nonmoral normative uncertainty, decision-making under, 124–125
Nozick, Robert, 164

objective moral theories, 74, 90
objective probabilities, 60, 63–64, 69–72, 94, 135
   uncertainty about, 63–64, 69–72
   using estimates of, 60
optimism-pessimism rule, 37
optimization, 50, 98–99
ordinal measurement
   of probabilities, 62–63, 71–72, 117–121, 135–136
   of value, 117–121
organ transplantation, 161
"overlap thesis," 8
overridingness thesis, 180 n

Parfit, Derek, 9
personal identity, 201 n
personhood, possible,   distinguished from potential personhood, 128
personhood issue, 53, 125–130, 132–133, 187–189 n
   and consequentialism, 56–57
   importance of, 53
   uncertainty about, 68–72, 187–188 n
Planned Parenthood v. Casey, 124
polio, vaccination for, 160
PR1
   defect in, 26
   objections to, 23–25
   stated, 23
PR2
   alternatives to, 30–34
   applying, 41–46, 50–63, 65, 67–68, 70–71, 73, 78, 82
   arguments against, 27–30, 35–41, 46–49
   argument for, 27
   conflicts with true moral principles and theories, 34
   reasons for adopting, 47
   stated, 26
PR3, 61–67, 71–72, 75–76
   applied to abortion decisions, 61–67, 71–72
   as not equivalent to PR2, 61–63

PR4, 82–83, 89–91, 95, 97–99, 109–111, 122, 134
   applying, 83, 89, 95
   defended, 90–91
   stated, 82
PR4J, 134, 136–137, 140
PR5, 89–90, 95–99, 109–111, 122, 134
   applying, 96
   stated, 95
PR5J, 134, 136, 139–140
practical guidance and moral uncertainty, 3, 9
prescriptivity, 104–105
Principle of Equity among Moral Theories (PEMT)
   applied, 84–86, 89
   arguments against, 86–87
   stated, 84
Principle of the Rights of Doubtful Persons (PRDP), 127–129
privacy, right to. *See* right to privacy
probabilities, objective. *See* objective probabilities
probabilities, ordinal measurement of. *See* ordinal measurement, of probabilities
probabilities, subjective. *See* subjective probabilities
probability of moral rightness
   notion of, 12–13
   as objective, 13
   as subjective, 13
probability, second-order, 61, 189 n
"prochoice" position, 73
"prolife" position, 73
prospective assessments of actions and persons, 47
Pybus, Elizabeth M., 100

quasi-supererogation, 105–107

radiography, 160
rank-order method, 89
"rational," as used in this book, 9–10
rational agent, life of the, 48
rationality
   and decision-making about abortion, 51
   and moral uncertainty, 9–16
Raz, Joseph, 100

reflective equilibrium, and judicial
reasoning, 141
regret, 46, 48
relativism, moral. *See* moral relativism
retrospective assessments of actions and
persons, 46–47
"reverence for life" principle, 54–55
Rhoden, Nancy, 130
right to life, 125, 130, 132–133, 137–
140
right to privacy, 125, 130–133, 137–
140
risk, decision-making under, 37
Roe v. Wade, 124–142
majority opinion, 125–133
romantic, life of, 48

safety lamp, 160
satisficing, 98–99
Schweitzer, Albert, 55
Singer, Peter, 100, 108
Sinnott-Armstrong, Walter, 39
"situation of moral uncertainty," 23
skepticism, ethical. *See* ethical skepticism
social harmony as a theme in utopian
literature, 165
Sophie's Choice, 39
spectator perspective, 101, 104
Styron, William, 39
subjective moral theories, 74, 76, 90,
192
subjective probabilities, 59–60, 94, 135,
189
measurement of, 59–60
subjectivism, moral. *See* moral
subjectivism
supererogation, 40–41, 54–55, 98–110,
170, 184–185 n, 194–195 n
and abortion, 54–55

supererogationism, 99–110
argument against, 107–108
supererogatory actions, essential
characteristics of
optionality, 102–103, 107
surplus moral value, 102–103, 107
surgery, 159

*Tarasoff v. Regents of the University of
California*, 112
technologies, development of, as means
of circumventing moral dilemmas,
159–163
technologies, morally dubious, 159–163
Thomson, Judith Jarvis, 53

Urmson, J. O., 99
utopia, 163–168
and political philosophy, 166–168
as unattainable by moral means, 163–
164
as world in which moral dilemmas do
not arise, 163–165
utopian imperative, 163

Varying Potential for Moral Rightness
(VPMR) thesis, 87–88, 145
virtue ethics, 20–21

Warren, Mary Anne, 128
Webster v. Reproductive Health Services,
124
White, Byron, 128
Williams, Bernard, 9–10, 46–49
Williamsian justification, 47–48
"winning is paramount" credo,
compared to "morality is
paramount" doctrine, 4
Winston, Morton, 113–118, 122–123